# EXPLORATIONS IN LOCAL AND REGIONAL HISTORY

Centre for Regional and Local History, University of Hertfordshire

and

Centre for English Local History, University of Leicester

SERIES EDITORS: KATRINA NAVICKAS AND ANGELA MUIR

## Previous titles in this series

# PRINCELY AMBITION

*Ideology, landscape and castle-building
in Gwynedd, 1194–1283*

CRAIG OWEN JONES

UNIVERSITY OF HERTFORDSHIRE PRESS

Explorations in Local and Regional History
Volume 10

First published in Great Britain in 2022 by
University of Hertfordshire Press
College Lane
Hatfield
Hertfordshire
AL10 9AB

British Library Cataloguing in Publication Data
A catalogue record for this book is available from the British Library

ISBN 978-1-912260-27-0

Design by Arthouse Publishing Solutions
Printed in Great Britain by Charlesworth Press

*Of course, none of the native Welsh castles can compare*
*with the scale and grandeur of Beaumaris, Caernarfon, Conwy*
*or Harlech, castles of the Edwardian conquest ...*
Stephen Friar, The Sutton Companion to Castles (2003)

*If something is forever like something else, it is never itself.*
Jonathan Meades, 1997

## Publication grant

Publication of this volume has been supported
by a generous subvention from the Marc Fitch Fund.

# Contents

# Illustrations

**Figures**

# Maps

# Tables

# Abbreviations

| | |
|---|---|
| AC | *Archaeologia Cambrensis* |
| AJ | *Archaeological Journal* |
| AW | *Archaeology in Wales* |
| AWR | H. Pryce (ed.), *The Acts of Welsh Rulers 1120–1283* (Cardiff, 2005) |
| BBCS | *Bulletin of the Board of Celtic Studies* |
| BUAS | Bangor University Archives Service |
| BYT Pen MS 20 | T. Jones (ed.), *Brut Y Tywysogyon* [Chronicle of the Princes] (Peniarth MS 20 version) (Cardiff, 1952) |
| BYT RBH | T. Jones (ed.), *Brut Y Tywysogyon* [Chronicle of the Princes] (Red Book of Hergest version) (Cardiff, 1973) |
| CMCS | *Cambrian Medieval Celtic Studies* |
| FHSJ | *Flintshire Historical Society Journal* (previously *Publications of the Flintshire Historical Society*) |
| FRO | Flintshire Record Office, Hawarden |
| GG | D. Stephenson, *The Governance of Gwynedd* (Cardiff, 1984) |
| JMHRS | *Journal of the Merioneth Historical and Record Society* |
| LlapG | J. Beverley Smith, *Llywelyn ap Gruffudd: Prince of Wales* (Cardiff, 1998) |
| LltG | R. Turvey, *Llywelyn the Great* (Llandysul, 2007) |
| MC | *Montgomeryshire Collections* |
| MP | D. Stephenson, *Medieval Powys: Kingdom, Principality and Lordships, 1132–1293* (Woodbridge, 2016) |
| NLW | National Library of Wales, Aberystwyth |
| NLWJ | *National Library of Wales Journal* |
| RCAHMW Archives | Archive of the Royal Commission of Ancient and Historical Monuments of Wales, Aberystwyth |
| SC | *Studia Celtica* |
| SHA | *Shropshire History and Archaeology* |
| THSC | *Transactions of the Honourable Society of Cymmrodorion* |
| WHR | *Welsh History Review* |
| WS | S. Davies, *War and Society in Medieval Wales 633–1283* (Cardiff, 2004) |

# Foreword

Anyone who writes on medieval Wales in the English language has to contend with the issue of how to render personal names. During the Age of the Princes (defined here as the period between Gruffudd ap Cynan's death in 1137 and the end of the war of 1282–3) the Welsh royal houses produced six men who styled themselves or were widely thought of as princes of Wales: Owain Gwynedd, Rhys ap Gruffudd, Llywelyn ab Iorwerth, Dafydd ap Llywelyn, Llywelyn ap Gruffudd and Dafydd ap Gruffudd. A further ruler, Dafydd ab Owain, exercised extensive power in Gwynedd prior to Llywelyn ab Iorwerth's succession. Where they share the same first name, distinguishing one from the other is usually accomplished by resort to their patronymics – a system that works very well, but takes some getting used to; the potential for confusion among casual readers unfamiliar with it is obvious. In the interests of accessibility for readers beyond Wales, I have therefore used regnal numbers throughout. This system, which is less commonly used than the above system, has the merit of being intuitive for the layperson, and has been used by historians including Glanville Jones, Keith Williams-Jones and even (on occasion) the father of modern Welsh historiography, J.E. Lloyd. I hope it will assist the reader unfamiliar with Welsh history in keeping straight the litany of Llywelyns and Dafydds whose names necessarily pepper this book's pages.

The title of this book should also be addressed. Although the scope of the book is limited to those castles built by the rulers of Gwynedd, the geographical extent of the book extends beyond Gwynedd's borders, including areas of Powys, Brecon and Shropshire in which the princes of Wales are known to have built or maintained castles. As the castles of Deheubarth were sponsored by the lords of that house, they are not considered in this volume.

I have accrued some substantial debts in the preparation of this book. David Hopewell of Gwynedd Archaeological Trust was endlessly obliging in fielding an array of questions concerning the recent excavations at Castell Carndochan, while Nigel Jones of Clwyd-Powys Archaeological Trust, Hugh Hannaford of Shropshire Council's Archaeological Service and Angharad Stockwell of Scottish Canals were similarly helpful in giving information and providing copies of site reports and articles. I would also like to thank Bill Britnell and Jeffrey Davies for their kindness in referring me to relevant literature on Roman roads, as well as Rachel Swallow of the University of Liverpool. Stephanie Hines, Teresa Davies and Bridget Thomas of the Flintshire Record Office, Ann Hughes and the staff at Bangor University Archives Service and Ywain Tomos and Adam Coward of the Archives of the Royal Commission on the Ancient and Historical Monuments of Wales in Aberystwyth were all instrumental in locating documents relating to native Welsh castles. The castle plans were drawn by Cath d'Alton (cathdaltonhome@btinternet.com) to a standard far exceeding that which I could have achieved.

I would also like to thank the University of Hertfordshire Press's series editors, Angela Muir and Katrina Navickas, for their support throughout the publishing process; Richard Jones and David Stephenson, for their comments on the manuscript; and particularly Jane Housham and Sarah Elvins, whose patience in dealing with a dilatory author has been exemplary. Lastly, this book was partly funded by a grant from the Marc Fitch Fund; I would like to sincerely thank the trustees, as well as the director, Christopher Catling, for their generosity.

COJ, Sacramento, California
417.64 ppm $CO_2$
Covid-19 case rate: 5.3
5 July 2021

# Series Editors' Preface

*Explorations in Local and Regional History* continues the series of 'Occasional Papers' of the University of Leicester's Department (now Centre) for English Local History, started in 1952. This succeeding series is published by the University of Hertfordshire Press with the Centre for Regional and Local History Research and the University of Leicester.

*Explorations in Local and Regional History* has three distinctive aims. First, the series seeks to open up new directions, prompt analysis of new sources and develop innovative methodologies in local and regional history. The series follows the fine tradition set by the universities of Leicester and Hertfordshire in empirical research into communities, place, landscape, demography, and social and economic change from the medieval era to the present day. But it also seeks new ways to reinvigorate the significance of local and regional history in the twenty-first century. Though local and regional history can be bounded physically by geography, it is not bounded by connections and networks that stretch over time and space. Local history drills down to find the meaning of place at all levels, from the micro to the global. We encourage both detailed studies of localities in Britain and Europe as well as comparative and more theoretical approaches.

The second aim of the series is to provide an outlet for mid-length studies in between research articles and full-length books, generally within the range of 40,000 to 60,000 words. Such works are hard to place with existing publishers, so our series offers a space for detailed, yet quicker to read, studies than standard monographs. We encourage innovative work from researchers at the start of their careers as well as from more established scholars.

Third, we hope this series is of interest to both academics and students, but also to researchers outside universities. Local heritage is a vital part of today's society and government: applied local history research enables community building through the commemoration of place, informs policies regarding conservation of both the built and natural environment, and of course helps to promote towns and regions for tourism. This series aims to provide historical context for these uses of heritage.

Angela Muir, University of Leicester
Katrina Navickas, University of Hertfordshire

**Key**

GWYNEDD  Welsh kingdom
*uwch Conwy*  region

⌘  Native Welsh
masonry castle

●  Selected other places
mentioned in the text

Native Welsh masonry castles mentioned in the text.

# Introduction

Writing this book would have been impossible fifty years ago. At the turn of the 1970s the field of castle studies was in its infancy, and something of a Cinderella in the academic sense. Castellologists were few in number, and the formation of the Castle Studies Group at Gregynog – the final development, perhaps, in lending the field undeniable academic legitimacy – lay over a decade in the future. The situation was especially parlous in Wales in general, and in reference to the native Welsh castles in particular. The documentary materials relating to them were in many cases yet to be discovered, or awaiting thorough analysis; several of the castles discussed here had not yet been subjected to modern archaeological scrutiny. Not for nothing did John Kenyon describe Wales as having once personified 'the poor man of British castle studies'.[1]

Since then, various aspects of the history of the Age of the Princes[2] have been the subject of sustained and in-depth analysis, but a scholarly, book-length study of the native Welsh castles has never appeared. Perhaps that is not all that surprising. The native castles have certainly not been neglected: several articles and archaeological reports have been published devoted to individual castles, as well as a spate of popular and well-written guidebooks published by Cadw. However, an overarching academic survey has been noticeable by its absence. And no wonder: at first glance they look like a very mixed bag indeed, with little to unify them in terms of architecture, siting or purpose. Treating them as cut from the same cloth seems perilous, and those who have done so have tended to issue generalisations about their purpose that spread more darkness than light (see below). To some extent this reflects the cultural bias – set in place principally by Gerald of Wales (d. 1223) and Matthew Paris, and parroted by generations of historians (including many Welsh ones) for centuries thereafter – to the effect that the Welsh under the princes were destitute of modern weapons, ignorant of the

---

1.  J. Kenyon, '"Those proud, ambitious heaps": whither castle studies?' AC, 166 (2017), p. 16.
2.  Defined for the purposes of this book as the period between the accession of Owain Gwynedd (the first ruler known to have used the style *princeps Wallie*, or prince of Wales) in 1137 and the victory of Edward I in the war of 1282–3.

principles of warfare and barbarous and duplicitous in character. The tendency of so many historians to offer generalities based on sources such as Gerald – who never knowingly left an axe unground where the Welsh were concerned – has not helped matters. The following passage, from the *Descriptio Kambriae*, is typical. Gerald begins by describing the Welsh approach to battle in positive terms, but his opinion is soon revealed to be less than admiring:

> In war the Welsh are very ferocious when battle is first joined. They shout, glower fiercely at the enemy, and fill the air with fearsome clamour, making a high-pitched screech with their long trumpets. From their first fierce and headlong onslaught, and the shower of javelins which they hurl, they seem most formidable opponents. If the enemy resists manfully and they are repulsed, they are immediately thrown into confusion. With further resistance they turn their backs, making no attempt at a counterattack, but seeking safety in flight.

Stopping for a moment to quote Horace – 'Although he may lack skill, only a coward flees' – Gerald goes on to question their tactical sense: 'Their sole idea ... is either to pursue their opponents, or else to run away from them.'[3] A subsequent compliment regarding the ability of the Welsh to carry out ambushes and night attacks is rather back-handed, as is his description of their fierceness in battle, but at least they were put into writing; compared with some contemporary commentators, Gerald was being charitable. Matthew Paris spoke of the reprehensible conduct of the Welsh in massacring the entire population of English towns they captured, while, later in the thirteenth century, Welsh soldiers were depicted as duplicitous, slovenly, drunken and many other things besides: at Falkirk in 1298, for example, a large contingent of Welshmen serving in Edward I's army against the Scots rioted, and eighty of them were killed by English cavalrymen sent to quell the unrest.[4] During the reign of Henry III – who at first opposed Llywelyn ab Iorwerth (r. 1194–1240; hereafter Llywelyn I) in Wales, and then his successors Dafydd ap Llywelyn (r. 1240–6; hereafter Dafydd II) and Llywelyn ap Gruffudd (r. 1246–82; hereafter Llywelyn II) – the Welsh were routinely described as crafty, 'traitorous', given to 'treachery' and living in 'bestial lairs'.[5]

Such depictions were part of a wider cultural discourse in England that racialised the Welsh. Commentators searching for ways to depict the Welsh invariably chose to highlight not points of commonality between the Welsh and

3. L. Thorpe (transl.), *Gerald of Wales: The Journey through Wales/The Description of Wales* (London, 1978), pp. 233–4.
4. M. Prestwich, 'Welsh infantry in Flanders in 1297', in R.A. Griffiths and P.R. Schofield (eds), *Wales and the Welsh in the Middle Ages: Essays presented to J. Beverley Smith* (Cardiff, 2011), p. 65.
5. M. Carlin and D. Crouch (eds and transls), *Lost Letters of Medieval Life: English Society, 1200–1250* (Philadelphia, PA, 2013), p. 118.

the Anglo-Normans and (later) English but their otherness – sometimes with malicious intent, sometimes not, but always with the result of simplifying the people and effacing nuances of custom, cultural norms and character. Rory Cox has recently re-presented this idea in terms of asymmetric warfare, noting that

> ethnic hatred on both sides of the Anglo-Welsh border was exacerbated by the sense among the Anglo-Norman troops that they were not fighting an honourable enemy, ... and therefore they afforded the Welsh none of the privileges normally extended to a typical symmetrical opponent.[6]

This included denying the Welsh any sense of propriety, acumen or wisdom where warfare was concerned. Over a century after Gerald put his thoughts on the martial abilities of the Welsh to paper, we have the following description from the *Vita Edwardi Secundi*: 'from the sayings of the prophet Merlin they [the Welsh] still hope to recover England. Hence it is that the Welsh frequently rebel, hoping to give effect to the prophecy; but because they do not know the appointed time, they are often deceived and their labour is in vain.'[7] The note of bemusement at the credence given to such foolish beliefs is palpable, and one that, even later, Shakespeare was also quick to sound in his depictions of several Welshmen in his plays, chief among them Owain Glyndŵr.[8] Stereotypes of the esoteric and gullible Welsh were easy to play on to audiences for whom such portrayals were both current and coherent.

This has implications for our understanding of the princes as castle-builders. What is true of perceptions of the medieval Welsh at war extends to native Welsh castles. They, too, have been maligned as peculiar, whimsical places, unsuited to the roles that have retrospectively been assigned to them. What follows is an attempt to correct that view. Before beginning, however, it is a worthwhile exercise to place the castles in their broader cultural and geographical context.

For many years the public's perception of Welsh castles has been informed by the Iron Ring, that remarkable collection of half a dozen or so castles that constitute Edward I's most important works along the north Wales coast. These 'magnificent badges of our subjection', to paraphrase the eighteenth-century Flintshire antiquarian Thomas Pennant,[9] are impressive for their sheer scale, are substantially intact and, between them, draw hundreds of thousands of tourists from across the globe each year. In every way, the castles of Rhuddlan, Conwy, Caernarfon, Beaumaris, Harlech and Aberystwyth are on show, at or near the centre of the towns in which they stand and towering above the two- and three-

---

6.   R. Cox, 'Asymmetric warfare and military conduct in the Middle Ages', *Journal of Medieval History*, 38 (2012), p. 108.
7.   N. Denholm-Young (ed.), *Vita Edwardi Secundi: The Life of Edward the Second* (Oxford, 1957), p. 69.
8.   See, for example, R.R. Davies, *The Revolt of Owain Glyn Dŵr* (Oxford, 1995), pp. 334–5.
9.   T. Pennant, *Tours of Wales*, 2 vols (London, 1778; repr. 1810), p. 404.

storey architecture that surrounds them; and, if the castle at Flint is not so readily accessible, tucked away behind a post-war housing estate as it is, like its more frequently visited cousins it is indeed magnificent.

Yet, throughout the history of tourism in the north, tugging at the coat-tails of the Edwardian castles has been a very different set of fortifications. The castles of the native Welsh princes occupy the summits of prominent hills and were seldom associated with towns. They are more remote and so are less frequently visited; and yet, from the standpoint of the historian, the archaeologist or the student of architecture, visits to these sites are singularly rewarding. The Edwardian castles are dissimilar enough to make their study interesting, but their peculiarities pale in comparison with those of their Welsh contemporaries. Rarely has a group of ostensibly similar buildings exhibited such heterogeneity of form and purpose. To a certain kind of eye, their lack of symmetry is disturbing; they seemingly have an air of improvisation about them; they are utile, but in ways that can escape the inattentive observer. To behold a native Welsh masonry castle is to see the Japanese principle of *wabi* at work. They are for the most part roughly hewn, austere places, constructed with a certain stolid pragmatism that left most of them all but bereft of decorative flourishes. In spite of the (albeit belated) excavation and consolidation of their remains, and the publishing of official guidebooks detailing their histories in common with their better-known English contemporaries, these castles suffer from an odd sort of neglect. In presenting them as destinations – for the Welsh citizen and the tourist alike – their essential remoteness must be contended with. The example of Cricieth aside, not a single native Welsh masonry castle has a visitor centre associated with it, in contradistinction to many of the Edwardian castles; at most, the best visitors can hope for is the odd bird-soiled interpretive board detailing the castle's history.

And yet this neglect stems from another, more fundamental neglect: that of the history of the native Welsh rulers, that extraordinary group of men and women who between them established and governed the nascent polities of Gwynedd, Powys and Deheubarth until the end of the thirteenth century. It is now over a century since J.E. Lloyd's landmark *History of Wales* (1911) pursued the stories of the native princes of Wales with the same diligence and verve previously reserved for their English-born successors. In its pages, Lloyd retraced the journey the Welsh made with quiet authority[10] – from a people unified under the impressive aegis of Gruffudd ap Llywelyn (d. 1064), perhaps the only Welsh ruler to fully deserve the style *rex Wallie*; to fragmentation following the interpenetration of the country by Anglo-Norman lords in the decades following the Norman Conquest; to the resurgence of Gwynedd under Gruffudd ap Cynan and the subsequent accession of his son Owain Gwynedd to the Venedotian throne in 1137. Then there followed that

---

10.  See H. Pryce, *J.E. Lloyd and the Creation of Welsh History: Renewing a Nation's Past* (Cardiff, 2011) for an assessment of Lloyd's contribution.

heady century and a half known today as the Age of the Princes, a period in Welsh history that Lloyd not only found immensely attractive but also implicitly elevated as the zenith of Welsh political achievement.[11] In it, he lionised Llywelyn I as Wales' great statesman, as canny in his dealings with King John and Henry III as with his enemies on the field of battle; while Llywelyn II's reign, though superficially more impressive – the Treaty of Montgomery, concluded in 1267, is notable as the only document signed by a king of England recognising the claims of a prince of Wales to rule over his principality[12] – was ultimately found wanting, as Gwynedd's debellation during the war of 1282–3 demonstrated.[13] The nation-building activities of the two Llywelyns, and also the prince whose reign is interposed between theirs, Llywelyn I's youngest son, Dafydd II, included the issuance of coinage; the expansion of the chancellery and the written documentation of royal governance more generally; the overhaul of the Welsh law codes; the initiation of diplomacy with France, Scotland and the Papacy; and, of course, the construction or augmentation of masonry castles across Gwynedd and the March.[14]

Since Lloyd's time, the princes' deeds have been subjected to increasingly detailed scrutiny by successive generations of Welsh historians determined to illumine what had hitherto been a poorly known path; but while names such as Huw Pryce, David Stephenson, J. Beverley Smith, Llinos Beverley Smith, R.R. Davies, John Davies, Ralph Griffiths, T. Jones-Pierce, Constance Bullock-Davies, Enid Roberts, Max Lieberman, Jenny Day and dozens of others have all raised the consciousness of this period of Welsh history, perceptions of medieval Welsh history among the public have remained, at best, partially informed.

The circumstances that gave rise to this state of affairs are complex and of longstanding. It is not enough to say that there has been a failure on the part of the academy to present Welsh history to the people of Wales in an engaging manner.

11.  As has been pointed out to exhaustion, it cannot be insignificant that the 'father of modern Welsh history' ends his *magnum opus* with the reduction of Wales by Edward I.

12.  For a recent assessment of the treaty, H. Pryce, 'Anglo-Welsh agreements, 1201–77', in Griffiths and Schofield (eds), *Wales and the Welsh*, pp. 1, 6–7.

13.  D. Stephenson, 'A Treaty too far? The impact of the Treaty of Montgomery on Llywelyn ap Gruffudd's Principality of Wales', MC, 106 (2018), pp. 19–32 somewhat endorses the view put forward by J. Beverley Smith that the onerous financial demands that fell on Llywelyn as a result of the treaty were instrumental in his fall from power, but also points out (p. 28) that several of the prince's pronouncements in the 1270s seem to indicate that Llywelyn was indeed in possession of substantial sums of money at that time (but see Chapter 3, below). Dr Stephenson has indicated (pers. comm.) that, in his view, Beverley Smith and Keith Williams-Jones may have underestimated the ability of Llywelyn's constituencies beyond Gwynedd to contribute to his payments under the terms of the treaty.

14.  For overviews of the reigns of the two Llywelyns, LltG and LlapG remain the standard accounts; in spite of a recent upsurge of academic interest in his short reign, a scholarly biography of Dafydd II has yet to appear. P.R. Davis' *Castles of the Welsh Princes*, 2nd edn (Talybont, 2011) comprises a most useful gazetteer of native Welsh masonry castles.

Though there is some truth in the allegation, the nature of the Welsh media constantly militates against such engagement. The fact that large swathes of the country spent most of the analogue era tuning in to English regional television channels – the old north-eastern county of Clwyd, along with a goodly portion of the north Wales coast, was not unfairly referred to as 'Granadaland' in the 1980s and 1990s[15] – hobbled attempts to educate by means of television series devoted to Welsh history, though many have tried. S4C's flagship series *Tywysogion* (Princes; 2007) and the BBC's *The Story of Wales* (2012) are salutary examples, and it was heartening to see both devoting significant airtime to native Welsh castles, even if they were primarily used as dramatic backdrops.[16] Similarly, the fact that there are only two national newspapers – the *Western Mail* and the *Daily Post* – meant that attempts at stimulating a national popular debate on Welsh history and its representations have been fitful.

Allied to this is the nebulous but lingering feeling that the Age of the Princes is a somehow unsuitable subject for public celebration. Here, the disreputability bestowed on the fifteenth-century rebel prince Owain Glyndŵr (d. *c*.1415) following the invocation of his name by Meibion Glyndŵr, a group responsible for scores of arson attacks on English-owned holiday homes in the 1970s and 1980s, cannot have helped.[17] Similarly, it was presumably the independentist rallies at Cilmeri – the place where Llywelyn II met his death in 1282 – that began in the 1950s that led John Gillingham to opine in earnest that that prince's ignoble, ultimate fate amounted to nothing more than 'becom[ing] a cult figure for some twentieth-century Welsh nationalists'.[18] The simplistic equation of the history of the Welsh princes with nationalist sentiment is significant. It is interesting that the recent blooming across Wales of St David's Day parades in many Welsh towns and cities are associated with Wales' patron saint, a safely distant historical figure shrouded in myth; persistent calls for annual events to be held on 16 September to celebrate what Welsh speakers refer to as 'Gŵyl Owain Glyndŵr' (Owain Glyndŵr Day) in observance of the anniversary of the beginning of the rebel prince's revolt in 1400 have gained far less traction.[19]

15. The term originally came into use as describing the catchment area of the ITV franchise in the 1950s; J. Medhurst, *A History of Independent Television in Wales* (Cardiff, 2010), p. 28. By the 1980s it was being employed in the Welsh example in a pejorative sense.

16. Both series saw the publication of popular accounts; see H. Pryce, *Tywysogion* [Princes] (Cardiff, 2006), J. Gower, *The Story of Wales* (Croydon, 2012). The former made use of computer-generated reconstructions to show how castles such as Dolforwyn would have looked during the medieval era.

17. E. Henken, *National Redeemer: Owain Glyndŵr in Welsh Tradition* (Cardiff, 1996), pp. 176–7.

18. J. Gillingham, 'The Early Middle Ages (1066–1290)', in K.O. Morgan (ed.), *The Oxford History of Britain*, rev. ed. (Oxford, 2001), p. 157.

19. Henken, *National Redeemer*, p. 182 refers to attempts to make the day a national holiday, 'a time for flag-waving and speech-making', spearheaded by 'political activist groups'. Tecwyn Vaughan Jones described 16 September as the province of 'Glyndŵr enthusiasts' as recently as 1998; see T.V. Jones, 'Review of *National redeemer: Owain Glyndŵr in Welsh tradition* by Elissa R. Henken', *WHR*, 19/1 (1998), p. 152.

There is a wider point to be grasped here. Even in the case of Glyndŵr – a revered historical figure whose name enjoys the widest currency of any native Welsh leader – there is no one well-known historical feat, no pithy exclamation or word of wisdom, on which the average person can rely. Most English people, and a great many Welsh, Scots and Irish for that matter, know that William the Conqueror won the battle of Hastings, or that Alfred burned the cakes (or is supposed to have done so). Ask the average Welsh citizen to name a feat in arms of Glyndŵr, however, and they will almost certainly flounder. Those acquainted with Shakespeare may recall that the prince claimed to 'call spirits from the vasty deep'; but, as R.R. Davies pointed out, such words placed in Glyndŵr's mouth said more about Shakespeare's sensibilities and the English need to reduce Henry IV's most steadfast opponent to an ineffectual chieftain, bumptious in manner and arcane in belief, and nothing about the prince as a statesman or a soldier.[20] References to Glyndŵr's landmark victories at Hyddgen (1401), Pilleth (1402) or Craig-y-Dorth (1404) would be thin on the ground; recollections of his diplomacy with France and Scotland, or his ambitious programme to establish Welsh universities and extend Wales' borders to the banks of the Mersey in the north and the gates of Bridgnorth in the east,[21] would be met with blank stares. Under such circumstances, attempts to locate Wales' 'usable past' can only continue.[22]

The corollary of this rueful state of knowledge is that the native Welsh castles, far from being points of interest for the Welsh citizen, are in fact *tabulae rasae*, unstoried and unnoticed. But the public perception of them is hardly helped by the fact that for almost a century – since they were first characterised as works of the native Welsh princes, in fact – two opposing schools of thought have emerged that, taken together, have served to confuse and stymie efforts to comprehend their significance.[23] In 1928 Wilfrid J. Hemp published his seminal article on the architecture of native Welsh castles, 'Ewloe Castle and the Welsh Castle plan'. Prior to its appearance, a great deal of hot air had been expended over the activities of the Welsh princes in the field of castle building. While much useful work had been accomplished by early archaeologists and historians on Castell Y Bere, Cricieth, Deganwy and elsewhere, scholarly understanding of the castles of the princes was to a great extent characterised by misconceptions, a result of the absence of reliable historical research and archaeological investigation. Hemp's achievement

---

20. Davies, *Revolt*, pp. 334–6. Earlier (p. 325) Davies makes a convincing case that it is not Glyndŵr's deeds but the man himself who has embedded in the Welsh popular consciousness.
21. Davies, *Revolt*, pp. 153–73.
22. N. Evans, 'Finding a new story: the search for a usable past in Wales, 1869–1930', THSC, new series, 10 (2004), pp. 144–62 explicates the notion of identifying and celebrating particular events and figures in order to serve a contemporary political or ideological need.
23. The following paragraphs are based on the introduction to C.O. Jones, 'How to make an entrance: an overlooked aspect of native Welsh masonry castle design', *Journal of the Mortimer History Society*, 1 (2017), pp. 73–89.

was to put clear water between Anglo-Norman and native Welsh castle design, identifying the principal characteristics of four castles he understood as typifying the latter: Ewloe, Deganwy, Y Bere and Carndochan.

Yet while Hemp's essay (and several less trumpeted publications that preceded it) succeeded in drawing attention to the princes as castle builders in their own right, it also put in place perceptions of their castles as outdated at best and ignorant of the most basic principles of defence at worst; and these ideas would dominate thinking on the matter for the next half-century. Hemp's principal subject, Ewloe, which stands a couple of miles inside the Welsh border in Flintshire, was revealed to be a castle whose plan was dictated by something approaching whimsy. While its circular tower is sited 'normally' – that is, on the curtain wall – the siting of the castle's other major feature, the Welsh Tower, behind rather than astride the curtain was viewed with barely concealed bemusement, while the position of the castle on a boss of rock that is largely overlooked at one end was 'exceptional' in the negative sense. According to Hemp, entrances to Welsh castles 'were of a primitive type', and emphasis was also placed on the almost total absence of 'mechanical luxuries' such as drawbridges and portcullises, being seemingly too 'elaborate', as Hemp had it, for the Welsh to countenance.[24]

Hemp's conclusions on the architectural details of native Welsh castles were very largely limited to the example at Ewloe, but the unfortunate circumstance arose that the criticisms behind his characterisation of what was, to a mind geared toward identifying aspects of its military function, a very oddly sited castle were applied by others to native Welsh castles more generally. Other scholars were kindlier, but were nevertheless swayed in their conclusions by a model that invariably categorised works of any sophistication at native Welsh castles as deriving from periods of English occupation.[25] R.R. Davies typified this view, stating in 1991 his opinion as to the rudeness of native Welsh castles of the twelfth and thirteenth centuries. While noting that the castles represented 'a not unimpressive response to changes in military strategy and fortification', Davies nonetheless damned the works with faint praise so comprehensively as to render the whole worthless:

24. W.J. Hemp, 'Ewloe Castle and the Welsh Castle plan', *Y Cymmrodor*, 39 (1928), pp. 4–19. A recent re-evaluation has been provided by D. Stephenson, 'A reconsideration of the siting, function and dating of Ewloe castle', AC, 164 (2015), pp. 245–53.

25. See, for example, L. Alcock *et al.*, 'Excavations at Castell Bryn Amlwg', MC, 60 (1967–8), pp. 8–27, in which the castle's gatehouse, since reasonably securely dated to the reign of Llywelyn II, is characterised as a feature 'of notably Edwardian plan', in spite of native Welsh exemplars at Cricieth and Dinas Brân that resemble it far more closely (p. 20). The most notorious example of this tendency is, of course, C.N. Johns' *Castell Cricieth/Cricieth Castle*, 2nd edn (1984; London, 1970), which erroneously ascribed Cricieth's most architecturally impressive feature – the inner gatehouse – to Edward I. The furore which followed is described by Richard Avent in *Criccieth Castle* (Cardiff, 1989), p. 10.

In design and construction they were very inferior in comparison with English castles built in Wales in this period, such as Montgomery, Cilgerran, Pembroke, or Whitecastle. Their overall design often appears haphazard; little attempt was made to integrate towers and curtain-walls into a sustained defence-system; and the quality of their masonry was frequently poor. Yet in their way these castles ... represent a not unimpressive response to changes in military strategy and fortification. ... Even at a technical level they were not without their merits – notably in the quality of their rock-cut ditches ... while the readiness of their builder to borrow and adapt contemporary English ideas in the art of fortification – such as the round tower at Dolbadarn or the gatehouses at Cricieth and Dinas Brân – speaks well for the imagination and receptiveness of the native princes.[26]

Anyone who has studied the designs of, say, the multi-ward layout of Dryslwyn, the handful of strongly built towers and barbican at Y Bere or Cricieth's concentric defensive system would have a hard time fathoming how the only technical detail felt worthy of mention by Davies was the castles' ditches; and, while the point about the 'imagination and receptiveness' of the princes is well made, in light of what precedes it it hardly counts for much. Such was for many years the prevailing attitude towards native Welsh castles. Even Richard Avent, whose sterling work in describing the works of the Welsh princes has done so much to raise the level of academic debate and educate the public alike, found cause to refer to the 'poor defensive quality' of native Welsh curtain walls as recently as 1994.[27]

However, an alternative view of the native Welsh castles soon developed, one that imbued the princes with far more in the way of architectural competency and military acumen. Its originator was Glanville Jones, a professor of historical geography at Leeds University, whose 'The Defences of Gwynedd in the Thirteenth Century' (1969), derived from his doctoral thesis, placed emphasis on the careful emplacement of masonry castles to defend or control strategically important passes and roads throughout Gwynedd and beyond. A second, equally important contribution was Jones' identification of vaccaries and havotries designed to supply the castles in times of peace, as well as his description of societal norms apparently designed to facilitate the swift movement of materiel into the mountains in times of war.[28] Jones' analysis had a great influence on the thinking of Welsh scholars; his theory of the concentric natural defences of Gwynedd was endorsed by David Stephenson in his landmark study of Venedotian administrative practices, The Governance of Gwynedd (1984), and by Sean Davies in

---

26. R.R. Davies, The Age of Conquest: Wales 1063–1415 (Oxford, 1991), pp. 255–6.
27. R. Avent, Dolwyddelan Castle/Dolbadarn Castle (Cardiff, 1994), p. 5. The point is repeated almost verbatim by L. Butler and J.J. Knight, Dolforwyn Castle/Montgomery Castle (Cardiff, 2004), p. 31.
28. G. Jones, 'The defences of Gwynedd in the thirteenth century', Transactions of the Caernarfonshire Historical Society, 30 (1969), pp. 29–43.

*War and Society in Medieval Wales 633–1283* (2004), and Roger Turvey among others accepted the notion of a Venedotian castle-building programme, while nationalist historians such as Gwynfor Evans embraced Jones' depiction of the considerable economic arrangements pursuant to the establishment of a masonry castle, and the organisational sophistication they implied, with much fervour.[29]

These more or less diametrically opposed views of native Welsh castle-building symbolise the confused characterisations of the castles of the princes that emerged in the twentieth century. Time and again, commentators struggled to discern the meaning behind their construction and resorted to approaches that incorporated one or other of these views, frequently glossing over the fine detail of their positioning, or their architectural style and dispositions, in the process. Indeed, Hemp's and Jones' articles are sundered by exactly this type of contradiction. Jones, for his part, makes the unspoken assumption – valid in the 1960s, but now suspect in light of the peregrinations of Charles Coulson, Oliver Creighton and others on the non-military uses of the castle – that the native Welsh castles were uniformly designed and emplaced solely with defence in mind. Ewloe again serves as a good example of the enormous problems of interpretation thrown up by this assumption. In Jones' imagining, Ewloe is situated to guard the north-eastern border with England – an assertion that would go unquestioned, and indeed be repeated, by many others.[30] And yet a cursory visit to the site reveals the essential soundness of Hemp's conclusions *vis-à-vis* Ewloe's siting within the wider landscape, and underscores how poorly equipped any garrison would be to offer more than circumscribed resistance against a determined siege party. To characterise it as constituting part of 'a coherent Welsh defensive policy [centred on] the outermost mountain rampart of Gwynedd [i.e. the Clwydian range]'[31] is misleading. Doubtless it merited some consideration in English invasion plans; indeed, the survival of what is apparently an English siegework speaks to this (see chapter 1). But during the war of 1276–7 it cannot have done very much to slow Edward in his stride; and, after its garrisoning by the English during the war of 1282–3,[32] it was tellingly left to decay.

Yet, while Jones' interpretation had its faults, not the least of which was the in some ways facile description of Gwynedd's natural defences – few mountain and hill ranges are quite so conveniently positioned for defence as Jones makes those of north Wales out to be, and one feels that the Clwydians would not be considered to constitute much of a barrier to Gwynedd given the wide, flat coastal strip to their north – it did at least have the merit of acting as a corrective to Hemp's allegations that the Welsh were unable to comprehend the basic principles of castle-building.

29.  GG, pp. 1–5; LltG, pp. 104–8; G. Evans, *The Fight for Welsh Freedom* (Talybont, 2000).
30.  See, for example, L. Butler, 'Dolforwyn Castle, Powys, Wales: excavations 1985–1990', *Château Gaillard*, 15 (1992), p. 74.
31.  Jones, 'The defences of Gwynedd', p. 37.
32.  J.E. Morris, *The Welsh Wars of Edward I* (Oxford, 1901), p. 161.

It borders on the ridiculous to imply, as Hemp did, that some, or even any, of the six men known to have assumed the title of prince of Wales in the century and a half prior to the Edwardian annexation[33] were militarily incompetent to the extent that they would sanction the expenditure of large sums of money on the construction of suboptimal or useless fortifications. The authors of medieval castles 'had far too much invested and took too much interest in their castles to make mistakes',[34] and we can be sure that the princes thought long and hard before deciding on a location and form for their fortifications.

Yet, if this is the case, why does Hemp's analysis continue to exert such a hold on the imagination? The answer lies in the fact that so many of the basic precepts of medieval castle-building appear to be flouted in the surviving Welsh examples. The most naïve student of military architecture cannot fail to be struck by this. It surely stands to reason that the angles in a curtain wall should ordinarily be capped by a tower, preferably circular in shape so as to stymie attempts at undermining; or that stretches of curtain of any length should be interrupted at regular intervals by towers or buttresses so that defenders may subject attackers to enfilading fire; or that castle entrances, being the most vulnerable spots on the curtain, should take the form of gatehouses, ideally complemented by barbicans or gate passages. And yet at Y Bere one finds the curtain wall replete with uncapped angles; at Dolbadarn and Dolwyddelan the lack of enfilading towers is plain to see; and, almost everywhere, gatehouses and barbicans are noticeable by their absence.

First impressions are inherently persuasive because we like to think that what we intuit is correct. In this case, however, we should resist that impulse. Our understanding of the form and function of native Welsh castles has, after all, been swept up in the more general recent debate on the relative importance of castles as indicators of status and prestige alongside their military value.[35] Accompanying this debate is a growing realisation that the Welsh princes were quicker to adapt to Anglo-Norman building practices (and, indeed, to adapt those practices to their own situation and needs) than has previously been assumed. In the context

---

33. Namely Owain Gwynedd, Llywelyn I, Dafydd II, Llywelyn II and Dafydd ap Gruffudd (r. 1282–3; hereafter Dafydd III). The sixth, the Lord Rhys (r. 1155–1197), was the leader of the house of Deheubarth, whose patrimony was centred on west Wales, particularly the regions corresponding to modern-day Carmarthenshire and Ceredigion. During the quarter-century of infighting in Gwynedd that followed the death of Owain Gwynedd in 1170, Rhys was the most powerful Welsh ruler and did indeed claim the title of *princeps Walliae* in the 1170s, later revising his style to *Walliarum princeps* [prince of the Welsh] by 1184. The title was, however, almost certainly aspirational; it is doubtful that the rulers of Gwynedd recognised Rhys' claim to overlordship. R. Turvey, *The Lord Rhys: Prince of Deheubarth* (Llandysul, 1997), pp. 90–3.

34. R. Liddiard, *Castles in Context: Power, Symbolism and Landscape, 1066 to 1500* (Macclesfield, 2005), p. 43.

35. See, for example, O. Creighton, *Castles and Landscapes: Power, Community and Fortification in Medieval England* (London, 2002).

of Gwynedd, Hugh Brodie and Rachel Swallow have led the way of late. The former has offered comment on the changing nature of the use of towers in native Welsh castles, linking the hitherto overlooked sequential development of first apsidal (or U-shaped) and then D-shaped towers to shifts in thinking over the inclusion of high-status accommodation in towers with a defensive function.[36] Swallow, meanwhile, has highlighted the close relationship between Llywelyn I and earl Ranulf of Chester in the years following the signing of Magna Carta.[37] Llywelyn's work at Cricieth has long been speculated to have emulated the designs of the gatehouses at Beeston, Montgomery and Whittington, all of which were in Ranulf's hands at one time or another and boasted twin D-shaped towers in that role; Avent dates Cricieth's construction to the 1230s accordingly, while Swallow suggests a slight revision to 1225–35.[38] However, Swallow also posits that Llywelyn adopted a policy of constructing castles such as Cricieth and Deganwy with the purpose of 'demarcat[ing] and consolidat[ing] lands for [his] heirs': 'The extent of the princes' power in the landscape was pinned down with the corporate design of emblematic castles of almost identical and innovative architecture.'[39]

Brodie and Swallow are but two of several writers who have begun the process of rescuing native Welsh castle architecture from the grave Hemp unwittingly dug for it. Few would argue with the view that the rudimentary nature of, say, the outer defences at early masonry constructions such as Dolbadarn, Dolwyddelan or even Carn Fadryn resulted from a lack of experience with the construction of castles in stone. However, with the benefit of a holistic view of each castle that incorporates its history, socio-economic and political contexts, and its builders as well as its architecture, examples dating from the thirteenth century increasingly look less like architectural incompetence and more like native responses to the ever-present problem of lack of resources, informed by often complex and nuanced political agendas. Ewloe once more provides a pertinent example. In a closely argued recent article, David Stephenson has succeeded in giving to this previously anonymous castle something of its history, identifying its use for negotiations between Dafydd II and Llywelyn II and their adversaries in the early 1240s and late 1250s respectively. More importantly, however, he convincingly argues that Ewloe's impressive and picturesque but otherwise peculiar siting was dictated by its symbolic value as the site of a famous victory by Owain Gwynedd over the invading forces of Henry II in what Lloyd called the battle of Coed Eulo in 1157. Almost certainly begun by Llywelyn I following his recapture of the north-east from King John in the early

---

36. H. Brodie, 'Apsidal and D-shaped towers of the Princes of Gwynedd', AC, 164 (2015), pp. 231–43.
37. R. Swallow, 'Gateways to power: the castles of Ranulf III of Chester and Llywelyn the Great of Gwynedd', AJ, 171 (2014), pp. 289–311.
38. 'Gateways to power', p. 306 and reference therein. Swallow further suggested that the start date might even have been slightly earlier, given that Montgomery castle – viewed as an important exemplar for Cricieth – was begun in 1223 ('Gateways to power', p. 306).
39. Swallow, 'Gateways to power', p. 307.

1210s, its prestige value as a construction 'intended to announce, and to symbolise in stone the restoration by a ruler of Gwynedd of enduring control of a territory that had seen a most memorable feat of arms by his forebears'[40] offers an entirely plausible explanation as to why its military function seems to play second fiddle to considerations of aesthetics and location (see chapter 1).

Idiosyncrasies can, of course, be observed at native Welsh castles, but we may seek explanations for them in places other than the supposedly ignorant or wayward impulses of their authors. Compared with English kings, or even the wealthier of the kings' magnates, the princes of Wales had limited means,[41] and sought to mitigate this problem using any and all methods at their disposal. Their choice of hilltop sites has most frequently been ascribed to this need, but the more unusual elements of the castles' architecture can likewise be put down to the necessity for making optimal use of limited resources. For example, as has long been realised, the aforementioned apsidal tower allowed the Welsh to kill two birds with one stone, having the floor space to provide accommodation while discharging a defensive function by dint of its semi-circular end, which was always sited either to dominate an approach to the castle or, on occasion, to provide enfilading fire.[42] In the same way, liberal use was made of rock-cut ditches as a cheap but effective way of bolstering a castle's passive strength and making an assault more difficult.[43]

Other features that in previous times were hailed as evidence of inadequacies in a castle's design can with hindsight be accounted for by a combination of careful consideration of the likely purpose of the castles and examination of the remaining archaeological evidence. The entrances to native Welsh castles built by the two Llywelyns have frequently been criticised on account of their slightness, but on reflection their unobtrusiveness would seem to be all of a piece with the defences of which they form a part. Traffic to many of these hill-top castles was unlikely to have been heavy, and several required points of entry to accommodate items no bigger than a horse or a cart. Entrances were therefore often small and relatively

40. Stephenson, 'A reconsideration', p. 253.
41. See LlapG, pp. 338–88 for a comprehensive overview of the political and financial strictures on Llywelyn II during the decade or so after the concluding of the Treaty of Montgomery in 1267.
42. For the dual function of apsidal towers see R. Avent, *Castles of the Princes of Gwynedd* (London, 1983), p. 11. Avent's reasoning has recently been enlarged upon by Brodie, 'Apsidal and D-shaped towers', pp. 238–9. The deployment of apsidal towers in a role dominating the main approach is particularly obvious at Carndochan and Y Bere, whose southern apsidal towers project beyond the curtain walls, commanding the paths leading up to the entrances. Y Bere's chapel tower enfilades the entire length of its eastern curtain, though King was of the opinion that this was coincidental; see J. Beverley Smith and Ll. Beverley Smith (eds), *A History of Merioneth Vol. 2: The Middle Ages* (Cardiff, 2001), p. 399 and reference.
43. Avent, *Dolwyddelan Castle/Dolbadarn Castle*, p. 5.

unheralded openings in the curtain.[44] Even so, the need to provide covering fire for them was nonetheless appreciated. At the largest castles, impressive twin-towered gatehouses guarded the entrances at Bryn Amlwg[45] and the first phase of works at Cricieth, as well as the Powysian castle of Dinas Brân,[46] while Y Bere boasted a barbican, a passage situated outside the castle ward through which attackers must pass, subjecting themselves to attack from above, in order to gain the castle entrance. The main entrances at Dolforwyn and Ewloe were overlooked by each castle's keep, while, of the smaller castles, recent excavations at Carndochan have at last pinpointed the location of the castle's long-lost entrance, nestled between the apsidal tower that dominates the site on the entrance's western flank and a D-shaped tower on its eastern flank, the two between them providing what must have been a very satisfactory enfilading effect.[47] Meanwhile, the irregular siting of towers that so impelled earlier generations of writers to excoriation is more easily understood in many cases as a feature resulting from the topography of these castles' locations. Placing towers at the angles of curtain walls would be impractical at sites whose summits require so many of them in order to provide an effective enclosure; but it was often also the case that approaches on some sides were so exceptionally steep as to allow for the construction of a curtain without incorporating a tower at all, as was the case, for example, at Dinas Brân.[48]

To an Anglo-Norman architect, unused to the uneven ground and practical restrictions incumbent on his Welsh counterpart, the results of such policies may have seemed odd to the eye. However, there is no doubting the effectiveness of many of these Welsh castles, and they left lasting impressions on those who beheld them, such as Henry de Lacy, who in 1277 wrote to Edward I that, in his opinion, there was no stronger castle anywhere in England or Wales than Dinas Brân, so much so that it was worthy of being retained.[49] Such personal opinions have but rarely come down to us, but other indications of the need to take seriously the business of investing and gaining possession of native Welsh castles can be discerned. In 1244 the justice of Chester was ordered to have four wooden towers built in the forest of the Wirral and to send two of them to the Welsh border for use by Henry III's army in Wales – an obvious acknowledgement of the perceived strength of native Welsh fortifications;[50] and the enormous armies sent to preside

44. D.J.C. King, 'Two castles in northern Powys: Dinas Brân and Caergwrle', AC, 123 (1974), p. 135.
45. This work has been identified as Welsh; see chapter 3.
46. David Stephenson has noted the likelihood that Dinas Brân was sponsored by Llywelyn II; see 'Potens et Prudens: Gruffudd ap Madog, Lord of Bromfield 1236–1269', WHR, 22 (2005), pp. 427–8.
47. D. Hopewell, 'High status medieval sites: Castell Carndochan Excavation Report 2015–16', Gwynedd Archaeological Trust (2016), p. 19.
48. King, 'Two castles in northern Powys', p. 123.
49. J.G. Edwards, *Calendar of Ancient Correspondence concerning Wales* (Cardiff, 1935), p. 83.
50. N.J.G. Pounds, *The Medieval Castle in England and Wales: A Social and Political History* (Cambridge, 1990), p. 112.

over the sieges at Y Bere during the war of 1282–3 and Dryslwyn and Newcastle Emlyn during the revolt of Rhys ap Maredudd in 1287–8, though perhaps primarily intended as shows of strength, are also surely reminders of the dangers these structures posed to invaders.[51]

Rehabilitation of the native Welsh castles as effective military installations is, as the above argues, long overdue. Up to a point, this book endorses the ideas of Colin Platt, for whom the perspective of Charles Coulson, who as long ago as the 1970s propounded the view that the chief function of a castle was to denote status rather than to act in a military role, has come to hold too much sway.[52] However, as Creighton and Liddiard noted in response, there can be no 'war or status' paradigm where castles of the thirteenth century are concerned:[53] this book was also written to integrate new perspectives and lines of evidence into a more balanced view of these castles that takes into consideration Coulson's thesis. Those looking for a concise and easy explanation of the locations and dispositions of native Welsh castles will be disappointed by this book. Some were raised with military objectives in mind. Some were built for largely symbolic reasons. Still others began life as one or the other, and were repurposed as time went on, according to the shifting agendas of successive princes; and yet acknowledgement of this kaleidoscopic collection of justifications for the ruins that lie before us is absent from the discourse on these works. Stephenson's recent call for 'reflection on the richness and variety of factors that might lie behind the construction of Welsh princely castles'[54] was prompted by this conceptual gap. All too often, native Welsh castles are assessed from a particular viewpoint – that formulated by consideration of Anglo-Norman methods of warfare – and found wanting, but we would do better if we took as our starting point the idea that the castles fulfilled some functions for certain rulers at certain times in history, and other functions at other times, and, indeed, that those functions themselves underwent modification. These changes in attitude towards the use of this or that castle can in some cases be inferred through careful analysis of the historical record. Combining elements of geospatial and topographical analysis with assessments of the nature and limitations of Venedotian power during the period under study, this book argues – pace Glanville Jones's analysis – that, where the construction of castles was concerned, there was no single 'defensive policy' espoused by the princes of Wales. Such an idea is rooted in the conviction that the security needs of a polity are both static and given equal weight from ruler to ruler. In the event, however, the first prince of Wales to raise castles did not inaugurate a defensive policy that was then handed down, as it

51. R.F. Walker, 'William de Valence and the army of west Wales, 1282–1283', WHR, 18 (1997), pp. 420–1; R. Griffiths, 'The revolt of Rhys ap Maredudd, 1287–88', WHR, 3 (1966), pp. 121–43.

52. C. Platt, 'Revisionism in Castle Studies: a caution', Medieval Archaeology, 51 (2007), pp. 83–102.

53. O. Creighton and R. Liddiard, 'Fighting yesterday's battle: beyond war or status in Castle Studies', Medieval Archaeology, 52 (2008), p. 161.

54. Stephenson, 'A reconsideration', p. 249.

were, from successor to successor. Instead, it makes more sense to conceive of the princes having followed several different policies.

The following seeks to show that the construction of castles was dictated by political needs that changed over time and, though constrained by the limited resources of the house of Gwynedd, incorporated architectural features in the castles appropriate to their siting and function. Often this function was to establish (or re-establish) authority in a given region; sometimes it facilitated the prince's wider aggrandisement. Only in the final phase of Venedotian castle-building – that inaugurated by Llywelyn II in the middle and later years of his principate – can we be reasonably certain that we are witnessing a prince seeing to the territorial defence of *pura Wallia*.

This notion of a succession of building policies, each with its own set of military, social and political imperatives, is borne out by a comparison of the reigns of the four leaders of Wales to assume the princeship during the thirteenth century. The position of prince of Wales was in some ways analogous to, say, that of the king of Scots. The two rulers enjoyed many of the same rights and exercised similar powers: they passed and amended laws, sanctioned the issuance of coinage and possessed the authority to conduct diplomacy with other countries. However, the smooth transition of power from the king to his successor seen in Scotland throughout the twelfth and thirteenth centuries (until the Great Cause of 1290–2, at any rate) has no parallel in Wales, where continuity may have been chronological, but was seldom institutional.[55] Dafydd II inherited his father Llywelyn's kingdom in 1240 and almost immediately was forced into accepting an inferior position as the price of support from Henry III owing to internal strife fostered by supporters of his half-brother and rival for the princeship, Gruffudd; for the first four years of his principate he styled himself merely as *princeps Norwallie*, a title not used since the earliest years of Llywelyn's reign.[56] His ability to exercise his authority beyond Gwynedd was obliterated by the terms of the Treaty of Gwerneigron, signed by him on Henry's successful expedition into Gwynedd in 1241, and the final two years of his life were spent waging war against Henry and the Marcher lords.[57] That war came to an end in defeat following his death, and his successor, Llywelyn II, had to rebuild the administrative machinery of Welsh royal government from this unpromising position; it is during his principate that changes in the make-up of that government can be discerned. Documents issued by his chancellery indicate the presence of magnates from beyond Gwynedd serving in his council in contradistinction to that of the first Llywelyn, and his network of local officials ballooned in the later years of his principate,[58] far outstripping anything his uncle

55. *LlapG*, pp. 274–9.
56. *AWR*, pp. 29, 78.
57. *AWR*, pp. 29–30, 78.
58. *LlapG*, pp. 255–60.

or grandfather might have put in place during their reigns. Finally, following the assumption of enormous monetary obligations after concluding the Treaty of Montgomery (1267) with Henry, the prince's finances were almost certainly more constrained than for any of his predecessors.[59] In other words, the nature of Welsh royal government in the thirteenth century was highly changeable, and it is scarcely to be wondered that the built heritage of the princes exhibits such enormous variations in form and role.

For the purposes of analysing these variations, two sets of terms are introduced. Firstly, the siting of castles is interpreted according to what shall be referred to here as considerations of *microlocation* and *macrolocation*. Microlocation is defined as pertaining to the immediate surroundings of a castle, loosely demarcated as the terrain within, say, a bowshot of its walls. This seems a relevant aspect to consider in the Welsh example because so much of what we see in the remains of native Welsh castles is dictated by the unique properties of each site. Such considerations are frequently underplayed, or omitted altogether, from surveys of castles in England and elsewhere, but this approach is surely warranted in Gwynedd: rarely has the reliance of military architecture on terrain been more marked. Macrolocation, meanwhile, refers to the more conventional assessment of function in relation to the area or region in which a castle stands; equally, however, I define this far more broadly than is usual, taking into consideration symbolic and historical reasons as well as strategic ones.

Taken in tandem with the surviving documentary and archaeological evidence, this approach allows us to begin to make sense of the native Welsh castles – to begin to understand why they were built, and how their authors perceived them. To assist in this, this book advances a tripartite model that defines the castles and, in some cases, discrete phases of construction according to three distinct building policies. For transparency's sake, the artificial nature of this model should be noted. No such chronology was instituted by the princes – at least, not that we know of – and this book is not an attempt to prove that they consciously conceived of the castles they raised in these terms. History is rarely so regimented, and the body of evidence is often simply too thin to admit either of definitive chronologies or paradigmatic shifts in thinking. Rather, the model is here used simply as a way of reconciling the observed characteristics of this exceptionally diverse set of structures with one another. When one sees gatehouses used in some castles but not others, or enfilading fire extensively made use of in one and entirely neglected in another, it is clear that the 'one size fits all' approach to the castles so often and unthinkingly used by historians will not suffice, and we have to theorise about them in a different way, even if it means our analysis must be based on the balance of probabilities.

The three policies advanced here, which it is suggested very roughly correspond to the early and late reign of Llywelyn I and the reign of Llywelyn II,

---

59. *LlapG*, pp. 309–19, 268–71, 361–5.

are defined as strategies of *emplacement*. The martial connotations of the term are deliberate for, even when it appears that a castle's primary function was to function as a symbol of prestige or to demarcate territory, one may nevertheless take the decision to build a masonry castle, as opposed to an opulent *maerdref* or unfortified princely residence, as a broad recognition of the need to establish a military presence within a particular area.[60]

The first of these strategies I refer to as *expeditionary emplacement*, which describes the policy of Llywelyn I in the early years of his reign, up to c.1220. The principal factor here in the deployment of castles is the fact that Llywelyn did not inherit a unified kingdom and so had to not only establish his right to such a kingdom by force but also define its extent. The castles he raised can be understood as demarcating the territory under his control, underscoring his pre-eminence in north Wales. Several occupy macrolocations well within Gwynedd's boundaries, disposing us to conclude that they were built to overawe and impress Llywelyn's competitors and rivals within the house of Gwynedd in the first instance. They also functioned as reminders of Gwynedd's supremacy and, by extension, Llywelyn's right to govern it. Dolbadarn, erected at the heart of an area of immense mythic importance within the Eryri massif, and Ewloe, emplaced at the site of a major battlefield victory over a king of England, functioned to connect Llywelyn's reign in the most intimate fashion with his people's history, and thereby foster the beginnings of a Venedotian political ideology.

The second policy dates from the final two decades of Llywelyn's reign, in which he was able to consolidate the gains he had made. This was a time of relative peace, and Llywelyn was doubtless aware that he had the opportunity and means to avoid the decades-long upheaval that followed the disputed succession of 1170; in these years he turned his attentions to securing the princely inheritance for his son, Dafydd.[61] At the same time he sought to elevate his position from that of head of the house of Gwynedd to ruler of all of native Wales. In his peerless introduction to *The Acts of Welsh Rulers 1120–1283* (2005, rev. edn 2010), Huw Pryce demonstrated how Llywelyn's style developed in the course of his reign to reflect the extent of his authority. Initially referred to as *princeps Norwallie* (prince of north Wales), by 1230 at the latest (and possibly as early as 1225) he had adopted a different style: *princeps de Aberffrau, dominus Snaudon* (prince of Aberffraw, lord of Snowdonia [Eryri]). The style referenced the tradition, then being actively drawn upon and indeed moulded by elements within Llywelyn's royal government, that the king of Aberffraw – that is, the ruler of the house of Gwynedd – enjoyed pre-

60.  See N. Johnstone, 'Llys and Maerdref: the royal courts of the Prince of Gwynedd', SC, 34 (2000), pp. 167–201 for an overview of the role of the *maerdref* in thirteenth-century Wales.

61.  For example, the flurry of diplomatic activity in 1226 designed to legitimise Llywelyn's consort Joan (a bastard child of king John), thereby removing any stigma attaching to her son, Llywelyn's heir Dafydd, is analysed in D. Stephenson and C.O. Jones, 'The date and the context of the birth of Dafydd ap Llywelyn', FHSJ, 39 (2012), pp. 21–32.

eminence over the other kings in Wales and, in turn, paid gold to the crown of London. This title, therefore, accomplished three things. Firstly, it functioned as an implicit challenge to the Treaty of Worcester, concluded between Llywelyn and the royal government of Henry III in 1218, which stated that Henry had the right to the homage of the other lords of Wales; secondly, it emphasised Llywelyn's right to overlordship of Powys and Deheubarth while avoiding the (possibly politically unacceptable) adoption of the style *princeps Wallie*; and, thirdly, the inclusion of *dominus Snaudon* restated Llywelyn's direct rule over Gwynedd.[62]

Such aggrandisement – and, indeed, the fact that it was tacitly accepted without Gwynedd – reflected the lofty orbit in which Llywelyn now moved. From 1218 he could count the earl of Chester, Ranulf de Blondeville – one of the most powerful magnates in England – as a trusted friend and ally. As Ranulf's lands abutted Llywelyn's in the north-east, the prince could consider himself safe from incursions on his territory from that direction; and with recognition of his pre-eminence at the courts of Powys and Deheubarth, his castle-building in this period seems to indicate a preoccupation not with authority but with influence. Following Rachel Swallow's perceptive analysis of this stage of Llywelyn's reign, his castles dating from the 1220s and 1230s – Cricieth, Y Bere and Deganwy[63] – are here described as examples of *corporate emplacement*. Unlike his earlier constructions they are comparatively large, incorporate several substantial towers and, at Cricieth and Y Bere, also include gatehouses. Most importantly, considerations of location are noticeably different from those pertaining at their older counterparts. While Deganwy was built on the site of an earlier timber castle first erected in the eleventh century, Cricieth and Y Bere were, it is suggested, deliberately chosen for their arresting command of the surrounding landscape (and seascape). Their purpose, then, was to amplify Gwynedd's supremacy to the lords under Llywelyn's aegis, but also to those from without. Cricieth and Deganwy did duty guarding the maritime approaches to Gwynedd, and they enjoyed special prominence, being highly visible to traders and visitors from beyond Welsh shores. Y Bere, meanwhile, is situated slightly inland, a little beyond the head of what would have been the Dysynni estuary in Meirionydd; if this location is rather less conspicuous, it resembles the other two in scale and, like Cricieth and Deganwy, also made abundant and conspicuous use of that typically Welsh innovation, the apsidal tower. As far as can be made out, these structures of aggrandisement were just that and, with one possible exception (see Conclusion), manipulation of their

62. This paragraph is heavily indebted to *AWR*; see Introduction for a comprehensive overview of princely styles in thirteenth-century Wales.

63. Our understanding of the very ruinous castle at Deganwy is far from complete; the last substantial excavations were carried out by Leslie Alcock in the 1960s, and so it is included tentatively here. However, there are good reasons for thinking Deganwy played a more important role in native Welsh society in peacetime during the early thirteenth century than its current remains seem to indicate. See chapter 2.

immediate environs did not extend to the surrounding landscape either for effect or for military reasons.[64] Nevertheless, the form of these castles pointed to native Welsh ingenuities and underscored the increasing resources commanded by a prince who was without peer among his countrymen and women.

The final policy was enacted during the reign of Llywelyn's grandson and namesake, Llywelyn II, who inherited the throne from his uncle, Dafydd II, in 1246 and ruled jointly alongside his brothers Owain Goch and (from 1252 onwards) Dafydd III until their defeat in the battle of Bryn Derwin in 1255 paved the way for Llywelyn to assume sole leadership of Gwynedd. By 1271 he ruled over what could, for the only time in the Age of the Princes, be accurately referred to as the Principality of Wales: a polity including all of Gwynedd, Powys and Deheubarth, as well as not insignificant portions of Shropshire conquered or otherwise occupied by the prince's men. *Defensive emplacement* is the term employed here to describe the policy of castle-building embarked on by Llywelyn during this period. Beginning in 1257, Llywelyn began modest restoration works at Ewloe, and he continued to strengthen existing castles or build new ones throughout the 1260s and into the early 1270s. Of the three policies outlined here, these works may be most easily understood as military in nature, with the appearance of several features designed to bolster defences at existing castles and castles on the borders of Wales acquired or raised with the seeming intention of commanding key routes into Llywelyn's kingdom. We cannot be emphatic on this point – the documentary evidence is too scarce – but analysis of microlocation and macrolocation appear to indicate that, in establishing these fortifications, consideration was given to the need to defend the Principality from attack. In this Llywelyn was forced to make hard choices. J. Beverley Smith has eloquently detailed the ways in which the prince's coffers were strained by the enormous sums of money he was bound to pay the English crown under the terms of the Treaty of Montgomery, and it is suggested below that his castle-building policy was not yet brought to fruition when Edward I waged war in Wales in 1276–7. Nevertheless, the replacement of apsidal towers with D-shaped towers during this period, a development Brodie associates with a greater emphasis on military function (see chapter 3), coupled with the possible appearance of the gate passage in Venedotian castle architecture during this period, speaks to Llywelyn's determination to dictate the strategy of invading forces as far as that was possible. These policies are compared in Table 0.1.

A note of caution should be sounded here. In the case of the native Welsh castles, the documentary evidence is extremely sparse. Of the eleven castles considered, none receives more than a dozen mentions relating to its usage by the princes in contemporary sources. Records of building costs, and fragmentary ones

---

64. For a refutation of the idea of a 'designed landscape' in medieval England, R. Liddiard and T. Williamson, 'There by design? some reflections on medieval elite landscapes', AJ, 165 (2008), pp. 520–35.

at that, exist for just one (Dolforwyn) during the period of Welsh occupation. Even dates of construction are lacking, with the beginning of works more or less securely dated only in the case of Y Bere (1221). What is advanced in the following pages is therefore informed to a substantial extent by extrapolations based on archaeological evidence, the patchy historical record and reasonable inferences about the dispositions of the Welsh rulers. In situations where (as at Dolbadarn) we cannot reliably identify the beginning of construction to within ten years, or are unable (as at Ewloe) to establish consensus on the castle's principal usage, we should be alert to the possibility of alternative interpretations for the features we see.

It also goes without saying that the above typology is a means to an end; doubtless neither Llywelyn I nor his grandson thought about their castles in quite so clinical a fashion. The characterisation of the castle-building policy of Llywelyn II as defensive is also at odds with the belief that the Welsh princes did not intend their castles to serve as defences against an attack by the English crown. My reasons for thinking that the idea of repelling – or rather, withstanding – an invasion by the king did in fact have some say in the castle-building policy Llywelyn II pursued are given in chapter 3; there can be no certainty on such an issue, but my feeling is that it is at least as likely as not. We should also acknowledge that we are missing large pieces of the puzzle where the Welsh attitude to castle-building is concerned. It smacks of hubris to think otherwise when there are so many oddities in the historical and archaeological record: for example, beyond their novelty we have no convincing explanation for the near-total absence of references to castles in the works of the princes' poets.[65] Our analysis is necessarily hobbled by the immense gulf that lies between the medieval mind and our own. As Tadhg O'Keefe and Margaret Coughlan put it in their discussion of a group of thirteenth-century castles in Ireland,

> Analysis of formal design is an essential part of archaeological enquiry, but we must be careful not to draw conclusions based on formal similarities without placing emphasis on conceptual similarities. ... we do not see [castles] as they were seen in the 13th century. We do not know whether the builders thought about the castles as conforming to a type. ... The ground plans, which we use to reduce the castles to two-dimensional entities in the pages of books, were not seen in the middle ages, so they do not necessarily articulate the way that interior or exterior space was perceived or experienced.[66]

Our task is made doubly difficult by the often scanty archaeological remains and the relative silence of the historical record on how these castles performed

---

65. In contradistinction to the relatively numerous references to walled fortifications occurring in early Welsh poetry; WS, p. 194.

66. T. O'Keefe and M. Coughlan, 'The chronology and formal affinities of the Ferns donjon, Co. Wexford', in Kenyon and O'Conor (eds), *The Medieval Castle*, p. 148.

Table 0.1 Native Welsh masonry castles of the princes of Wales – a typology of emplacement.

| Type of emplacement | Period | Chief roles | Typical microlocation | Typical macrolocation | Architectural features | Examples |
|---|---|---|---|---|---|---|
| Expeditionary | 1194–c.1220 | Delimitation of territory; prestige and expression of power to Welsh lords | Inland hilltop site | At junctions of roads/defiles; also symbolic locations | Single ward; rectangular keep | Dolwyddelan, Dolbadarn, Ewloe, Carndochan |
| Corporate | c.1220–40 | Prestige; expression of power to English/continental observers; attempt to delimit sphere of influence(?) | Coastal hilltop site; estuarine hilltop site | Overlooking trade routes; emplaced for maximum visibility | Prominent gatehouses; increasing use of apsidal (U-shaped) towers | Cricieth (first phase), Y Bere, Deganwy (Welsh phase) |
| Defensive | 1246–82 | Attempt to render the Principality defensible/influence the strategy of an invading army | Inland hilltop sites (new builds) | At junctions of roads/defiles near border of the Principality (new builds) | Switch from apsidal to D-shaped towers | Cricieth (second phase), Dinas Brân, Dolforwyn, Sennybridge, Bryn Amlwg, Y Bere (south tower)? |

Note: Although built by Dafydd III from 1277 onwards, Caergwrle castle is not considered here, as Dafydd built it for his own seat, and it would appear never to have figured in the plans of the princes of Wales.

in times of peace and war. One sees a castle in its true colours in the context of conflict, but for the duration of the Age of the Princes the masonry castles of the princes were very seldomly besieged and to our knowledge never served as mustering points. In times of peace many of the usual techniques for analysing the ways in which the castles were utilised cannot be applied in the Welsh example. The nomenclature of the various components of these castles is lost (the towers of the only important exception, Cricieth, bear names given to them after the Edwardian conquest). Analyses of the interactions of these castles with the morphology of adjacent towns cannot be carried out because such settlements have either yet to be excavated or postdate the castles' construction; and, because almost all of the towers and internal buildings are either badly ruined or reduced to their footings in all but a couple of instances, attempting access analysis is futile.[67] Some readers will also doubtless find fault with some of the attributions of authorship and dating put forward here. All that can be said in response is that these problems are endemic where the princes' castles are concerned, such is the poverty of the written sources and the incompleteness of the archaeological investigations, and that every care has been taken to provide convincing warrants for each claim. In spite of these difficulties, there are reasons for thinking that the princes' works are nevertheless pervious to an analysis that takes into account the shifting agendas of each of their authors as their reigns developed. In approaching the princes' works in this way we may transcend the problems of scarce documentary evidence with which so many historians have had to contend in the past, and come a little closer to resolving the seeming contradictions thrown up by their existence.

---

67. Dolforwyn is a notable exception; L. Butler, 'Dolforwyn Castle: prospect and retrospect', in Kenyon and O'Conor, *The Medieval Castle*, p. 158. Even this, however, requires some imagination, and offers only speculation as to the internal layout of the now vanished upper levels of the towers.

# 1

## The early castles of Llywelyn I ab Iorwerth (1194–c.1220)

Llywelyn I ab Iorwerth entered the fraught world of Venedotian politics early and in earnest. Born around 1173 at Dolwyddelan, of his father, Iorwerth Drwyndwn, virtually nothing is known beyond the likelihood that his claim to the throne was denied following his father Owain Gwynedd's death in 1170, perhaps due to medieval objections to physical deformity in rulers (Drwyndwn translates into English as 'flat-nosed').[1] Iorwerth died around 1174, but he apparently held Nant Conwy, the southern portion of the commote of Arllechwedd in which Dolwyddelan castle stood, on the south-eastern edge of the Eryri massif.[2]

Llywelyn's mother, Marared, was a daughter of Madog ap Maredudd (d. 1160), under whose leadership the house of Powys had undergone a remarkable resurgence after its eclipse the previous century. Styled *rex Powissensium* ('king of the Powysians'),[3] during a thirty-year career Madog unified his fractious house and had even annexed the lordship of Oswestry to Powys by 1149.[4] While Llywelyn's childhood went unrecorded, it has been persuasively argued that he was brought up in the Powysian royal court,[5] in accordance with the precedent that heirs were often sent to be reared at the courts of allies. Such an upbringing would naturally yield a certain sympathy with the Powysians – a theory that may also go some way toward explaining his keen interest in the politics of neighbouring Shropshire during his reign.

Llywelyn was enough of a presence to have been noticed by Gerald of Wales on his 1188 tour of Wales preaching the Crusade. Gerald described him as having begun to challenge the positions of Dafydd I ab Owain (hereafter Dafydd I) and Rhodri, both of whom had played prominent roles in the leadership of Gwynedd

---

1. LltG, pp. 22–3.
2. J.E. Lloyd, *A History of Wales* (London, 1911), p. 587.
3. D. Stephenson, 'Madog ap Maredudd, *rex Powissensium*', WHR, 24 (2008), p. 21.
4. BYT RBH, p. 129. Stephenson, 'Madog ap Maredudd', p. 9 makes the important observation that Madog had annexed the lordship by 1149 (in which year he is recorded as raising or repairing the castle at Oswestry), and not necessarily in 1149.
5. Lloyd, *History of Wales*, p. 587; LltG, p. 29; MP, p. 297.

since Owain Gwynedd's death, and who apparently shared power for a period in the 1170s and thereafter.[6] The former has long been understood as the effective successor to Owain. His usage of styles such as *rex Norwallie* and *princeps Norwallie* is a matter of record; his prestigious marriage to Emma of Anjou in 1174 was without precedent for a Welsh ruler; and his presence before Henry II at Oxford in 1177 alongside the Lord Rhys, prince of south Wales, has been interpreted as evidence of pre-eminence.[7] In fact, his writ may not have run in quite so unencumbered a fashion within Gwynedd.[8] Nevertheless, it is clear that any attempt by Llywelyn to gain power in the troubled kingdom would involve dealing with Dafydd and Rhodri.

Llywelyn came of age around 1187, and the following decade or so has been described as Llywelyn's 'wilderness years', not because of any perceived wayward streak but because the period is so opaque: very few sources survive and those that do tend to contradict one another.[9] We may reasonably speculate that Llywelyn was being touted as a potential leader of Gwynedd from an early stage. His claim to the throne was certainly credible, more so in some ways than those of his rivals, as his father was Owain Gwynedd's only legitimate son;[10] and, if the praise poetry addressed to him is any indication, Llywelyn clearly distinguished himself in arms at an early age.[11] It has been surmised that his supporters may have gone so far as to adopt various strategies for promoting his succession in the late 1180s and early 1190s, including the issuance of Welsh coinage from the mint at Rhuddlan.[12] These may, perhaps, even have included commissioning elements of the prose works later known as the *Mabinogion* in order to present stories detailing a legitimate scion's rise to power that could be understood allegorically by their

6. C. Insley, 'The Wilderness Years of Llywelyn the Great', *Thirteenth Century England*, 9 (2003), p. 165, wherein the unique complexities of this interpretation are also discussed.

7. *AWR*, pp. 24, 75; A.J. Roderick, 'Marriage and politics in Wales, 1066–1282', *WHR*, 4 (1968), p. 14. Insley, 'The Wilderness Years', p. 165 offers a different interpretation of Dafydd's presence before Henry in 1177, suggesting that Dafydd met with the king in order to gain his support against his Welsh enemies.

8. Insley, 'The Wilderness Years', pp. 165, 166–9.

9. Insley, 'The Wilderness Years', pp. 165, 166–9.

10. *LltG*, p. 24.

11. E.M. Jones (ed.), *Gwaith Llywarch ap Llywelyn 'Prydydd Y Moch'* [The Work of Llywarch ap Llywelyn 'Prydydd Y Moch'] (Cardiff, 1991), poem 18, which celebrates the prince's feats in arms, was probably written to commemorate his coming of age.

12. See E. Besly, 'Short Cross and other medieval coins from Llanfaes, Anglesey', *British Numismatic Journal*, 65 (1995), pp. 46–83, especially p. 55. Besly plausibly ascribes the issuing of coinage at the Rhuddlan mint at the end of the twelfth century to Dafydd I. C.O. Jones, *The Revolt of Madog ap Llywelyn* (Llanrwst, 2008), p. 36, n. 9 suggests that the imitative Short Cross issues may conceivably have continued to have been commissioned by or on behalf of Llywelyn in an attempt to legitimise his claim to the throne. According to M. Allen, the Rhuddlan mint 'made a significant contribution to the local currency of north Wales'; 'Silver production and the money supply in England and Wales, 1086–c.1500', *Economic History Review*, 64 (2011), p. 125.

audience.[13] Adopting the trappings of power – striking coins, commissioning works of literature and so forth – may have acted in the febrile times in which the young Llywelyn lived as a way, so to speak, of waging war against his fellow claimants to the throne by other means.

This argument rests on circumstantial evidence, and it would be unwise to place too much weight on it. However, the erection of fortifications would fit well into the pattern of aggrandisement it indicates. The building of castles was begun by Welsh lords in the 1110s and the historical record is studded with scattered references to castles throughout that century. Examination of the confirmed and conjectured sites of these early castles show that most were constructed out of timber. However, that the ability to raise masonry castles – or masonry *towers*, at any rate – had evolved among the sons and grandsons of Owain Gwynedd is surely indicated by the appearance of a flurry of such sites datable to the last quarter or so of the twelfth century, including the well-known fortifications at Dinas Emrys, Prysor, Deudraeth and Aber Iâ. The authorship of this collection of towers is in most cases unknown, but they clearly operated not only as outposts meant to guard important roads and defiles but also, by dint of their novelty in Gwynedd, as indicators of prestige through which claimants to the throne could underscore their authority and might.

Llywelyn's accession to the throne of Gwynedd is normally dated to 1194. According to the most important and well-informed of the native Welsh chronicles, *Brut Y Tywysogyon* (The Chronicle of the Princes), in that year Llywelyn fought and won a resounding victory at the battle of Aberconwy on the fringes of Gwynedd uwch Conwy, defeating the forces of Dafydd I.[14] The next twenty years saw, with one exception, a succession of military and diplomatic successes that cemented Llywelyn's position as ruler in the north: his capture and banishment of Dafydd to England in 1197–8;[15] a further battlefield victory at Mold in 1199, this time against the forces of the earl of Chester – an exploit so spectacular to his contemporaries that he would be lauded for it in verse;[16] the peace treaty concluded with King John in 1201;[17] his securing of lands on the Llŷn peninsula

13. W. Parker, 'Gwynedd, Ceredigion and the political geography of the Mabinogi', NLWJ, 23 (2002), pp. 365–9.
14. BYT Pen MS 20, p. 190. The nature in which the various strands of evidence for the battle conflict with one another is described by Insley, 'The Wilderness Years', p. 166.
15. It was presumably Dafydd's capture that recently prompted David Crouch to reassign the beginning of Llywelyn's reign to the former year: *Medieval Britain c. 1000–1500* (Cambridge, 2017), p. 292.
16. See Llywarch ap Llywelyn's poem to Llywelyn, where it is implied that the castle there was burned to the ground by the prince: 'No delusion, since Mold, wolf-pack fortress/Rhun's descendant's triumph:/Towers burnt, each one gutted,/Mighty flame, Alun's [the neighbourhood in which Mold stands] folk in flight.' J.P. Clancy, *Medieval Welsh Poems* (Dublin, 2003), p. 160.
17. Pryce, 'Anglo-Welsh agreements', pp. 2–3.

and in Eifionydd from his final significant opponent in Gwynedd, Maredudd ap Cynan;[18] the highly advantageous marriage with John's illegitimate daughter, Joan (Siwan), around 1205;[19] and a successful incursion into southern Powys in 1208 that resulted in its effective annexation, at least temporarily.[20] By the end of 1215 – the year in which Llywelyn appeared as one of the very few non-English individuals named in Magna Carta[21] – the borders of his realm extended as far south as Ceredigion and as far east as Shrewsbury. Only three years later, his position was fortified by the Treaty of Worcester, in which the minority government of Henry III recognised his authority and granted him custodianship over the king's castles at Carmarthen and Cardigan.[22] The undisputed overlord of Powys and Deheubarth, a feared aggressor in the March and an ally of Ranulf de Blondeville, earl of Chester and Philip Augustus of France, by the end of the decade Llywelyn could with justification be said to have firmly woven himself into the fabric of Anglo-Norman, and indeed western European, politics.

Llywelyn began his career as an author of masonry castles in this way. On the one hand, he was faced by the need to define the boundaries of his kingdom in Wales – to mark out his borders and delimit the reach of his Welsh and Marcher neighbours. On the other hand, there was the need – surely recognised from the moment he emerged as a prospective leader of Gwynedd – to achieve recognition of his status in the eyes of the king of England, who projected his power in the southern half of Britain with a long and mighty arm. At this early stage in his career, this meant impressing his will to power on the English crown's proxies, namely the Marcher lords, and such native Welsh rulers as drifted into English orbits. Llywelyn's military and architectural initiatives in the first half of his reign were set in motion with these goals in mind. The four castles considered in this chapter reflect Llywelyn's modest means at the beginning of his principate. All four are constructed on a small scale and bear the hallmarks of compromises and tensions resulting from suboptimal siting, methods of construction and layout. They nevertheless fulfilled Llywelyn's expeditionary purpose well enough, serving to establish his aegis and project his power in their respective districts. Hopewell's description of Carndochan, which could well be applied also to Dolbadarn,

---

18. AWR, p. 26. Maredudd's discomfiture was gradual; he had been expelled from his lands on the Llŷn peninsula by Llywelyn in 1201, and lost Eifionydd in 1202.

19. LltG, p. 47. By far the best treatment of Joan's life and career is L. Wilkinson, 'Joan, wife of Llywelyn the Great', *Thirteenth Century England*, 10 (2005), pp. 81–94.

20. LltG, p. 51. The annexation occurred at the expense of easy relations with John, however; C.O. Jones, 'A rupture, sudden and unaccountable? King John's Welsh incursion of 1209 reconsidered', WHR, 30 (2020), pp. 1–18.

21. See J. Beverley Smith, 'Magna Carta and the Charters of the Welsh Princes', *English Historical Review*, 99 (1984), pp. 344–62, particularly pp. 345–6, for review of the three clauses pertaining to Wales within the charter.

22. LlapG, pp. 21–2; Pryce, 'Anglo-Welsh agreements', p. 9.

Dolwyddelan and Ewloe – that it is 'impressive in a local context' only[23] – cannot be improved upon.

## The timber castles, the masonry towers, Dolbadarn and Dolwyddelan

What was the nature of the built inheritance Llywelyn gained when he came of age? His father had, it seems, been in possession of Nant Conwy, which contained Tomen Castell in Dolwyddelan, Llywelyn's reputed birthplace. Excavations carried out in the early 1960s were inconclusive as to the nature of the rectangular tower that graced the mound; the foundations were discovered and found to be made out of stone, but the lack of mortar was interpreted as indicating that the rooms above were probably made of timber.[24] By 1202, by which time the prince had cleared Gwynedd of challengers to his position, other fortifications had fallen into his possession. Dinas Emrys, the Norman fortification at Aberlleiniog and several others came under his aegis. Any discussion of what, if anything, Llywelyn did with these sites is purely speculative, but it is at least conceivable that some were made defensible, or that Llywelyn undertook to maintain the defences already in existence. It certainly stands to reason that, once he gained possession of them, questions of form and function became important ones. The decade-long presence of Normans in the north during the 1080s and 1090s[25] had left a permanent reminder in the spate of castles dotted along the coast: mottes at Prestatyn, Rhuddlan, Caernarfon and Nefyn had long since been abandoned by their builders, but their utility in monitoring the maritime approaches to Gwynedd must have been obvious. Elsewhere, mottes were found at *maerdrefi* and functioned as local administrative centres and also as residences for the itinerant Welsh court. The impressive motte at Rhuddlan was certainly in use when Llywelyn came of age; Gerald of Wales stayed there as a guest of Dafydd I on his journey through Wales in 1188,[26] and it is clear that the site was maintained by Llywelyn on his accession, as coins were minted there throughout the early part of his reign and perhaps even later.[27] The early history of the nascent Welsh towns at Caernarfon and Nefyn are frustratingly poorly documented, but, given Llywelyn's interest in fostering trade at ports such as Llanfaes during his reign, one is sorely tempted to wonder whether the mottes in those places were refortified by Llywelyn as the settlements grew. Rachel Swallow has recently argued that the royal *llys* at Caernarfon was not situated at Llanbeblig, to the south of the modern-day town,

---

23. D. Hopewell, 'Castell Carndochan: survey and excavation 2014–17', AC, 169 (2020), p. 205.
24. J.E. Jones and A. Stockwell, 'Tomen Castell, Dolwyddelan, Gwynedd, North Wales: Excavations at an early castle site', AW, 54 (2015), pp. 73–90.
25. Lloyd, *History of Wales*, pp. 357–99.
26. L. Thorpe (transl.), *Gerald of Wales: The Journey through Wales/The Description of Wales* (London, 1978), p. 196.
27. Besly, 'Short Cross and other medieval coins', p. 55; see also C.O. Jones, 'Gwenwynwyn, the silver mine at Carreghofa, and the supremacy of Powys', CMCS, 79 (2020), pp. 47–59.

as has long been considered to be the case, but immediately adjacent to the motte that was subsequently incorporated into the later Edwardian castle.[28] That motte was certainly garrisoned by the Welsh during the war of 1282–3, when an English force was dispatched to seize the location; the fact that that force was detained there for over ten weeks has been presented as evidence that a siege was required in order to capture it.[29] Prydydd Y Moch's glowing reference to the llys there, written around 1215, and the issuance at Caernarfon of a grant to Ynys Lannog priory in 1221, make clear its importance to the prince.[30] Refortification of the motte may have played a part in bulwarking that status.

The more compelling lesson, however, was surely the effectiveness of castles when they were placed beside roads. Dylan Foster Evans' recent study has done much to overturn the long-held notion that roads and ways in medieval Wales were rare, of poor quality and badly maintained, making use of fragmentary but persuasive references to the maintenance of roads by Llywelyn's contemporary the Lord Rhys of Deheubarth (d. 1197) and, possibly, by Llywelyn himself.[31] Stand-alone masonry towers that were (one presumes) in existence prior to Llywelyn's accession, such as Dinas Emrys, were emplaced with the intention of guarding vital roadways into Gwynedd. Others, such as that at Prysor, may have been raised by Llywelyn in the early years of his reign. Though we can only speculate, the late date of Llywelyn's assumption of overlordship in Meirionydd (1202) is worth noting, and it is not beyond the realms of possibility that Prysor's masonry tower, which has been dated to after 1220 on typological grounds,[32] may in fact have been built earlier as part of a series of small fortifications that included Tomen-y-Mur, Aber Iâ and perhaps an initial phase of construction at Carndochan.[33] In the unstable political environment of late twelfth-century Gwynedd the importance of securing internal communications was doubtless of immense importance to Llywelyn, and we should bear this in mind when considering his emplacement of his earliest masonry castles.

28. R. Swallow, 'Living the dream: the legend, lady and landscape of Caernarfon Castle, Gwynedd, North Wales', AC, 168 (2019), pp. 153–95.
29. A.J. Taylor, *The King's Works in Wales 1277–1330* (London, 1974), p. 369.
30. Jones, *Gwaith Llywarch ap Llywelyn*, poem 25, line 17; AWR, p. 411.
31. D.F. Evans, 'Conquest, roads and resistance in medieval Wales', in V. Allen and R. Evans (eds), *Roadworks: Medieval Britain, Medieval Roads* (Manchester, 2016), pp. 277–302.
32. H.N. Savory, 'Excavations at Dinas Emrys, Beddgelert (Caern.), 1954–56', AC, 109 (1960), p. 13; Martin de Lewandowicz, 'A survey of Castell Prysor, Meirionnydd', AW, 38 (1998), p. 40.
33. Prysor is not likely to date from as late as 1220, as the military reasons for erecting it would no longer apply, and while it has been speculated that its appearance coincided with the promotion of Prysor to the status of a llys (de Lewandowicz, 'Castell Prysor, Meirionnydd', p. 41), such masonry structures cannot typically be found at other similar sites. Though the detail can hardly be used for diagnostic purposes, it is worth noting that the revetment below the summit at Prysor was mortared using seashells as an ingredient (de Lewandowicz, 'Castell Prysor, Meirionnydd', p. 40), as was the case at Carndochan.

The relative absence of dating information makes it impossible to establish a definitive chronology for Llywelyn's early castle-building policy. However, it is generally accepted that the works at Dolwyddelan and Dolbadarn were among the earliest – if not in fact the earliest – castles (as opposed to any stand-alone towers that may have been his work) he raised. The castles have much in common. Both are realised on a modest scale, featuring a single ward and with only one tower of any size, which functioned as the keep. Both keeps are found on the curtain wall, rather than being enclosed by it, and – Dolbadarn's later round tower notwithstanding – rectangular towers are the dominant feature at both sites. However, while Dolwyddelan makes multiple appearances in the historical record during the twelfth and thirteenth centuries, those same records are comparatively reticent about Dolbadarn. The two castles are described by Beverley Smith as being 'sited for strategic reasons',[34] but over and above their value as bulwarks of the mountain passes they overlook, what can be said about the wider implications of their positioning in the Eryri landscape?

Given its proximity to the coastal routes and centres of power of north-west Gwynedd, it is in some ways curious that Dolbadarn is, as has been noted, by far the more elusive of the pair. Just three explicit references to it can be found dating from the thirteenth century, all from the very end of its existence as a Welsh fortification. The first is in a trio of letters issued by Dafydd III and Gruffudd ap Maredudd ab Owain on 2 May 1283 from 'Llanperis' – a reference, surely, to Dolbadarn; the village of Llanberis lies just adjacent to it – during the final weeks of his principate, addressed to various recipients and asking them for military assistance in the face of Edward I's advances.[35] The second derives from a May 1284 document issued by Edward's royal government, instructing one Master Richard the Engineer to remove timbers from the castle and take them to Caernarfon.[36] The final reference is in a group of letters from Edward I himself, dated June–July 1284 at 'Baladeulyn' – probably a reference to Dolbadarn, though the identification is not quite certain.[37] An additional strand of evidence worthy of note, in spite of its lateness, is Leland's remark that Llywelyn II imprisoned his brother Owain Goch at the castle.[38]

---

34. LlapG, p. 229.
35. For 'Llanperis', see, for example, the text of Gruffudd ap Maredudd's letter in *AWR*, pp. 213–14; LlapG, pp. 572–3 gives useful commentary.
36. The Royal Commission on Ancient and Historical Monuments in Wales (RCAHMW), *An Inventory of the Ancient Monuments in Caernarfonshire II: Central* (London, 1960), p. 167.
37. The isthmus on which Dolbadarn stands was known as Baladeulyn. However, RCAHMW, *Caernarfonshire II: Central*, p. 168, n. 1, notes that another place called Bala Deulyn, in Nantlle, a few miles to the west, has been suggested as Edward's residence during this time by several writers, including Pennant in his *Tours of Wales* (1778).
38. L.T. Smith (ed.), *The Itinerary in Wales of John Leland* (London, 1906), p. 84.

The documentary evidence for Dolwyddelan's military career likewise derives from the late thirteenth century, but it is sufficient to establish that, of the two castles, it had a far more vigorous existence. A letter of 1278 from Rhys Wyndod of Deheubarth regarding the homage of one Madog ap Trahaearn ap Madog was issued from Dolwyddelan,[39] presumably in the presence of Llywelyn, and J.E. Morris speculated that Llywelyn's successor, Dafydd III, convened a *parlement* of Welsh nobles at the castle in December 1282 to discuss the prosecution of the war against the English following Llywelyn's death earlier that month.[40] Edward I certainly viewed the securing of Dolwyddelan as a necessary first step in his reduction of Eryri during the war of 1282–3. Michael Prestwich convincingly argues that the castle's constable, Gruffudd ap Tudur, defected to the English court in December 1282, allowing Edward to swiftly capture the castle with his connivance.[41] Morris' suggestion that the castle was besieged in early January 1283 is compatible with this notion; a short siege followed by a quick surrender may have saved face among certain of the Welsh garrison unhappy at the prospect of being seen to yield one of the prince's few remaining castles so readily. In any case, by 18 January the castle was in English hands and work was started immediately on a second tower to complement the keep.[42] The castle was still in use by the English in 1290, but its military role appears to have ceased shortly thereafter; it was not garrisoned during Madog ap Llywelyn's revolt of 1294–5.[43]

Seen in the context of the other Welsh masonry castles that we know of, their modest size, their location within the Eryri massif and their limited military usefulness invites the supposition that Dolbadarn and Dolwyddelan represent Llywelyn's first constructions, and that they were built within a few years of one another. The current consensus is that the first phase of works at Dolbadarn belongs to the beginning of the thirteenth century, and the only substantial addition, the round tower, has been dated to anywhere between 1210 and 1240 (see below).[44] The conclusions of the RCAHMW on their initial survey of Dolwyddelan in the 1950s were that the castle's keep could be dated to the late twelfth century and the curtain walls appeared in the thirteenth, but more recently the Commission revised this conclusion, placing both keep and curtain early

---

39. *AWR*, pp. 239–40.
40. Morris, *Welsh Wars of Edward I*, p. 185. Morris notes that the source – the chronicle of Pierre de Langtoft – puts this meeting at Denbigh, but that the settlement there was already in English hands by Christmas, and it may be a garbled reference to a meeting held to plan the revolt the previous year; see A.D. Carr, 'The last and weakest of his line: Dafydd ap Gruffydd, the last Prince of Wales', *WHR*, 19 (1999), p. 391.
41. M. Prestwich, *Edward I* (Berkeley, CA, 1988), p. 195 and n. 102.
42. A. Taylor, *The Welsh Castles of Edward I* (Oxford, 1986), p. 44.
43. A.D. Carr and G. Carr, *Cestyll Gwynedd* [Castles of Gwynedd] (Cardiff, 1985), p. 11.
44. D. Williams, *Dolbadarn Castle* (Cardiff, 1990), p. 2 suggests a date between 1216 and 1240.

in the thirteenth century.[45] Avent also suggests a construction date of between 1210 and 1240 for both.[46] Determining which castle came first with certainty is not possible, but when Dolbadarn's scarce presence in the historical record is compared to the plethora of evidence relating to Dolwyddelan, it seems clear enough that the latter was the more important stronghold of the two in military terms. It appeared on the itinerary of Llywelyn II, and a persistent tradition supported by documentary evidence from the later part of his reign places the prince's treasury there.[47] The fact that Edward I saw fit to prioritise its capture, seemingly laying siege to it in January 1283, reveals much about its reputation as a regional focus for the prince's authority.

In spite of this, however, and *pace* the earlier suggestion of the RCAHMW, it is suggested here that Dolbadarn was built first, for two reasons. First, any need for a fortified presence at Dolwyddelan would seem to have been met during the earliest years of Llywelyn's reign by Tomen Castell, located less than a mile to the south-east of Dolwyddelan castle. The need for a fortification in the Lledr valley was obvious and of longstanding. Rising from the valley floor to the south-west was the road that led over Bwlch Y Gorddinan (Crimea Pass) and into the commote of Ardudwy. Emplacing a castle in the valley would effectively guard this route (see Map 1.1). It would also allow the Bwlch-y-Groes pilgrimage route to be monitored. This ran on a south-east–north-west alignment that ultimately led into Dyffryn Edeirnon and intersected with the course of the Dyfrdwy to the east, and continued due west of Dolwyddelan, affording travellers – and indeed small skirmishing parties – access to the Nant Gwynant valley through the pass at Bwlch yr Ehediad; it crossed the Lledr less than a mile from Tomen Castell's location.[48] Unfortunately, excavations carried out there in the 1960s failed to unearth any finds, so it is at present not possible to advance a sequence of occupation.[49] However, the motte did have a rectangular tower raised (in part at least) in stone at its summit, and so might well have been viewed by Llywelyn – initially, at any rate – as sufficient for the task of guarding routes through the valley.

The tradition that Llywelyn was born at Tomen Castell should not be entirely discounted, for there is every chance that, being a major undertaking for a lord with such limited lands and resources as Llywelyn's father Iorwerth Drwyndwn was, the castle and its appurtenances came to constitute his seat. Throwing up a motte in this location (or, indeed, refortifying an abandoned Norman one) may

---

45. Royal Commission on the Ancient and Historical Monuments of Wales, *An Inventory of the Ancient Monuments in Caernarfonshire I: East* (London, 1956), p. 80; <https://coflein.gov.uk/en/site/95299/details/dolwyddelan-castle> (accessed 14 February 2020).
46. R. Avent, *Dolwyddelan Castle/Dolbadarn Castle/Castell Y Bere* (Cardiff, 2004), p. 11.
47. *LlapG*, p. 231, n. 206 and references therein.
48. D. Elis-Williams, 'St. Gwyddelan's Church and the medieval geography of Dolwyddelan', *AW*, 54 (2015), pp. 109–24.
49. Jones and Stockwell, 'Tomen Castell', pp. 88–9.

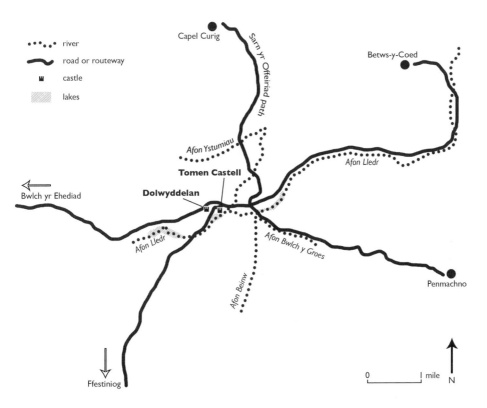

•••••• river

⌒ road or routeway

♜ castle

▨ lakes

Capel Curig

Betws-y-Coed

Sarn yr Offeiriad path

Afon Ystumiau

Afon Lledr

Tomen Castell

Bwlch yr Ehediad

Dolwyddelan

Afon Lledr

Afon Bwlch y Groes

Afon Beinw

Penmachno

Ffestiniog

0 _____ I mile    N

Map 1.1 Macrolocation of Dolwyddelan and Tomen Castell, Dolwyddelan.

well have been deemed a necessary expenditure by Iorwerth Drwyndwn after the death of Owain Gwynedd placed rivals for the princely patrimony on all sides. Bwlch Y Gorddinan was (and remains) the principal northern inland route from Ardudwy, and if, as Nerys Ann Jones and Esther Feer suggest, Cynan ab Owain was in possession of Ardudwy,[50] the erection of a tower in stone at Dolwyddelan may have been viewed by Iorwerth as an essential precaution. What little we know of Cynan shows him to have been an impressive, and most belligerent, warlord. First attested in 1145, when he sacked Cardigan with his brother Hywel, Cynan was one of the lynchpins of the Welsh victory at the battle of Coed Eulo in 1157,

50.  N.A. Jones and E. Feer, 'A poet and his patrons: the early career of Llywelyn Brydydd Y Moch', in H. Fulton (ed.), *Medieval Celtic Literature and Society* (Dublin, 2005), p. 132.

and must have enjoyed considerable standing thereby.[51] He was also considered sufficiently dangerous that his father Owain had cause to imprison him in 1150.[52] The construction of a masonry tower may therefore have been conceived as a wise investment for security reasons; if still standing and defensible at the time of Llywelyn's rise to power, it would have made further works redundant until slightly later.

The second factor that seems to antedate Dolbadarn's construction to some time before Dolwyddelan's is its architectural style. The later insertion of its impressive round tower notwithstanding, the drystone construction of its curtain walls is unique among masonry castles of the thirteenth-century princes of Wales; the nearest comparisons are with the earlier strongholds of Carn Fadryn on the Llŷn peninsula and Castell Deudraeth at Portmeirion, whose small military importance is underscored by the lack of certain references to either of them after Gerald of Wales noticed them on his travels through Wales in 1188.[53] At that time, both castles were newly built, and it is natural to conceive of the architectural thinking at Dolbadarn as, if not following their example in terms of plan, then at least deriving from the same mindset. Indeed, at least one author has suggested a pre-1200 date for the curtain on these grounds,[54] and it is not difficult to envisage construction beginning in the late 1190s, following the drystone methods of construction favoured at Carn Fadryn.

The positions and architectural features of Dolbadarn and Dolwyddelan are worth examining. Both are placed adjacent to routes that traverse important mountain passes. Dolwyddelan, for example, is situated in the final settlement the westbound traveller arrives at prior to ascending Bwlch Y Gorddinan, which towers impressively over Blaenau Ffestiniog, and which crosses a col separating the commotes of Arllechwedd and Ardudwy. In addition to its role monitoring traffic over the pass, then, it (or more accurately, the tower at neighbouring Tomen Castell) may also have performed an important political function during, say, the 1170s, at a time when the border between the commotes served as the dividing line between rival patrimonies. It may be that the influence the macrolocation exerted on the mind was such that Llywelyn saw fit to retain the strategic position, merely relocating the stronghold from Tomen Castell to a more prominent microlocation – the nearby boss of rock on which Dolwyddelan stands, within a few hundred metres of the road leading to the pass – at some point soon after achieving

51. Although J.G. Edwards, 'Henry II and the fight at Coleshill: Some further reflections', WHR, 3 (1967), p. 256 endorses King's reasonable inference that Cynan (and his brother Dafydd) were not acting on their own initiative, but had in fact been posted in a position of ambuscade by their father Owain Gwynedd prior to the battle.
52. Turvey, *The Lord Rhys*, p. 35.
53. Thorpe, *The Journey through Wales/The Description of Wales*, p. 183. Edward I may have visited Deudraeth in the early 1280s; see chapter 3.
54. J. Pettifer, *Welsh Castles* (Woodbridge, 2000), p. 34.

Figure 1.1 Dolbadarn's round tower; a light in the upper wall is visible.

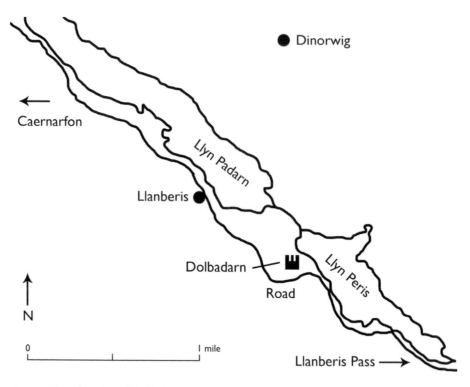

Map 1.2 Macrolocation of Dolbadarn.

supremacy in Gwynedd. Dolbadarn's strategic function is similarly clear-cut. It is emplaced to guard the Llanberis Pass to the south; the road passes just a few hundred metres from its position (see Map 1.2).[55]

Thus far, the impression given is of a pair of compact masonry castles, conventionally sited to command important routes and situated to take advantage of the terrain to enhance both their visibility and their defensibility. However, further inspection reveals several features that fly in the face of the basic precepts of military architecture. At Dolbadarn, the round tower – far and away the strongest point in the defences – has lights, not slits for the loosing of arrows, in its upper walls (see Fig. 1.1);[56] angles at both castles are left exposed; most importantly, there is a complete lack of recognition of the importance of the enfilade. Only at Dolbadarn is such an effect produced, and then seemingly by happenstance; neither the round tower nor the west tower was sited to project very far beyond the curtain wall (see Figs 1.2 and 1.3).

Three obvious possibilities come to mind when trying to account for these architectural indiscretions. Either they are signs of Llywelyn and his architect's lack of familiarity with the mechanics of castle-building, or the enfilade was

55. RCAHMW, *Caernarfonshire I: East*, p. 80; RCAHMW, *Caernarfonshire II: Central*, p. 165.
56. RCAHMW, *Caernarfonshire II: Central*, p. 167.

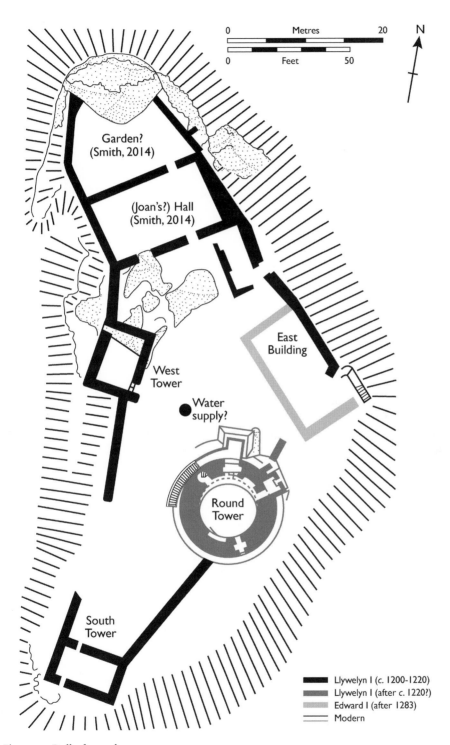

Figure 1.2 Dolbadarn, plan.

Figure 1.3 Dolbadarn's round tower, as seen from the south. The off-centre positioning of the curtain wall produces a poor enfilading effect.

simply not accorded the same military importance in Gwynedd as in England, or the castles were not intended to be held in the event of a siege. However, none of the three seem viable. The third option is unlikely, given that the builders were at pains to make so many other aspects of the castles' construction as defensible as possible (though the adequacy of water supply at both sites is questionable).[57] The second option is also difficult to maintain, given the almost always adequate (and often fine) enfilade effects achieved at the necessary points in the circuit at almost all native masonry castles constructed later. One might seek an explanation in a belated recognition of the enfilade as one of the rudiments of castle-building, though it is hard not to feel one does the Welsh soldier poor justice if one adheres to that belief. During the twelfth century Welsh soldiers had served outwith Wales on many occasions. A contingent of infantry under Owain Gwynedd's brother Cadwaladr had fought in England as early as 1141 with Queen Matilda's army at the battle of Lincoln,[58] and would have had ample time to observe the siege of the castle there in progress and absorb the lessons offered by watching (or even experiencing) the effect of enfilading fire in practice.

Though it can only ever be conjecture, there is a further possibility that may explain these idiosyncrasies: for all the soundness with which they were emplaced, it may be that Dolbadarn and Dolwyddelan were, so to speak, experiments in stone, built to fulfil a certain didactic function. Though similar, there are also important differences that may suggest incremental progress toward an incipient native Welsh architectural style. Dolbadarn looks impressive today solely on account of its exemplary round tower, which is almost certainly a later addition, built following the example of similar round keeps that can be found in the Marches;[59] there is a good circumstantial case to be made for its erection marking Dolbadarn's transition to a high-status residence of a member of the house of Gwynedd during Llywelyn's later reign (see chapter 2). If the tower is removed from consideration the remains look paltry indeed, and show up in stark relief the deficiencies of raising castle walls in drystone (see Fig. 1.4): in places, the curtain

---

57. No well is mentioned in any of the published accounts of Dolbadarn, but a water source identified as such was apparently found in the ward a few yards due north of the round tower during a site visit in June 1933 and noted on a sketch plan drawn at the time; RCAHMW Archives 8M/1214/05/1. No well is visible at the spot, but a natural water supply in this location in medieval times, which natural upwelling the surveyors of the 1930s had sight of, is conceivable. Although E. Neaverson opined that 'water ... is probably not copious in the slate or grit outcrop' (*Medieval Castles in North Wales* (Liverpool, 1947), p. 33), it may have been so during the Medieval Warm Period. Neaverson noted the presence of natural springs at Dolwyddelan in 1934 (*Medieval Castles*, p. 32).

58. J. Gillingham, 'The context and purposes of the *History of the Kings of Britain*', Anglo-Norman *Studies*, 13 (1990), pp. 115–17; WS, p. 137.

59. The date range for the tower is very broad; no timber has survived for dendrochronological analysis and excavation produced no finds; RCAHMW, *Caernarfonshire II: Central*, p. 167. The suggestion (RCAHMW, *Caernarfonshire II: Central*, p. 167) that the ward and tower were constructed simultaneously by Welsh and English builders respectively seems doubtful on logistical grounds.

Figure 1.4 Dolbadarn's south tower; the fragmentary nature of the remains is evident.

approaches the flimsy in terms of thickness and foundation, and it is surely not coincidental that this type of walling was eschewed at every castle subsequently built by the princes of Wales. Close inspection of the castle shows that in several places the circuit is untidy. The north-eastern curtain wall and the hall do not quite meet up, and neither does the southern curtain wall and the south tower, and there are several variations in wall thickness throughout. Even if one invokes multiple phases of construction, between them these give the impression of a castle whose construction was not as orderly an affair as was the case with later castles. There is also the matter of the castle's awkward northern end, which, in spite of its strong natural disposition – the outcrop drops off very sharply here – is nevertheless poorly defended, being capped by neither a tower nor a buttress (though the remaining curtain wall does thicken somewhat towards the end). The open space beyond the hall has recently been characterised as a garden intended for the use of Llywelyn's consort Joan;[60] if this is correct, it is instructive that at no subsequent castle did a prince allow such a function to override defensive considerations. This archaeological evidence may suggest that Dolbadarn was the very first masonry construction of any size that Llywelyn attempted.

Seen from this perspective, Dolwyddelan represents a distinct improvement. Its curtain and keep are both more robustly constructed; their walls are thicker,

60. S.G. Smith, 'Dolbadarn Castle, Caernarfonshire: a thirteenth-century royal landscape', *AW*, 53 (2014), p. 69.

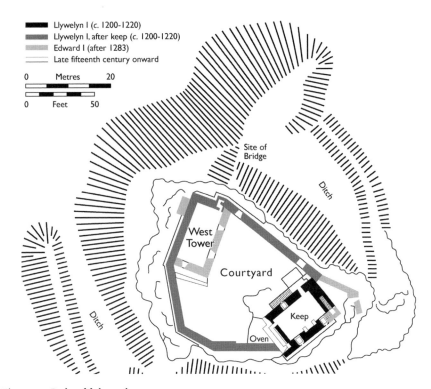

Figure 1.5 Dolwyddelan, plan.

and far more consistent in that thickness throughout. Writing decades before the nineteenth-century renovations that did so much to form impressions of Dolwyddelan in Victorian minds, Pennant was entirely justified in describing the castle as well built: 'The materials of this fortress are ... well squared, the masonry good, and the mortar hard.'[61]

It is also possible to discern in Dolbadarn and Dolwyddelan the beginnings of what Hemp called 'the Welsh castle plan'. At both castles the entrance is small and unobtrusive, lacking a gatehouse or portcullis (see Fig. 1.5). In addition, both display a characteristic that hitherto has been only intermittently recognised as symbolic of native Welsh masonry castles: the summits of the hilltops on which they are constructed are entirely enclosed by their curtain walls.[62]

61. Pennant, *Tours of Wales*, p. 302.
62. Dolbadarn seems to violate this principle, as its south-eastern curtain wall, on which the round tower sits, was laid some way in from the edge of the summit. However, it has been plausibly argued that the wall on the south-east did indeed run along the edge of the summit originally, and was dismantled and replaced by the present wall prior to the round tower's construction (RCAHMW, *Caernarvonshire II: Central*, p. 168). This left two narrow segments of the hilltop unenclosed but, as they were immediately overlooked by the round tower, the risk to the castle of leaving them beyond the walls was presumably deemed to be very small.

There is also an important ideological aspect that disposes us to think of Dolbadarn and Dolwyddelan as Llywelyn's earliest military builds of importance. While Llywelyn's initial power base beyond Nant Conwy was established in Gwynedd is Conwy, in the area between Eryri and the English border known as the Perfeddwlad, the importance of the Eryri massif to Venedotian power is a matter of record. Gerald of Wales' comment that all the livestock of Wales could be brought to pasture on the slopes of Eryri's mountains is merely the most famous report of the importance of the region to the Venedotian agrarian economy.[63] However, over and above its importance for food supply, the immense psychological relevance of north Wales' many ranges of mountains and hills to the relationship between native and Anglo-Norman as forming a natural stronghold that had proved impregnable to over a century of Norman incursions can hardly be doubted. The characterisation of the topography of the north as forming a system of natural obstacles arranged in concentric fashion – the Clwydian hills to the east, the Berwyns further west, and Eryri in the heart of Gwynedd[64] – is too neat to be accepted without qualification in the case of the low-lying Clwydians, but it is sound in outline with reference to Eryri itself. English invasion armies were indeed deterred from taking inland routes into Wales almost without exception during the Age of the Princes, preferring a coastal route that was more easily secured and which offered the possibility of easy movement between areas of Gwynedd by ship, as occurred during Henry II's invasion of 1157.[65]

It is no wonder, then, that the princes of Wales took advantage of Eryri's reputation as a formidable region at every opportunity. It looms large in praise poetry devoted to the princes,[66] and it is surely instructive that when Llywelyn I sought to claim his right to rule Wales the style he chose included the description *dominus Snaudon*.[67] The effectiveness of the allusion is supported by the fact that the title stuck. It is true that Dafydd II reverted to the style *princeps Wallie* (last used in the late twelfth century by Owain Gwynedd) during the latter stages of his troubled principate (1240–6). However, subsequent reuse of *dominus Sn(ow) don(ie)* by Llywelyn II from the late 1250s onwards, and again by both Dafydd III in 1283 and Madog ap Llywelyn during his revolt of 1294–5, as well as the title *domina Snaudon* by Llywelyn II's consort, Eleanor de Montfort, from 1279 to her death in 1282 may be taken as a ringing endorsement of the rhetorical power the connection to Eryri held.[68]

---

63. Thorpe, *The Journey through Wales/The Description of Wales*, p. 230.
64. Jones, 'The defences of Gwynedd', pp. 34–6.
65. W.L. Warren, *Henry II* (Berkeley, CA, 1977), p. 70.
66. Cf. Prydydd Y Moch's reference to Llywelyn I as being 'o hil eryron o Eryri' (from a line of lords of Eryri); Jones, *Gwaith Llywarch ap Llywelyn*, poem 25, line 44.
67. See *AWR*, pp. 75–9 for an invaluable and comprehensive overview of the princes' styles, on which this analysis relies.
68. *AWR*, p. 79.

That resonance extended beyond Wales. Contemporary chroniclers were quick to incorporate the mountainous landscape of Eryri into their narratives where the native princes of Wales were concerned. Whether writing of King John's invasion in 1211, the war of 1244–6 or the war of 1282–3, annalists in Chester, Lanercost and elsewhere all characterised Eryri in ways that implied its centrality to Venedotian power. For the former, for example, the war of 1282–3 was at an end when all the castles of Eryri were captured in 1283 (*capta sunt omnia castella Snawdonie*); the only other event during that final year of war deemed worthy of note was the capture of Dafydd III himself.[69] The Lanercost annalist offers a brief and somewhat garbled account of the revolt of Madog ap Llywelyn in 1294–5, but in its portrayal of him retreating into Eryri after destroying English castles elsewhere it is typical of the slant placed on English narratives where the Welsh of the north are concerned.[70] Writing of the war of 1282–3 in the 1290s, meanwhile, Pierre de Langtoft made Eryri a fortified bastion of the princes, but also imbues it with something of the supernatural – prospective conquerors would find even the weather worked against them, in ways that defied nature:

> Grievous is the war, and hard the suffering;
> When elsewhere it is summer, it is winter in Wales.
> Snowdon[ia], which is so strong, Llewellyn causes to be guarded,
> So that king Edward knows not where to make entrance.[71]

Such was Eryri's reputation as a fastness of formidable proportions; and this point leads us to consider one final, tantalising strand of evidence underscoring Eryri's vast importance. It stands to reason that the regions of a prince's kingdom where princes are found most often are those which are the most important or meaningful to them; and in this respect Eryri, particularly its northern reaches, has an intriguing story to divulge. An initial survey of the historical record shows that references to the presence of the princes in the vicinity of the Carneddau, Eryri's northernmost mountain range, are spotty at best. Several references to their presence in Aber, in which place there was a *maerdref* that commanded considerable resources in the thirteenth century, when other *maerdrefi* are seen to be in retreat, are indicative of its importance.[72] Both princess Joan and Dafydd II were at Aber when they died, in 1237 and 1246 respectively;[73] and Llywelyn II's

69. R.C. Christie (ed.), *Annales Cestrienses: Chronicle of the Abbey of S. Werburg, At Chester* (London, 1887), <http://www.british-history.ac.uk/lancs-ches-record-soc/vol14/pp102-121> (accessed 16 February 2018).

70. H. Maxwell (ed.), *The Chronicle of Lanercost 1272–1346* (Glasgow, 1913), p. 107.

71. T. Wright (ed.), *The Chronicle of Pierre de Langtoft*, Vol. 2 (Cambridge, 2012), p. 177.

72. T. Jones Pierce, 'Aber Gwyn Gregin', *Transactions of the Caernarvonshire Historical Society*, 23 (1962), pp. 38–9.

73. BYT Pen MS 20, pp. 104, 107.

famous riposte to Archbishop Peckham's peace offer in the autumn of 1282, variously known as the Garth Celyn Declaration, the Declaration of the Nobles or the Reply of the Welsh, was issued from Aber.[74] Otherwise, however, and apart from the aforementioned isolated records demonstrating the presence of Dafydd III and Llywelyn II at Dolbadarn and Dolwyddelan respectively, it is not possible to demonstrate the presence of any of the princes at particular moments in Eryri.

Where documentary evidence fails us, however, it may be possible to infer something from the rich and largely unstudied topography of oral tradition relating to the princes that was current in northern Eryri during the early modern period. Map 1.3 shows the locations various princes of Wales are reputed to have visited at some point during the late twelfth and thirteenth centuries.[75]

The persistence, and demonstrable falsity, of the tradition locating the burial of William de Briouze – the infamous lover of Llywelyn I's wife Joan, who was hanged by the prince in May 1230 near Y Bala – in Aber parish, in a cave at a location given as 'Cae Gwilym Ddu' (Black William's Field),[76] testifies to the perils of accepting oral traditions at face value, and no attempt is made here to systematically weigh the relative merits of each of the reports listed above. One of them, at least, is highly suspect on tactical grounds if nothing else; it is hard to envisage the military advantage conferred on any force stationed at the summit of Gyrn, which is poorly sited with respect to both the coastal and Nant Ffrancon routes in and out of Gwynedd.[77] In the same way, the surviving structure at Hafod Gelyn dates from the eighteenth century and so we must invoke the earlier remains on which it was built if nineteenth-century traditions of medieval occupation are to retain any credence at all.[78]

---

74.  For the Declaration of the Nobles, LlapG, pp. 543–6.

75.  RCAHMW, *Caernarfonshire II: Central*, p. 84 (though 'Gwaith Hywel ab Owain Gwynedd', in K.A. Bramley et al. (eds), *Gwaith Llywelyn Fardd I ac Eraill o Feirdd y Ddeuddegfed Ganrif* (Cardiff, 1994), p. 159, retains an open mind on the presence of a motte at Dwygyfylchi); John Fisher (ed.), *Richard Fenton's Tours in Wales* (*Archaeologia Cambrensis* supplement, 1917), p. 205; H. Hughes and H.L. North, *The Old Churches of Snowdonia* (1908; repr. Capel Curig, 1984), pp. 99, 149, 150; H.D. Hughes, *Hynafiaethau Llandegai a Llanllechid* [Antiquities of Llandegai and Llanllechid] (1866; repr. Groeslon, 1979), p. 20.

76.  References abound from the early nineteenth century; see, for example, T. Jones, *A History of the County of Brecknock*, Vol. 1 (London, 1805), p. 130. A 'Kay gwylyn dy' is noted in the parish of Llanllechid – in which a field of the same name stands today, a few hundred yards from the border with Abergwyngregyn parish – in the Penrhyn manuscripts from *c.*1560, and a further reference from *c.*1499 may refer to the same field; see Archif Melville Richards database, Place-Name Research Centre, Bangor University, search term 'Cae Gwilym Ddu' (<http://www.e-gymraeg.co.uk/enwaulleoedd/amr/cronfa_en.aspx> (accessed 17 February 2018).

77.  But see chapter 3 for an assessment of the princes' military dispositions at the mouth of the Nant Ffrancon valley.

78.  But RCAHMW, *Caernarfonshire I: East*, p. 4 only tentatively suggests even a documentary reference dating from as recently as 1648.

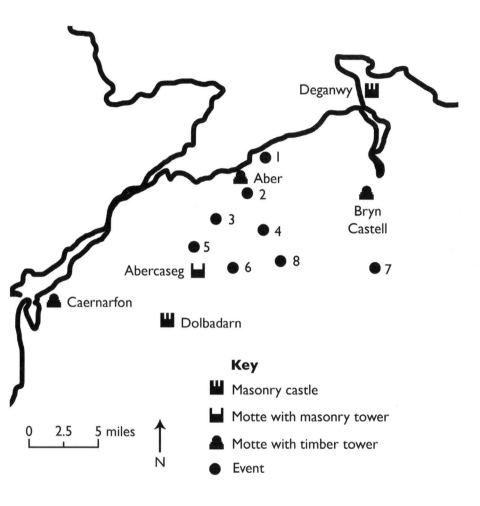

Map 1.3 Oral traditions and bardic references regarding the princes of Wales in northern Eryri.

Key
1. Headland at Penmaenmawr; Llywelyn I's reputed base during King John's burning of Bangor (1211)
2. Probable fortification at Dwygyfylchi; mentioned in poem by Hywel ab Owain Gwynedd (1170?)
3. Gyrn; supposed location of a camp of an army of Llywelyn II (1282–3?)
4. Hafod Gelyn; ruins of a supposed residence of the Princes of Wales (thirteenth century)
5. Dôl Ddafydd; reputed location of a training camp for Welsh soldiers (1282–3)
6. Cerrig Henllys; reputed camp of Dafydd III (1283)
7. Trefriw; parish church reputedly built by Llywelyn I for the use of his princess Joan (1230s?)
8. Nanhysglain; reputed place of capture of Dafydd III (June 1283)

Collectively, however, these traditions may have some merit, inasmuch as they support the idea that Eryri signified to the princes, and indeed to the Welsh, in a way that demanded they form the heart of what would under Llywelyn II become the Principality of Wales. The most interesting of them are the trio of reports relating to the movements of Dafydd III during the final months of the war of 1282–3. The references recorded by the antiquarian Hugh Derfel Hughes in the mid-nineteenth century to a training camp at Dôl Ddafydd (Dafydd's Meadow) in Bethesda, and hiding from the English at Cerrig Henllys on the slopes above the village,[79] are of interest, particularly as the tradition detailing his capture at Nanhysglain above Aber Falls less than five miles to the east recorded by the eighteenth-century antiquarian William Williams Llandegai is among the more persuasive of those listed here.[80] The oral traditions that speak most clearly to the region's importance, are, of course, the names of the mountains Carnedd Llywelyn and Carnedd Dafydd, the former of which is second only to Snowdon in height, and which are attested by the Elizabethan antiquarian William Camden in the sixteenth century.[81] Taken together, the case may be made for Eryri, over and above even the manor at Aberffraw on Ynys Môn, perhaps, as constituting the backbone of Welsh political ideology in the thirteenth century.

## Carndochan

To Llywelyn's roster of castles erected during the early years of his reign we might add the enigmatic fortress of Carndochan. This site, neglected like no other of comparable size in north Wales – the first modern excavations were begun in 2014 – is absent from the historical record until the early modern period.[82] Given its neglect, even today it is too poorly understood to allow even a rudimentary history to be established. In 1955 Hogg was confident enough to ascribe a mid-

---

79. The site Hugh Derfel Hughes refers to as 'Cerrig Henllys' in *Hynafiaethau Llandegai a Llanllechid* is clearly Cerrig Cenllysg, a natural grouping of large stones near the source of Afon Cenllysg on the north-western slopes of Carnedd Dafydd (E. Owen, 'Arvona Antiqua', *AC*, 22 (1867), p. 106).

80. D.G. Jones (ed.), *Prydnawngwaith Y Cymry a gweithiau eraill gan William Williams* [*Prydnawngwaith Y Cymry* and other works by William Williams] (Bala, 2011), p. 60. *Prydnawngwaith Y Cymry* was published in 1822, but the passage in question appeared in barely modified form in an earlier work, *Observations on the Snowdon Mountains* (1802).

81. Hywel Wyn Owen and Richard Morgan propose that the nearby mountain Carnedd Dafydd was named after Dafydd II, and not his nephew Dafydd III as most traditions have it; *Dictionary of the Place-Names of Wales* (Llandysul, 2007), pp. 72–3.

82. The earliest reference is from an indenture of 1522; D. Hopewell, 'High status medieval sites: Castell Carndochan Excavation Report 2016–17', Gwynedd Archaeological Trust (2017), p. 29. According to G. Davies, 'Traddodiadau a Hynafiaethau Llanuwchllyn' [Traditions and antiquities of Llanuwchllyn], *JMHRS*, 3 (1958), pp. 151–2, an oral tradition then current held that the farm named Tŷ Cerrig immediately adjacent to the castle was given to the ancestor of the then owner for the bardic recitations he gave for the castle's inhabitants; Davies implies this to have occurred at the time of Rhirid Flaidd, a local lord mentioned in late twelfth-century praise poetry.

thirteenth century date to the fortification,[83] and speculation as to its authorship has accordingly focused on Llywelyn I and Llywelyn II. Carndochan's extreme dilapidation, the result of a combination of more severe weathering than usual due to its very exposed position on a tall outcropping of rock commanding the southern end of the Lliw valley and the use of poor-quality mortar,[84] has thwarted attempts at interpretation until recently. Even more frustratingly, finds have been rare and resistant to dating beyond very broad limits that are consistent only with a date of construction during the reigns of either Llywelyn.[85] The relative lack of finds also defies attempts to interpret the remains.

All that will be hazarded here is that the earlier Llywelyn authored much of the castle in the 1200s or 1210s, presumably beginning at some point in the decade or so after 1202, when Penllyn, the commote in which Carndochan stands, came into his possession.[86] If the idea that a line of castles and towers was erected along the border with Meirionydd prior to Llywelyn's annexation of that region in 1202 is true (see above), there may be a case for treating the square tower as a first phase of works (see below).

The reasons for surmising a construction date in the first two decades of the thirteenth century for the castle as a whole are ideological and topographical rather than architectural. Carndochan's siting seems to owe more to the principles of expeditionary emplacement than it does to, say, the more plainly military principles of defensive emplacement. As an expression of Llywelyn's will to power in a commote that had been the site of a tug-of-war between Gwynedd and Powys, and, latterly, Anglo-Norman lords, for decades – Penllyn contains the remains of half a dozen mottes – Carndochan could hardly be bettered. Figure 1.6 comprises a viewshed analysis for Carndochan.[87] When standing to full height, the castle would have been visible from the Dyfrdwy valley at the point where Cwm Cynllwyd debauches into it, directly opposite the entrance to the Lliw valley.[88] Travellers traversing the latter to the east would have been presented with its most impressive aspect; its long axis is parallel to the valley bottom, ensuring maximum visibility from the road below.

83. A.H.A. Hogg, 'Castell Carndochan', JMHRS, 2 (1955), p. 180.
84. Hopewell, 'Excavation Report 2016–17', p. 1.
85. Hopewell, 'Excavation Report 2015–16', p. 13 and Appendix 1.
86. Brodie, 'Apsidal and D-shaped towers', p. 234; Hopewell, 'Excavation Report 2016–17', p. 7. The square keep may well be the oldest part of the castle, and may be another masonry tower dating from the end of the twelfth century. It has been suggested that the apsidal tower was built later in his reign (Hopewell, 'Excavation Report 2016–17', and references therein). I believe it probably dates from the same period as the curtain walls, but can advance no very convincing warrant for this.
87. All viewshed analyses were created using ArcGIS, using the castle's keep as the central point. Observer location is arbitrarily defined at six feet above ground level; the lines of sight from the taller parts of the castles, such as the battlements and keep, would in many cases be slightly longer than shown.
88. Hopewell, 'Excavation Report 2016–17', pp. 6–7.

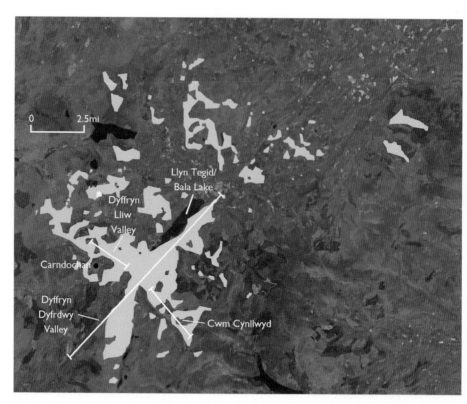

Figure 1.6 Carndochan, viewshed analysis. The castle dominates the crossing point of the upper Dyffryn Dyfrdwy/Dee Valley and the lower Dyffryn Lliw Valley; longer sightlines are impeded by the surrounding hills. Analysis created using ArcGIS; height above ground at origin set at six feet; north is at top.

Yet, while its macrolocation is admirable, its microlocation is not. Sightlines due south are significantly impeded by a low, wooded spur about half a mile distant that blocks the view of the road south into Meirionydd. Far more worrying, however, is the disposition on the south side of the spur on which Carndochan sits, where the military crest lies well below the topographical crest, meaning that assailants assaulting the castle from this side do so to their advantage, being in dead ground, obscured from the view of archers on the castle walls, until they are relatively near. Finally, the approach from the west, along the crest of the ridge whose eastern end Carndochan occupies, is quite flat (Fig. 1.7).[89]

While the terrain on this side presents obvious problems for the attacker, being boggy, the rock-cut ditch in front of the castle here was clearly viewed as a necessity rather than an additional layer of protection.[90] These shortcomings do

89.  Hopewell, 'Excavation Report 2015–16', p. 1.
90.  Hopewell, 'Excavation Report 2015–16', p. 1.

Figure 1.7 Carndochan as seen from the west; the approach is relatively flat. The top of the rock-cut ditch in front of the apsidal tower is visible. Photograph courtesy of David Hopewell, Gwynedd Archaeological Trust.

not render the position indefensible, but they do significantly complicate the task of the defender and it is unsurprising that no other native Welsh masonry castle in Gwynedd is so emplaced.

In terms of layout, Hogg's preliminary survey and brief analysis (1955) has held up surprisingly well. The earliest construction on the site was almost certainly the square tower, which is of lighter build than the rest of the castle, and probably yet another of the stand-alone towers of the late twelfth century, perhaps built by Llywelyn in the late 1190s.[91] Presumably the curtain wall then followed, and perhaps the apsidal tower appeared at the same time. The 'round tower' at the castle's eastern extremity, characterised as possibly unfinished by Hogg, and his 'semi-circular tower' in the southern curtain wall[92] have since been revealed as an apparently complete circular tower and a D-shaped tower,[93] overlooking the castle's northern curtain wall and the castle's entrance respectively. The former is built on top of the curtain wall itself and the latter is connected to the curtain by a butt joint, so it appears that both were later additions, but no firm conclusions can

91.  Hopewell ('Excavation Report 2015–16', pp. 4–5) notes the tower's resemblance to Dinas Emrys and postulates authorship by the sons of Cynan ab Owain.
92.  Hogg, 'Castell Carndochan', p. 179.
93.  For the D-shaped tower, Hopewell, 'Excavation Report 2016–17', p. 4. Excavations during the 2017 season supported, but did not prove, the existence of a round tower at the castle's north-eastern end (Dave Hopewell, pers. comm.).

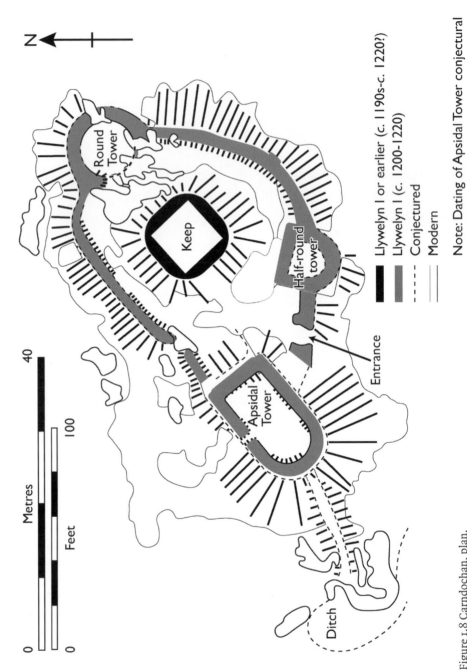

Figure 1.8 Carndochan, plan.

Figure 1.9 Evidence of galletting at Carndochan. Photograph courtesy of David Hopewell, Gwynedd Archaeological Trust.

be arrived at due to a lack of dating evidence.[94] In the same way, the relationship between the curtain wall and the site's dominant feature, the apsidal tower jutting out to the south-west, is not currently known.

For all the uncertainty over Carndochan's authorship, however, it can be said with some confidence that in its final form (Fig. 1.8) it represents an improvement in construction style and layout over Dolbadarn and Dolwyddelan. It is more heavily fortified, boasting no less than four towers, and there is increasing use of the enfilade, particularly in the vicinity of the entrance, which is flanked by the apsidal tower and the D-shaped tower. The entrance itself is awkwardly built – its strangely tapering form has been plausibly interpreted as either a product of overly hasty building or a bodged repair after a collapse[95] – but this is one of the few weaknesses in a plan that overall may be taken as an indication that native Welsh methods of castle wall construction were maturing. In various parts of the castle walls have been raised using galletting, a masonry technique meant to minimise the amount of mortar exposed to the elements by inserting smaller stones into big gaps between larger, unshaped pieces of stone that would otherwise be filled by mortar (see Fig. 1.9).

94. Dave Hopewell, pers. comm.
95. Hopewell, 'Excavation Report 2016–17', p. 20.

However, excavations of the wall of the castle's strongest point, the apsidal tower, have revealed that the lowest courses were carefully built using only very large stones with no large mortared gaps between them – a method that has been interpreted as indicating that the builders were aware of the need to deter attackers from attempting to undermine the tower's walls.[96] This appreciation of Anglo-Norman siege practices, and the evolution (or adoption) of innovative building techniques to counteract them, says a great deal about the increasing abilities of the prince's architects and masons.

## Ewloe

By the end of the first decade of the thirteenth century Llywelyn could count himself well pleased with the progress he had made since his ascent to power. However, by 1210 his cordial relationship with John had soured. Following a successful campaign in Ceredigion in the autumn of 1208 Llywelyn overran the territory of southern Powys. He did so in the absence of Gwenwynwyn, who had been imprisoned by John that October.[97] It was an overreach on Llywelyn's part, and John's seizure of Llywelyn's castle at Ellesmere on 18 December precipitated a spate of urgent communication between prince and king. The situation was salvaged, it appears, only by a face-to-face meeting between the two men on the Welsh border around 29 January the following year; and, although Llywelyn dutifully attended the English court on a further three occasions in 1209, even serving with the king on his expedition to Scotland that summer, it is clear that John now considered Llywelyn's allegiance to be suspect.[98] An incursion into Gwynedd by Ranulf, earl of Chester, as far as Deganwy in the summer of 1210 was followed in November by an even more ominous move by John himself, who reinstated Gwenwynwyn to the lands in Powys Llywelyn had annexed two years before.[99] The reasons for this sudden *volte-face* have never been conclusively determined. A possible alliance between Llywelyn and William de Briouze has been suggested, and, given the close links between Gwynedd and the de Briouzes later in Llywelyn's reign – the bishop of Hereford, Giles de Briouze, may well have negotiated on Llywelyn's behalf with the king of France prior to the concluding of the Franco-Welsh treaty of 1212; a son of de Briouze married Llywelyn's daughter Gwladus in 1215; and Llywelyn's son Dafydd married Isabel de Briouze in 1231[100] – this notion may have some merit. The *Brut*, meanwhile, ascribes John's policy more simply to retaliation for Llywelyn's repeated attacks on John's lands.[101]

96. Hopewell, 'Excavation Report 2016–17', p. 14. There is some evidence of galletting at Dolwyddelan, albeit on a smaller scale; Neaverson, *Medieval Castles in North Wales*, pp. 32–3.
97. MP, pp. 91–2.
98. For a full examination of this often overlooked episode, Jones, 'A rupture'.
99. Lloyd, *History of Wales*, p. 633.
100. LltG, pp. 58, 76, 90.
101. BYT Pen MS 20, p. 85.

Worse was to come. After splitting most of Llywelyn's Welsh allies off from the prince with promises of land and favour, in May 1211 John assembled an army and invaded Gwynedd.[102] An unfortunate gap in the administrative records detailing John's itinerary for this year prevents a detailed examination of the king's dispositions, but it is known that John and his army marched westward as far as Deganwy, which had been rebuilt by Ranulf following Llywelyn's slighting of it the previous year.[103] Llywelyn's response was to avoid battle, and the Welsh chronicles recount a massive movement of men and materiel into the fastnesses of Eryri ahead of the English advance. On his arrival at Deganwy John found there was no enemy to confront and an army to feed – the latter ultimately proving a task that taxed the resource of the adjacent countryside beyond breaking point; according to the *Brut* the army was reduced to eating horseflesh, and by the end of May John was back in England.[104] But in the summer the king returned, and this time pushed well to the west, burning Bangor – and, we are told, seizing the bishop of Bangor even as he stood before the high altar in the cathedral – and forcing Llywelyn's capitulation.[105]

The agreement signed between king and prince on 12 August 1211 was an object lesson in humiliation.[106] Three clauses in particular are remarkable for their severity. Aside from being forced to pay the enormous tribute of 10,000 head of cattle, Llywelyn was required to yield the Perfeddwlad – the four *cantrefi*[107] that constituted north-east Wales – to John. Though a reference in the text to the preservation of 'Llywelyn's right in Tegeingl' does at least suggest that the prince

102. BYT *Pen MS 20*, p. 85; LltG, pp. 54–5.
103. This, the culmination of Ranulf's expedition, is recorded in the chronicle *O Oes Gwrtheyrn* [From the Time of Gwrtheyrn]; see O. Jones, 'Historical writing in medieval Wales', PhD thesis (Bangor, 2013), p. 419.
104. BYT *Pen MS 20*, p. 85. Quite why John had such trouble finding provender has never been satisfactorily explained; Lloyd is uncharacteristically facile in positing that 'John was baffled by the special difficulties of Welsh warfare' (*History of Wales*, p. 635). One source has Llywelyn attacking the English army's supply train, but, even so, John does not appear to have been besieged in Deganwy, and so the surrounding countryside was presumably available to him, making the army's privations all the more inexplicable. One possible explanation may lie in the exigencies created by the weather. References to crop yields in the accounts of the bishop of Winchester show that grain prices spiked in 1211 compared to the last available year (1209) and the following year. This strongly points to a protracted period of wet weather the previous autumn and winter that would not have been conducive to the growing of crops (J. Titow, 'Evidence of weather in the account rolls of the Bishopric of Winchester 1209–1350', *Economic History Review*, 12 (1960), p. 365). If the situation in Winchester was replicated in Wales it, combined with the Welsh strategy of moving goods of value to the mountains – including, one must assume, livestock and perhaps grain also – might more convincingly account for John's troubles.
105. Lloyd, *History of Wales*, pp. 635–6.
106. Pryce, 'Anglo-Welsh Agreements', p. 8; AWR, p. 26.
107. The term *cantref* corresponds with the English term *hundred*, but its application over time was noticeably more fluid.

was able to salvage some sort of jurisdictional concession from John in that *cantref*,[108] the loss must have been grievous in terms of prestige as well as revenue. But even these stipulations paled in comparison to John's final demand: in the event that Llywelyn died without an heir by Joan, Gwynedd was to escheat to the English crown.[109] John could not have known that Joan was pregnant at the time of the agreement's signing with the son who would ultimately inherit Llywelyn's kingdom, Dafydd, but even so, the threat to Gwynedd was palpable: now, a simple riding accident or an untimely illness could reduce the house to nothing.

In the winter of 1211 and into the spring of 1212 Llywelyn bided his time; and, before long, his patience began to reap dividends. The Welsh lords of Powys and Deheubarth who had been enticed to John's side, wearied as they must have been by years of Venedotian aggression since Llywelyn came to power, doubtless saw swearing allegiance to the king as the lesser of two evils, but this impression abruptly changed when it became clear that the king's intent was to permanently reduce Wales by means of an extensive castle-building programme.[110] Among his more egregious missteps was the retention of the castle at Llanbadarn (Aberystwyth), a decision that angered the sons of the Lord Rhys who had formerly been in possession of it. Attacks against Llanbadarn masterminded by Rhys' progeny commenced even before 1211 was out,[111] and Llywelyn took note. After spending Easter 1212 with the king at Cambridge[112] he returned to Wales a few days later. Joan was by now heavily pregnant and was brought to child-bed at Castell Hen Blas, a motte-and-bailey castle in Tegeingl that had presumably remained in Llywelyn's possession under the clause protecting his rights there in the 1211 agreement. Llywelyn's second son, Dafydd, was born shortly thereafter.[113] The campaign that followed in July must have been as ferocious as it was all-encompassing: at the head of an alliance of Welsh lords Llywelyn regained all of the lands lost under the terms of the 1211 agreement with the exception of the English castles at Deganwy, Rhuddlan and Holywell. By 1213 these too had fallen to the Welsh,[114] and Llywelyn could once more claim the leadership of native Wales. In diplomacy he had shown considerable acumen, allying in the summer of 1212 with Philip Augustus of France,[115] and his hand was strong enough within Wales to allow him to call an assembly at Aberdyfi in 1216 to receive the homage

---

108. *AWR*, pp. 387–8.
109. *AWR*, pp. 387–8; *LltG*, p. 56.
110. *LltG*, p. 57.
111. *AWR*, p. 10.
112. Stephenson and Jones, 'The date and context', p. 30.
113. Stephenson and Jones, 'The date and context', p. 32; a date within a week or two after 25 March – at which time Llywelyn and Joan were still in Cambridge – seems most likely.
114. *BYT Pen MS 20*, p. 87; T. Jones, '"Cronica de Wallia" and other documents from Exeter Cathedral Library MS. 3514', *BBCS*, 12 (1946), p. 35.
115. R.F. Treharne, 'The Franco-Welsh Treaty of Alliance in 1212', *BBCS*, 18 (1958–60), pp. 60–75.

of the lords of Wales and to preside over the partition of Deheubarth among the feuding sons and relatives of the Lord Rhys.[116]

By that time, Llywelyn had already experienced his *annus mirabilis*. His campaigning against John had been suspended in 1213 by a two-year truce,[117] but in 1215 the king was beset by serious opposition by his disgruntled barons, who took the field and secured several key strategic points, including London. Llywelyn saw his chance and moved again, this time into England itself. In a campaign of extraordinary audacity, a Welsh army swept through the Oswestry salient and marched on Shrewsbury. The town yielded in May 1215 and remained in Welsh hands for the next year and more, along with a sizable chunk of north-western Shropshire.[118] It represented an extraordinary feat of arms for a prince whose direct rule probably did not yet extend to as many as 100,000 people; and, if Shrewsbury was to be shortly returned to English control, several lordships in the Oswestry salient remained in the hands of the princes of Wales for most of the next half-century.[119]

The campaign of 1215 firmly established Llywelyn as a presence to be reckoned with in the March, and began a pattern of occupation of lands in Shropshire that would continue until the loss of Welsh independence. By 1218 Llywelyn's pre-eminence was such that he was able to sign the Treaty of Worcester: in return for his homage, Llywelyn received English recognition of his rights to the lands he had conquered.[120] If the treaty fell short of his expectations, not least in its implicit assertion that the homage of the Welsh lords could only ever be done to the English king, as Huw Pryce has recently argued,[121] in its recognition of Llywelyn's pre-eminence in Wales it did at least represent a very significant improvement on

---

116. Davies, *The Age of Conquest*, p. 243.
117. Lloyd, *History of Wales*, pp. 641–2.
118. For the 1215 campaign, Lloyd, *History of Wales*, p. 643; Lloyd dates the fall of the town to some point after 17 May. When these territories reverted to English control is not easy to determine. King John embarked on a military expedition to the March in the summer of 1216 and was present at Shrewsbury and Oswestry in early August, at which point he burned the castle of the latter (Lloyd, *History of Wales*, p. 650, n. 195). Lloyd interprets the latter action as a punitive move against the Fitzalans, but the mere fact that the castle was burned does not necessarily suggest it was back in Marcher hands at this time; neither, given the febrile conditions in the March, can we conclude that John's expedition resulted in the return of the lordships Llywelyn had seized to men who remained in opposition to the king. Shrewsbury was not mentioned under the terms of the treaty of Worcester (1218), by which we may infer that Llywelyn had indeed yielded control of the region by that time.
119. See, for example, D. Stephenson, 'Fouke le Fitz Waryn and Llywelyn ap Gruffudd's claim to Whittington', SHA, 77 (2002), pp. 26–31; 'Llywelyn the Great, the Shropshire March and the building of Montgomery castle', SHA, 80 (2005), pp. 52–8.
120. AWR, pp. 398–401.
121. H. Pryce, 'Negotiating Anglo-Welsh relations: Llywelyn the Great and Henry III', in Weiler (ed.) with Rowlands, *England and Europe in the Reign of Henry III*, p. 16.

the conditions imposed on him seven years earlier. Certainly Llywelyn's erstwhile Welsh enemies perceived it that way, for, although his principate endured for another two decades, that period saw no serious challenge to his power from Powys or Deheubarth. Llywelyn's position was, for the moment, secure.

It is in this context that we should seek to situate the conception and construction of Ewloe castle. Nestled in woodland in the north-eastern extremity of Wales, less than five miles from the English border, Ewloe's history has proven extraordinarily resistant to scrutiny and it was only with the breakthrough provided by David Stephenson's recent analysis (2016) that much could be said about it. Briefly noticed by Leland in the 1530s as the 'ruinus castelet' of 'Castell Yollo',[122] the castle was first described in any detail by Thomas Pennant, whose *Tours in Wales* (1778) contains the following description, melancholic and pregnant with romantic possibilities:

> It is a small fortress, consisting of two parts: an oblong tower, rounded at the side, and guarded on the accessible places by a strong wall at some distance from it: an oblong yard with the remains of a circular tower at its extremity, forms the other part. The towers are now finely over-grown with ivy, and command the view of three wooded glens, deep and darksome, forming a most gloomy solitude.[123]

An 1828 notice published by the Metropolitan Cambrian Institution largely derived from Pennant notwithstanding,[124] the next useful overview followed in 1891, when Ewloe's then owner, T.B. Davies-Cooke, undertook a survey of historical references to the castle. Following Henry Taylor, Davies-Cooke drew attention to what for many years was thought to be the only near-contemporary source to mention the castle, the Chester plea rolls of 1311, in which he asserted that the castle was recorded as being 'built' by Llywelyn II in the year 1257.[125] We shall hear more of this document shortly. In 1912 the castle was listed as part of the RCAHMW's survey of historic buildings and monuments. The poor state of the site as surveyed was matched only by the deficiencies in this initial characterisation. The sketch plan included with the Commission's volume on

---

122. Smith, *Itinerary*, p. 93.
123. Pennant, *Tours of Wales*, Vol. 1 (1778), p. 116.
124. Anon., *Transactions of the Cymmrodorion*, 2 (1828), pp. 366–7.
125. T.B. Davies-Cooke, 'Ewloe Castle', *AC*, 5th series, 8 (1891), p. 3. For Taylor's discovery of the 1311 document, *Wrexham and Denbighshire Advertiser*, 27 May 1882, p. 6, which notes Taylor's reading of a paper on the castle to a meeting of the Chester Natural History Society earlier that month; his *Historic Notices of Flint* (London, 1883) contains the first complete published reference to the 1311 document (p. 41, n.). The town clerk of Flint, Taylor's principal contributions to Welsh history were *Historic Notices of Flint* and his dogged and ultimately successful advocacy of conservation efforts at Flint Castle; see C.O. Jones, '"Ho, oh! What castle is this": Flint and the quincentenary of Richard II's arrest', *FHSJ*, 41 (2018), pp. 145–57.

Flintshire monuments includes many inaccuracies and the suggestion that the west tower was the first of the castle's two towers to be completed was soon discredited.[126] However, the survey did at least fix the castle as being of thirteenth-century date, correcting the earlier misconception that it may have been the work of Henry II.[127]

It was not until a comprehensive clearance and consolidation effort was made in the 1920s that archaeologists began to make good sense of the site. By 1926 enough had been cleared of the undergrowth to reveal the castle's basic outline, and Hemp's landmark survey of the castle was published in 1928.[128] At this time, and in spite of Hemp's doubtful identification of the possible vestiges of a platform for a theorised twelfth-century motte on the site,[129] it was understood, on the basis of the 1311 document alluded to above, that the castle was built by Llywelyn II. Thanks to Stephenson's investigations, this is now known to be wrong; the incorrect translation of a single word in the French text misled historians into thinking that the prince 'built' the castle, whereas 'restored' or 'strengthened' are more accurate renderings, implying the existence of a fortification at Ewloe prior to 1257.[130] Given the distinctive two-ward form of the castle, it has been considered possible that what became the upper ward, containing the archetypal apsidal keep named the 'Welsh Tower' by Hemp, represents an initial phase of works, and the lower ward, with its second, smaller tower, followed in 1257,[131] but this is almost certainly wrong (see below).

Dating the onset of construction is difficult. There are references to the castle dating from 1259 and 1260 as a meeting place for delegations of Welsh and English envoys, and a meeting of a similar sort held in the early 1240s, assuming the castle existed at that time, as is likely, may be considered the formal *terminus ante quem*.[132] However, we may postulate a rather narrower date range for construction. Even taking into account the relatively sheltered environment in which it stands, the castle's state of preservation is impressive, and indicates a date after the experiments in drystone walling at Dolbadarn. Llywelyn I came into possession of Mold, and (one presumes) the rest of Tegeingl in 1199, but it is doubtful that

126. RCAHMW, *An Inventory of the Ancient Monuments of Wales and Monmouthshire II: Flint* (London, 1912), p. 38.
127. RCAHMW, *Flint*, pp. 37–9.
128. Hemp, 'Ewloe Castle', *passim*.
129. Hemp, 'Ewloe Castle', pp. 11–12. Renn and Avent (*Flint Castle/Ewloe Castle* (Cardiff, 2001), p. 6) dismiss the suggestion on grounds of topography and lack of evidence.
130. Stephenson, 'A reconsideration', p. 249. Stephenson is cautious on this point, merely admitting the possibility of earlier work, but a construction date in the late 1250s can be safely discounted on other grounds; see below.
131. Hugh Brodie tentatively speculates ('Apsidal and D-shaped towers', p. 233) that the Welsh Tower may be of a different phase to the curtain wall that surrounds it on architectural grounds; but see *infra*.
132. Stephenson, 'A reconsideration', pp. 247–9.

works could have begun at Ewloe until at least 1201, when his treaty with King John confirmed him in the lands seized in the warfare of the previous few years.[133]

However, another strand of evidence – the recent pinpointing of Dafydd II's birth in 1212 – disposes us to assign Ewloe a slightly later date. The link between Dafydd's birth date and Ewloe may not be obvious at first glance, but it is in fact instructive with regard to Ewloe's origins because of *where* he was born. While birth dates of 1206, 1208 and 1215 have all previously been advanced, it seems all but certain that Dafydd was in fact born in the spring of 1212, shortly after Llywelyn and Joan's return from their meeting with John at Cambridge.[134] The survival of a 1305 petition by the monks of Basingwerk abbey detailing the history of the chapel at Coleshill allows us to pinpoint Dafydd's birthplace with uncommon precision for a Welsh prince. By 1305 services had not been held at the chapel for some time, and so the discomfited monks wrote to the abbot of Basingwerk to ask for remedy. Part of their petition entailed a brief but comprehensive history of the chapel, which, it was asserted, was built by Llywelyn in celebration of the birth of his son Dafydd at Castell Hen Blas, the motte-and-bailey castle situated around five and a half miles north-east of Ewloe.[135] We now know this particular reference to Coleshill to be synonymous with Hen Blas, which, combined with an exceptionally unusual flurry of diplomatic activity intended to achieve papal dispensation for Dafydd's mother's illegitimate status in early 1226, leaves us with the circumstance that Dafydd was about to come of age at that time, meaning he was born around April 1212 in the castle.

This, however, invites a most important question: why not Ewloe? As Llywelyn's first-born son by his consort Joan, Dafydd's arrival was clearly regarded by the prince as auspicious, as his construction of the chapel – a gesture unique in the history of the native princes – indicates. There are indications that Hen Blas was, at least for a time, a high-status site, as the recovery of several items indicative of that status, including an ornate roof finial in the shape of a lion, surely a reference to the prince's coat of arms, demonstrates.[136] We should be alert to the possibility that Hen Blas was thought of highly despite the fact that no masonry castle was built there.[137] Nevertheless, it seems inconceivable to envisage the prince bringing Joan to child-bed in a wooden motte-and-bailey castle, no matter how comfortable, if a brand-new masonry castle, with all the connotations of wealth and aggrandisement it carried, were available a couple of miles away. Such symbolism was alluring even to English monarchs: seventy years later, Edward I would have his queen Eleanor conveyed to Caernarfon to deliver his son,

133. *AWR*, p. 26.
134. Stephenson and Jones, 'The date and context', p. 32.
135. For a full explication, Stephenson and Jones, 'The date and context', pp. 22–3, and references therein.
136. G.B. Leach, 'Excavations at Hen Blas, Coleshill Fawr, near Flint – Second Report', *JFHS*, 18 (1960), pp. 30–3 (note by G.C. Dunning).
137. R. Higham and P. Barker, *Timber Castles* (Exeter, 2004), p. 11.

described by Prestwich as resembling little more than a 'building-site' at the time, owing to the site's imperial Roman connections.[138]

Ewloe would have constituted even more attractive a spot for Dafydd's birth if Stephenson's analysis of its microlocation is correct. In seeking an explanation for the castle's markedly suboptimal siting, with high ground to the south and restricted sightlines on three sides, Stephenson has plausibly argued that the castle was built on the site of the battle of Coed Eulo (1157), in which an army led by Henry II was ambushed and defeated by a Welsh force led by the sons of Owain Gwynedd.[139] The reverse was insufficient to check Henry's progress entirely, but the battle's outcome, combined with the Welsh victory over an Anglo-Norman invasion force at Moelfre on the north-eastern coast of Ynys Môn during the same campaign,[140] was surely responsible for Henry's decision to bring Owain to terms early and to depart Wales having secured territorial concessions rather than the more comprehensive reduction of the prince's kingdom that he had surely first envisaged.[141] As such, Owain's fame spread far and wide, and it does not overstate matters to suggest that the victory attained substantial symbolic importance.[142] Ewloe may well have been built where it was to commemorate that victory. Its suitability as a birthplace for the prince's child is plain. That it did not function as such argues very strongly against its existence at the time of Dafydd's birth.

All this suggests a start date between Easter 1212 and the early 1240s for the initial works at Ewloe. But, while no firm conclusions can be drawn, examination of Llywelyn's relations with his contemporary rulers and what we know of his castle-building activities elsewhere may allow us to further refine the probable period of construction. For many years Llywelyn had endured an antagonistic relationship with his eastern neighbour, Ranulf III, earl of Chester, but in 1218 the two men made peace.[143] The circumstances were propitious. Ranulf, about to go on crusade, was desirous of securing the western border of the palatinate of Chester, which abutted Tegeingl, while Llywelyn may have been anxious to smooth relations with one of his most dangerous opponents. The exact nature of this rapprochement is poorly attested. If it was ever written down, no copy survives, and the only source to make explicit reference to it is *Annales Cestrienses*. The entry, though brief, very clearly implies that it was initiated by Ranulf; the only

---

138. Prestwich, *Edward I*, p. 226.
139. Stephenson, 'A reconsideration', p. 253. In so doing, Stephenson finessed a suggestion first put forward by J.G. Edwards ('Henry II and the fight at Coleshill', pp. 251–63) that the battle took place in the Ewloe area, who was himself interrogating the long-held belief that the battle occurred in the vicinity of Castell Hen Blas.
140. This battle receives the briefest of mentions in the *Brutiau*, but was fulsomely described in contemporary poetry; see, for example, Clancy, *Medieval Welsh Poems*, p. 136.
141. BYT RBH, p. 137; Lloyd, *History of Wales*, pp. 498–500.
142. Stephenson, 'A reconsideration', p. 247.
143. Swallow, 'Gateways to power', p. 299 and references therein.

other event recorded as having occurred in the year 1218 is Ranulf's departure on crusade, which is explicitly described as having taken place the following week.[144] The prevailing view is that the two men were at that moment engaged in armed conflict of some description, but this is an unsound conclusion, for no such conflict is recorded in any contemporary source. Indeed, this narrative is entirely unsupported by the *Brutiau*, which, despite containing unusually full and detailed entries for 1216, 1217 and 1218, make no mention of conflict in the north-east and ignore the agreement of 1218 completely. Evidently it was of less importance in Welsh circles than in Ranulf's, which leaves us floundering for an explanation as to why it came to pass in the first place; the explanation tentatively advanced by Ranulf's biographer James W. Alexander – that the agreement was a response to Welsh opposition to the king, opposition that was at that point at least two years in the past – is slender at best.[145] It is reasonable to assume that Ranulf feared the possibility of an aggressive move by Llywelyn in his absence – the accounts in the *Brutiau* describe in heady detail Llywelyn's vigorous campaigning in 1216 and 1217 in particular[146] – and sought to forestall such a move. The two men had reason to fear one another, having come to blows during Ranulf's inconclusive Welsh expedition in the summer of 1210; and, indeed, Ranulf almost certainly had an eye-witness to draw upon for Llywelyn's more recent campaigns in mid-Wales, in the guise of Gwenwynwyn, a Powysian lord who fled to Cheshire in 1216 after having been dispossessed of his lands in Powys as the result of Llywelyn's forays that year.[147] But, given that the prince's campaigning took place in southern Powys, the region around Brecon and south Wales, what reason would Ranulf have to suspect Llywelyn wished to open a second front, so to speak, in the north-east? Perhaps the earl merely saw what Llywelyn was doing elsewhere and worried that his lands would be next. But it becomes a great deal easier to understand his trepidation if we postulate that the prince's works at Ewloe had lately commenced.

After 1218 a sustained period of cordial relations between Llywelyn and Ranulf ensued. The peace between the two men endured and, as Rachel Swallow has argued, relations were so harmonious that it may even be permissible to speak of a nascent 'power bloc' in north Wales and Cheshire at this time;[148] indeed, in 1222 the friendship was further strengthened when Ranulf's heir John the Scot married one of Llywelyn's daughters, Elen.[149] The border between Gwynedd and England in the north-east would doubtless have been perceived by Llywelyn as stable and, in the end, it proved so until the end of

144. Christie, *Annales Cestrienses*, <http://www.british-history.ac.uk/lancs-ches-record-soc/vol14/pp50-59> (accessed 8 January 2020).
145. J.W. Alexander, *Ranulf of Chester: A Relic of the Conquest* (Athens, GA, 1983), p. 77.
146. BYT RBH, pp. 207–19.
147. Lloyd, *A History of Wales*, pp. 649–50.
148. Swallow, 'Gateways to power', p. 303.
149. Swallow, 'Gateways to power', p. 300.

Figure 1.10 Ewloe as viewed from the south-west, showing the Welsh Tower and upper ward revetment.

Llywelyn's reign. It then becomes insupportable to envisage Ewloe as having been built after this point, because it would have served no purpose. I can find no warrant for the recent suggestion – made from a (perfectly understandable) impulse to account for the seeming disjunction between the castle's *relative* weakness and its military effectiveness – that Ewloe's primary function was as 'lordly accommodation with a level of security'.[150] Not only does it violate Occam's razor, given Castell Hen Blas's position as readily available fortified accommodation less than half an hour's ride to the north-west,[151] but it also requires the dismissal of the very substantial building work carried out at Ewloe to make the position a defensible one. The castle's most impressive technical accomplishments are arguably not the walls of the Welsh Tower at all, but the massive revetment that underpins the curtain wall and the rock-cut ditches that are adjacent to it on three sides (Fig. 1.10).[152]

This feature is nowhere paralleled at any of the sites Llywelyn is known to have fortified up to this point – work of this sort at Dolwyddelan is far less substantial, and the revetment at Prysor more poorly erected – and must have significantly increased the outlay on the castle's defences, far beyond that expected to lend the position a mere 'level of security' (Fig. 1.11).

This argument is lent further support by the probability that the works at Ewloe were all authored by Llywelyn I. For many years it has been assumed that the castle was built, either in part or in its entirety, by Llywelyn II in 1257. As noted above, the document on which this theory rests in fact records nothing more than a restoration or strengthening occurred at that time, and Brodie's recent suggestion that work carried out that year extended to nothing more than a replacement of roofs or floors that had fallen into disrepair[153] is almost certainly correct. Llywelyn's situation and the course of events in 1257 do not readily support the idea that the prince embarked on substantial work there that year or subsequently. For one thing, the reconquest of the Perfeddwlad is likely to have taken many months, and was probably ongoing in 1257;[154] the construction of an entire castle, or even the lower ward and west tower that is often represented as a possible second phase, is unlikely to have been accomplished under such

---

150. Brodie, 'Apsidal and D-shaped towers', p. 233. The analysis presented above in turn makes Brodie's suggestion that Ewloe was probably built between 1221 and 1237 – that is, during a time of cordial relations between Llywelyn and Ranulf – less likely; see below.

151. As noticed by Stephenson, 'A reconsideration', p. 250, n. 3. Nor was Llywelyn's use of Hen Blas in 1212 exceptional; the castle was still in use thirty years later, when Dafydd II appears to have signed a charter there, strongly suggesting that Hen Blas and Ewloe were meant to fulfil differing roles and that the latter was not meant to replace all the functions of the former (Leach, 'Excavations at Hen Blas', p. 59).

152. Renn and Avent, *Flint Castle/Ewloe Castle*, p. 30.

153. Brodie, 'Apsidal and D-shaped towers', p. 234.

154. Stephenson, 'A reconsideration', p. 250, n. 2.

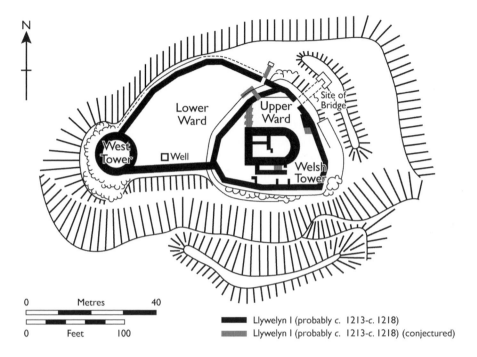

Figure 1.11 Ewloe, plan.

conditions.[155] Secondly, Roger de Montalt did not come into possession of Ewloe until after he was made justice of Chester in late May, which presupposes that Llywelyn took possession at some point in the year after that, giving insufficient time to build an entire ward and a tower before the end of the building season in the autumn. (Even if we assume that a programme of works continued until 1259 – by which time Ewloe was in use as a meeting place, and such construction may reasonably be thought to have been completed – the great famine of 1258 would have acted as such a drain on manpower that it stretches credulity to think such work could have been successfully brought to completion.) Thirdly, Henry III's campaign in north Wales, which left Chester in August, appeared to devote no time at all to the reduction of Ewloe – a peculiar omission if that castle had been recently extended; the king would surely have wished to seize and destroy such works for symbolic reasons if not military ones. Finally, there is the probability that Llywelyn's financial resources were being spent on military campaigns in 1257: aside from the prince's operations in the north-east, a major campaign was embarked on in south Wales, culminating in the rout of an English army under

155. For the rationale behind this theory, Stephenson, 'A reconsideration', p. 250, n. 2.

Stephen Bauzan at Cymerau in June.[156] None of this lends credence to a major construction programme in 1257: on the contrary, it tends to give more weight to the idea that Ewloe was abandoned on Roger de Montalt's repossession of the region after the war of 1244–6, and that Llywelyn made a point of restoring Ewloe to its former glory in order to impress upon de Montalt – a thorn in the side of his predecessor Dafydd II – the emergence of a new power in the region. It would seem, however, that that was the extent of his work, and that the castle was conceived, commenced and completed by his grandfather.[157]

The most recent date range given for Ewloe's construction is between 1221 to 1237: that is, a period when relations between Llywelyn and the earl of Chester were cordial, thus endorsing the interpretation that Ewloe had no *a priori* military purpose.[158] However, this idea of Ewloe's function is more difficult to sustain than it appears. For one thing, the castles we know Llywelyn was building in the 1220s, Y Bere and Cricieth, were of an entirely different character in both form and function, being bigger, more massively built and emplaced for maximum visibility. Secondly, both boasted sophisticated entrances incorporating gatehouses and portcullises, and Y Bere in particular made increasing use of the enfilade. It is true that these details are not found universally in castles built subsequently by the princes, but that fact that none of them are found at Ewloe is odd if it was Cricieth's and Y Bere's contemporary. For Llywelyn to embark on construction of a castle there without these innovations seems like a retrograde step.

There remains, however, the question of Llywelyn's residence at nearby Hen Blas. If Ewloe was meant to act as princely accommodation in the area, Hen Blas' continued occupation until well into the later thirteenth century, as is attested by documentary and archaeological evidence, makes no sense. Regardless of the inadequacies of Ewloe's siting and its subsequent usage as a meeting place, then, we are left with the notion that the castle was envisioned as a military installation in the first instance, with an overt expeditionary role. All the indications are that it was built to underline Llywelyn's renewed grip on Tegeingl after 1212, and its microlocation would seem to have been the product of a compromise between the demands of a nascent political ideology and simple military expediency. While hardly boasting the passive strength of Cricieth or Dinas Brân, its dispositions are by no means neglected. Its defences face east – that is, toward the earl of Chester's territory. The existence of a (now vanished) linking wall connecting the Welsh Tower with the curtain wall demonstrated an increasing attentiveness to internal

---

156. LlapG, pp. 98–9.
157. This refutation of 1257 as Ewloe's date of construction derives from C.O. Jones, 'Further thoughts on Ewloe castle', *Archaeologia Cambrensis*, 170 (2021), pp. 237–50.
158. Brodie, 'Apsidal and D-shaped towers', p. 233.

communications;[159] and, for all the criticism of the Welsh Tower's siting, its sheer strength and height must have made it a formidable keep. Much has been made of the imposing counterscarp that overlooks the castle on its southern side, but we must endeavour to imagine how the position would have looked without this in place. Although Ken Lloyd Gruffydd's suggestion that this feature is a fourteenth-century addition designed to demarcate the extent of the deer park created by the Black Prince[160] is not sound, equally its existence in the 1210s would have made a mockery of Llywelyn's works, and the suggestion that it represents a siegework of Edward I is probably correct.[161] All in all, Ewloe's position was as well prepared as could be imagined – if it was indeed built on the site of the victory at Coed Eulo as a constant reminder to Llywelyn's English adversaries of the dangers of underestimating Welsh military power, its builders could only make the best of the terrain at their disposal. It is certainly difficult to see how this microlocation could have been fortified any more effectively.

However, Ewloe's military role would only have obtained during Llywelyn's reign for as long as Tegeingl lay adjacent to a hostile neighbour. Once relations with Ranulf were normalised in 1218, securing that border by means of a castle or castles would accordingly have slipped down Llywelyn's list of priorities. At the same time, postulating a date of construction in the early 1220s is unlikely, for in 1221 Llywelyn is recorded as having begun construction work at Y Bere, and works at Cricieth were almost certainly begun a few years later; it is difficult to

159. This feature – marked in grey on the diagram in the Cadw guidebook – is strangely elusive in descriptions of the castle. It is not presently visible on the surface, and nor is there any indication of a joint with either the curtain wall or the north-western corner of the Welsh Tower. Clearly, some sort of wall was present here, however, and a substantial one at that: Hemp's 1928 plan shows a wall of the same thickness as the Welsh Tower's walls very distinctly, running north to south into the tower's corner, and it also appears on a RCAHMW plan of 1926 (albeit with a slightly different north-west–south-east alignment). Hemp was in no doubt that it once existed, but was now 'entirely lost' (*Ewloe Castle* (London, 1929), p. 9). At present, the only possible indication of the wall's existence is the presence of the left-hand side of a door jamb in the ruinous northern end of the Welsh Tower's west wall. Renn and Avent speculate (p. 34) that this either gave onto a short passage affording access to the top of such a wall or turned east, into an intramural passage in the north wall, possibly leading to a latrine. The current writer sees no reason why this passage could not have done both. If so, it demonstrates that the linking wall rose to at least first-floor height and, aside from joining the Welsh Tower and the curtain, would also have faced the castle's entrance, exposing anyone gaining access to the ward there to fire at close range. Similar dispositions at Cricieth and Dolforwyn arguably underline a hitherto unsuspected native Welsh awareness of and attention to the weakness of the Welsh style of castle entrance, which often constituted a simple, narrow opening in the curtain; see chapter 3. There is a superficially similar feature at Carndochan, but it lies atop the fallen remains of the castle, and Hogg's theory that it is of a later date has recently been confirmed (D. Hopewell, pers. comm.).

160. FRO NT/833.

161. Ken Lloyd Gruffydd suggested that Ewloe fell between 16 November and 15 December 1276; FRO NT/833.

imagine the prince placing unnecessary strain on the royal coffers by building three substantial castles at once.[162] One final possibility is that the castle was built after Ranulf's death in 1232, but Llywelyn's relations with Ranulf's successor – the prince's son-in-law, John the Scot (d. 1237) – were at least nominally friendly, and there are no indications of tensions on the border at this time.[163] The balance of evidence, then, requires us to ascribe Ewloe's first phase to a period between, say, the cessation of hostilities between Llywelyn and John in mid-1213 and the concluding of peace between Llywelyn and Ranulf in 1218.[164]

Ewloe's aspect and microlocation would seem to fit very well with the political realities faced by Llywelyn at this time. While Llywelyn was clearly in possession of Castell Hen Blas at the time of Dafydd's birth in 1212, his grip on the remainder of Tegeingl was still open to question. In 1212 the prince re-emerged following John's humiliation of him the previous year, but Llywelyn did not regain his former authority throughout Tegeingl until the following year. In 1213, as has been noticed already, Welsh forces under his aegis captured the motte-and-bailey castles at Rhuddlan and Holywell, securing the northern coastal route from England as far east as Hen Blas. If this advance halted a few miles further to the east, it becomes entirely credible to view the building of Ewloe as an example of expeditionary emplacement.

As such, however, Ewloe was almost certainly meant to announce Llywelyn's presence rather than act as the lock and stay of the north-east. As events during the second half of the thirteenth century demonstrated, Ewloe was ultimately unsuited to act as an effective bulwark against incursions by armies of the English crown from the east; we take liberties with both its defensibility and its positioning if we pretend otherwise. As time wore on, the expediency of possessing a stronghold in Tegeingl that was both able to withstand determined assault and so emplaced as to be able to command the coastal route increasingly favoured by English invasion armies would force the princes of Wales to seek ever more elaborate ways to meet the need.

162. Avent, *Dolwyddelan Castle/Dolbadarn Castle*, p. 5 emphasises the enormous drain the construction of a masonry castle must have been on the prince's finances: 'Construction would not have begun without a clear purpose in mind.'

163. A construction date after 1237 seems to conflict with indications of Llywelyn's decreasing rigour in his final years; LltG, p. 134.

164. One objection to this dating is architectural. The castle is formed from yellow sandstone which, in the opinion of Renn and Avent, was sourced from local Coal Measures (*Flint Castle/Ewloe Castle*, p. 29). However, the Welsh Tower features red sandstone in its surviving door jambs and dressings (Brodie, 'Apsidal and D-shaped towers', p. 233). No such deposit was known about in the vicinity on the Welsh side of the border. The closest source was Burton Point on the Wirral peninsula, but presumably this would not have been available to the builders of Ewloe during the suggested period of construction because Llywelyn and Ranulf were at that time in conflict. One possible explanation may be that a supply of red sandstone from the Wirral was already in Welsh hands. The same stone is found at Castell Hen Blas, the builders of which may plausibly have sourced a quantity of the stone in early 1212, in the hiatus after the peace agreement of 1211 but before hostilities recommenced in the summer.

# 2

## The later castles of
## Llywelyn I ab Iorwerth (c.1220–40)

Much like history itself, the lives of great men and women rarely divide themselves into neatly organised periods, and Llywelyn I's life is no exception. His rise to power was incremental and – the surrender of 1211 and the triumphs of 1215 aside – his reign was not distinguished by any very swift rise or fall in his status. Those looking for a sudden change in his castle-building policy – some moment at which the modes and principles of construction and emplacement detailed in the previous chapter were discarded in favour of a new agenda – will search in vain.

And yet it is possible to discern a subtle change in Llywelyn's approach during the later years of his reign. It was partly occasioned by the adoption of new theories regarding castle-building and partly by, as we may surmise, an increase in the funds available to Llywelyn by dint of the swelling numbers of territories under his control and the gradual advent of a cash-based economy. These factors allowed him to begin works at Cricieth, Deganwy and Castell Y Bere of greater proportions and sophistication than any of his other castles. It is also true that, as his position became secure, Llywelyn expended increasing amounts of effort on attempting to ensure his patrimony passed unhindered to his chosen *edling*, Dafydd, his son by his consort Joan.[1] The construction of one of these castles, Cricieth, if not occasioned by the need to accommodate the circumstances and ambitions of Dafydd's elder but illegitimate brother, Gruffudd, may have at least been partially informed by this necessity. However, the advent of this collection of corporate castles also constituted a change of emphasis regarding function. Carndochan, Dolwyddelan and their ilk were emplaced to articulate Llywelyn's claim to princely power, to stamp authority on the regions in which they were raised and to see to the internal security of his kingdom once it was established. By contrast, the interaction of Cricieth and Deganwy with the landscape shows that they contributed little to Gwynedd's *internal* security during Llywelyn's later reign. On the contrary: they were sited to allow the maritime approaches to Gwynedd to be monitored, and Y Bere, though a little way inland, likewise overlooked a navigable waterway in the

---

1.   Lloyd, *History of Wales*, p. 656; Stephenson and Jones, 'The date and the context', pp. 28–9.

Dysynni valley and, as Hemp put it, 'afford[ed] easy access to the harbour at the mouth of the Dysynni river'.[2] What these castles did that the smaller castles of Llywelyn's early reign did not do was to underline his authority at points of entry into his kingdom, in much the same way that the formidable castles at Dover and Portchester did for the king of England, and they did so in a far more impressive and dramatic fashion than any fortification he had yet commissioned.

The importance of Wales's maritime links during the early thirteenth century has yet to be fully appreciated, mostly because concrete evidence of maritime trade and movement by sea, so abundant for Wales in the fifteenth century and relatively so for the fourteenth, is thin on the ground for the period of Llywelyn's reign. However, a great deal of circumstantial evidence exists suggesting that these links were as abundant (or nearly so) during Llywelyn's reign as they were in these periods. The nascent town at Nefyn had been in existence in some form since the days of Llywelyn's grandfather Gruffudd ap Cynan (d. 1137), and was attracting merchant settlers – such as one Stephen, who also owned a burgage in Drogheda on the Irish coast opposite Nefyn – in the very earliest years of Llywelyn's reign.[3] The earliest mention of the town at Llanfaes on Ynys Môn dates from 1209; the context suggests a port that was already well known and being frequently visited by foreign merchants (see below).[4] Further south, it has been plausibly argued that the monks of Cymer abbey in Meirionydd cultivated a lively trade in wool; a Cae Llong ('Field of Ships') in the vicinity of the abbey seems to speak more directly to such a trade.[5] Timber, too, may have been exported from Gwynedd: R. Andrew McDonald has made a convincing case for such a trade between Wales and the Isle of Man.[6] The Welsh laws made extensive references to procedure that should be followed in the event of shipwrecks and, indeed, referred to the sea as 'the King's [i.e. the prince's] packhorse'; archaeological finds of thirteenth-century French pottery at Y Bere testify to the importation of wine, presumably by ship, datable to the late thirteenth century; and there also exist several references to the existence of something akin to a navy or, at the very least, the ability to fit out ships for military purposes, in Llywelyn's time.[7] Wales was indeed a maritime nation in the early thirteenth century. What responsible prince would have neglected its seaward defences – or indeed have failed to capitalise on the possibilities for personal and national aggrandisement

2.    W.J. Hemp, 'Castell Y Bere', AC, 97 (1942), p. 121.
3.    D. Stephenson, 'Events at Nefyn c. 1200 – the plundering of King John's Irish hounds and hawks', CMCS, 75 (2018), pp. 39–43.
4.    Jones, 'Historical writing in medieval Wales', p. 419.
5.    J. Burton and K. Stöber, Abbeys and Priories of Medieval Wales (Cardiff, 2015), pp. 84–5.
6.    R.A. McDonald, Manx Kingship in its Irish Sea Setting, 1187–1229 (Dublin, 2007), p. 106.
7.    D. Jenkins (ed. and transl.), The Law of Hywel Dda (Llandysul, 2000), p. 112; for the find of French pottery in a likely Welsh context at Y Bere, L.A.S. Butler, 'Medieval finds from Castell-Y-Bere, Merioneth', AC, 123 (1974), p. 83; for Llywelyn's ships, K.L. Gruffydd, Maritime Wales in the Middle Ages: 1039–1542 (Wrexham, 2016), p. 10.

that the advertisement of power in the form of a well-sited, strongly built masonry castle overlooking his principal shipping routes would afford him?

This aspect of castle-building in thirteenth-century Gwynedd has been sorely neglected. Though Lawrence Butler moved a little way in this direction, according Llywelyn the epithet of 'protector of the coasts' by dint of his works at Cricieth and Deganwy,[8] Rachel Swallow's plausible suggestion that these castles, along with the substantial motte at Twthill (Rhuddlan), may have constituted part of 'a coastal line of Llywelyn's castles demarcating his territory'[9] represents the beginnings of an attempt to formulate a sustained response to this gap in our understanding of Llywelyn's military dispositions. Perhaps the most pressing need along the northern coast was to monitor traffic in and out of the Menai straits. This need was appreciated by the Anglo-Normans who interpenetrated Wales in the 1090s, and who were the likely authors of the mottes at Caernarfon and Aber. Both were maintained and utilised by the Welsh in the thirteenth century, the latter as one of Llywelyn's two most important *llysoedd*. To this list we might add Deudraeth, which was in existence at the time of Gerald of Wales's progress around Wales in 1188; the motte at Cymer; and Cynfal.[10]

Llywelyn's new builds at Cricieth and Y Bere and his likely refortification in stone of Deganwy (see below) were the most prominent of these castles. That they were meant to control (or at least monitor) the coast is clear, but their 'symbolic' purpose[11] cannot be underestimated; in their grandiosity they are unlike any of the castles under his control elsewhere in Gwynedd. At the peripheries of his territory, for example, Llywelyn contented himself with the castles that came into his possession as he expanded his kingdom and influence. The Oswestry salient provides several important examples. Ellesmere was given to Llywelyn on his marriage to King John's daughter Joan in 1205; the castle was seized from the prince in late 1208, but returned early the following year, after which he enjoyed almost uninterrupted possession of it until 1231.[12] Similarly, in 1223, Llywelyn

8.   L. Butler, 'The castles of the Princes of Gwynedd', in Williams and Kenyon (eds), *Impact of the Edwardian Castles*, p. 29.

9.   Swallow, 'Gateways to power', p. 307.

10.   Ynys Môn, by contrast, is almost entirely destitute of castles of either Welsh or Anglo-Norman construction; the few exceptions – Aberlleiniog, the later castle at Beaumaris, and a (conjectured) motte in the vicinity of Moel-y-don (Royal Commission on the Ancient and Historical Monuments of Wales, *An Inventory of the Ancient Monuments in Anglesey* (London, 1937), p. cxlvi) – all overlook the Menai straits.

11.   Butler, 'The castles of the Princes of Gwynedd', p. 29.

12.   On 27 June 1231 the sheriff of Shropshire was ordered to take the manor of Ellesmere into the king's hand and keep it safely until the king orders otherwise; <https://finerollshenry3.org.uk/content/calendar/roll_030.html> (accessed 28 March 2021). I am grateful to David Stephenson for bringing this reference to my attention. For a full examination of the circumstances behind the bestowal of Ellesmere, as well as its subsequent loss and recapture by Llywelyn in the 1210s, C.O. Jones, 'Prydydd Y Moch, Ellesmere, and Llywelyn ab Iorwerth's Shropshire campaigns', AC, 169 (2020), pp. 165–76.

seized the castles at Whittington and Kinnerley, apparently holding the latter for the remainder of his reign.[13] These castles in north-west Shropshire are themselves deserving of further study. They were held in high regard by Llywelyn and his people – the references to Ellesmere's opulence in the praise poetry of Prydydd Y Moch (d. *c*.1220), no less than Llywelyn's strenuous efforts to recapture the castle in 1212 and 1215,[14] testify to its centrality in his thinking regarding the strategic situation in the Oswestry salient.

However, these castles were opposed by mottes thrown up and garrisoned by Marcher lords and, as such, their symbolic importance was limited. The reduction of such timber-framed castles as these was well within the grasp of both Llywelyn and the Marcher lords.[15] Llywelyn did not augment them by building masonry castles in their stead surely because he had neither the financial resources nor the political capital necessary to embark on that work. In this way we may account for his apparent retention of the masonry castle at Alberbury until as late as 1226, and his sustained interest in Whittington lordship, in which a substantial masonry castle was being built on the initiative of Fulk fitz Warin from the mid-1220s onward; his manoeuvrings over the lordship may indeed have crystallised into a formal claim following his marriage to Fulk fitz Warin's daughter, Eva, in 1239.[16]

By the mid-thirteenth century masonry castles were also beginning to speak more resoundingly to a different level of power, wealth and authority, and the appearance of such castles at Cricieth, Deganwy and Y Bere is indicative of changing priorities in the latter part of Llywelyn's reign. Aside from their superior size and architecture, their macrolocations in coastal areas are the most emphatic demonstration of this. Evoking J.E. Lloyd's observation of the silence of the Welsh law books on the subject of maritime travel, B.H. St John O'Neil averred that 'there is no evidence that the Welsh princes of the thirteenth century took any interest in the sea'.[17] However, references exist that attest to the increasing importance in Gwynedd and Deheubarth of travel by and exploitation of the sea in the thirteenth century, particularly from the 1210s and 1220s onwards. Internal communications were certainly facilitated by boat and ship. The existence of ferries conveying passengers and goods across the Menai straits and the Conwy estuary is well known; three were in existence serving the former in 1282 and, of these, at least one – that of Llanfaes – almost certainly existed in Llywelyn's time.[18] Additionally, limestone probably derived from Ynys Môn in the mortar used to

13. Stephenson, 'Fouke le Fitz Waryn', p. 26; D. Stephenson, 'Welsh lords in Shropshire', SHA, 77 (2002), p. 34.
14. Jones, 'Prydydd Y Moch'.
15. D.J.C. King and C.J. Spurgeon, 'The mottes in the vale of Montgomery', AC, 114 (1965), p. 84.
16. Stephenson, 'Fouke le Fitz Waryn', p. 27.
17. B.J.St.J. O'Neil, 'Cricieth Castle, Caernarvonshire', AC, 98 (1944–5), pp. 2–3.
18. As is suggested by the conveyance of the body of Joan to Llanfaes from Aber in 1237; Lloyd, History of Wales, p. 686.

build Carndochan castle almost certainly arrived by sea, as Dave Hopewell has convincingly suggested.[19]

There is also evidence that the Welsh of Llywelyn's kingdom embarked on sea voyages to places further afield and received those making the reciprocal journey. Envoys were probably sent to Rome by the prince in 1226, as they were by Dafydd II in 1244 and by Llywelyn II in the 1270s, and although the earliest inarguable evidence for a papal representative visiting Wales during the Age of the Princes dates from the mid-1260s,[20] it is not inherently unlikely that earlier visits occurred. As noted above, archaeological finds of French pottery at Y Bere supports the idea that there was a lively trade for those items at high-status sites, and Kathryn Hurlock's recent investigations of Welsh participation in the Crusades has revealed that numbers of Welsh are recorded as having travelled to the Holy Land; doubtless those numbers were higher than is recorded in surviving documents.[21] Still others travelled to sites of pilgrimage. Katharine Olson's study of the presence of the Welsh in Rome in the later medieval period makes clear that the abundance of late medieval pilgrims had its corollary in earlier groups of *Romipetae* who travelled from Wales in Llywelyn's time, and whose exploits were obliquely referred to by the prince's poets.[22] These strands of evidence do not necessarily constitute proof of direct maritime links with mainland Europe. French trade items could have arrived via Bristol or Chester, for example, and, in the same way, we also know that travel to mainland Europe via England was an option for Welsh travellers during times of peace.[23] However, there are so many examples of contact between Wales and mainland Europe occurring in situations where English involvement was unlikely or impractical that it seems Anglocentric in the extreme to invoke travel or trade via English ports in every circumstance. Direct contact between Gwynedd and the French court was established in 1212 and again in 1241 – that is, at times when open conflict, or at least hostility, between Wales and England rendered travel via England unfeasible; indeed, the latter report, made by John Lestrange, of the presence of envoys of Dafydd II at the

19. The limestone was probably conveyed to Meirionydd by ship and brought up the Mawddach before arriving at Carndochan and being processed on site. Personal communication with the author, 4 December 2019.

20. B. Jones, 'Documents relevant to Wales before the Edwardian conquest in the Vatican archives', in P. Skinner (ed.), *The Welsh and the Medieval World: Travel, Migration and Exile* (Cardiff, 2018), p. 223.

21. K. Hurlock, *Wales and the Crusades c. 1095–1291* (Cardiff, 2011).

22. K. Olson, '"Ar ffordd Pedr a Phawl": Welsh pilgrimage and travel to Rome, *c.* 1200–*c.* 1530', *WHR*, 24 (2008), pp. 5, 10–11.

23. A good example of this is provided by Llywelyn's *distain* [seneschal] Ednyfed Fychan, who in 1235 was reported to be embarking on a crusade to the Holy Land. Whether he got there is not certain, but he certainly seems to have begun his journey, as Henry III understood that he had stopped in London *en route* and gave orders to have him sought out and presented with a silver cup as a token of his affection (Hurlock, *Crusades*, p. 218; *GG*, p. 208).

court of Louis IX around 1241 is couched in tones of startlement, suggesting a lack of foreknowledge of a Welsh diplomatic mission to the French royal court.[24] One might also recall the rumour recorded by Matthew Paris of an alliance between the Welsh and the Scots, supposedly concluded during the early 1230s.[25] We do not know the veracity of this report, but its significance lies in the fact that Llywelyn was in conflict with Henry III's Marcher lords at the time, presumably making travel between Gwynedd and Scotland via England an unattractive proposition, and that Paris was clearly under the impression such an alliance could have been concluded without English knowledge of it.

Wales may have been perceived as geographically isolated and economically backward; in the twelfth century it was certainly the latter. By the later years of Llywelyn's reign, however, it was becoming markedly less so. The move from a render-based to a cash-based economy was slow, but it was indisputably under way by the first decade of the thirteenth century. It was aided by the exploitation of silver deposits in Gwynedd and Powys by Llywelyn and Gwenwynwyn respectively, the former using Flintshire silver to strike his own imitative issues of the Short Cross penny at Rhuddlan, and the latter selling silver mined at the works at Carreghofa to the Shrewsbury mint across the border.[26] Accordingly, trade with foreign merchants began to pick up. The prosperity of Llanfaes is suggested by the fact that it was attacked by Viking raiders in October 1209. The raiders, led by one Erlendr Pikr, seem to have gone out of their way to do so, apparently sailing from Iona in Scotland. On landing at Llanfaes they were defeated, and Erlendr killed, by a Welsh force apparently led by Llywelyn himself.[27] The discovery of substantial numbers of coins on the site of the settlement in the mid-1990s, coupled with evidence of the presence of a goldsmith,[28] underlines the attractiveness of the port as a target for the Vikings, and by implication awareness of its existence outside the British Isles.

Situating castles along the coasts, particularly in close proximity to ports, was therefore becoming expedient in the later period of Llywelyn's reign. Castles so emplaced fulfilled a dual purpose. Firstly, they allowed the maritime approaches to Gwynedd to be monitored and important economic centres to be defended. We can see instances of this most clearly in the refortification of Norman mottes at Aber and Caernarfon – that is, at opposite ends of the Menai straits and therefore positioned to monitor traffic in and out of the straits. The former overlooked the port at Llanfaes, while the latter appears to have been adjacent to the royal *llys* and

24.  Edwards, *Calendar of Ancient Correspondence*, p. 22.
25.  R. Oram, *Alexander II, King of Scots 1216–1249* (Edinburgh, 2012), p. 136.
26.  Jones, 'Gwenwynwyn'.
27.  Jones, 'Historical writing in medieval Wales', pp. 426–7; for Llywelyn's likely presence at Llanfaes, Jones, 'Prydydd Y Moch'.
28.  Besly, 'Short Cross and other medieval coins', *passim*; M. Redknap, 'Some medieval brooches, pendants and moulds from Wales: a short survey', *AC*, 143 (1996), p. 122.

settlement there.[29] The motte at Nefyn, if it was indeed reused by the Welsh,[30] provided another such site, with a prominent position immediately adjacent to the port and commanding views of Bae Caernarfon, and the motte at Prestatyn, which was considered sufficiently important for it to be invested by a combined force of men from Gwynedd and Deheubarth in 1167,[31] did the same duty for its Norman occupants in regard to the approaches to Liverpool Bay in the mid-twelfth century. It is not quite safe to follow C.P. Lewis's lead and assume that the surviving mottes on the Gwynedd's shores were constructed because 'a [Norman] strategist of genius had understood how Gwynedd could be dominated from a few vital points on the coast'[32] – the possibility that mottes such as that at Tomen Fawr on the southern coast of the Llŷn were erected by local Norman lords not as part of some grand strategic plan for regional subjugation but to defend their own estates, as part of what Creighton describes as 'an unrivalled boom in private defence' in the late eleventh century, cannot be ruled out.[33] However, there is no denying their utility as positions from which sea traffic could be monitored, and that their later counterparts were raised to fulfil the same function. Cricieth – less than three miles from Tomen Fawr – overlooked Bae Tremadog and Cardigan Bay more generally; Castell Deudraeth, identified reasonably securely as the motte south of modern-day Portmeirion, allowed for the observance of traffic in and out of the Dwyryd estuary; and Deganwy's position at the mouth of the river Conwy commanded Bae Conwy and the opposite shore of Ynys Môn.

Secondly, these castles were situated in places where they would be seen by outsiders. The passage of ships to and from Welsh ports brought with it opportunities not only for trade but also for aggrandisement. As such, the castles erected by Llywelyn exuded extraordinary symbolic value, all the more so for a prince who, as Butler so aptly put it, had reached a point in his accrual of power where he felt them necessary 'to reflect his status and meet the expectations of his new-found peer group'.[34] The contention that these castles were 'almost identical' in architectural terms[35] forces the point somewhat, but in general there is far more about the castles of this period of Llywelyn's reign that is broadly similar than is different. Direct comparison of their layouts is of limited utility, not least because one of them – Deganwy – has yet to be fully excavated. But the three castles characterised here – Cricieth, Deganwy and Castell Y Bere – have several features

29. Swallow, 'Living the dream', pp. 173–4.
30. T. Jones Pierce believed it was; see 'The Old Borough of Nefyn 1355–1882', *Transactions of the Caernarfonshire Historical Society*, 18 (1957), p. 38.
31. BYT RBH, p. 149.
32. C.P. Lewis, 'Gruffudd ap Cynan and the Normans', in K.L. Maund (ed.), *Gruffudd ap Cynan: A Collaborative Biography* (Woodbridge, 1996), p. 70.
33. Lewis, 'Gruffudd ap Cynan and the Normans', p. 70; Creighton, *Castles and Landscapes*, p. 46.
34. Butler, 'The castles of the Princes of Gwynedd', p. 32.
35. Swallow, 'Gateways to power', p. 307.

in common in terms of their location, their relationship to the landscape and the role they played in Llywelyn's Gwynedd. They were indeed, as Rachel Swallow has so convincingly demonstrated, gateways to power.

## Cricieth (first phase)

The castle at Cricieth stands as one of the most impressive architectural achievements of the house of Gwynedd, but in spite – or perhaps because of – that status it has been subject to a great deal of wrong-headed thinking since historians first began to contemplate its origins. Thought by Victorian antiquarians to be a construction of King John,[36] Harold Hughes' excavations in the early 1900s began the task of determining its nature and extent in earnest.[37] B.H. St John O'Neil's investigations in the 1940s completed the bulk of this work. O'Neil revealed a castle built according to an irregular concentric plan. The large rectangular keep and massive twin towers of the inner ward – the gatehouse that so exercised the mind of William Turner when he painted the castle in 1835–6 – were complemented by the discovery and excavation of a substantial outer ward previously largely hidden from sight, consisting of two rectangular towers and an outer gatehouse, that was constructed in a second phase of building works. O'Neil further suggested that a third phase of works followed the castle's seizure by the forces of Edward I in 1283, including the addition of an extra floor to the inner gatehouse.[38] C.N. Johns' rather wayward 1970 reassessment spread far more darkness than light, asserting on the slenderest of grounds that the inner ward and not the outer ward constituted the second phase of building; this view was comprehensively demolished by Colin Gresham in 1973.[39] More recently, it has been postulated that a previously overlooked feature in the outer ward may represent the remains of a gate passage (see chapter 3),[40] but otherwise, barring one or two details, the architectural history of the castle has been established.

The start date of works at Cricieth is not known. Unlike Y Bere (see below), no documentary reference survives pertaining to it, and it cannot be conclusively linked with any known conflict. It has been suggested that Cricieth was to be equated with the 'Deudraeth castle' noted by Gerald of Wales in 1188, but there is no warrant for this.[41] Richard Avent dated Cricieth's construction to the 1230s,[42] and there are some grounds for accepting this premise. The first securely dated

36. F.G.W. Chapman, 'Notes on the castles of Harlech and Cricieth', *Journal of the British Archaeological Association*, 34 (1878) p. 165.
37. H. Hughes, 'Criccieth Castle', *AC*, 60 (1905), pp. 200–10.
38. O'Neil, 'Criccieth Castle, Caernarvonshire', pp. 18–20.
39. Johns, *Castell Cricieth/Criccieth Castle*; C. Gresham, 'The development of Criccieth Castle', *Transactions of the Caernarfonshire Historical Society*, 34 (1973), pp. 14–22.
40. Jones, 'How to make an entrance', *passim*.
41. A.F.L. Beeston, 'In the steps of Gerallt Cymro', *THSC* (1988), p. 23.
42. Avent, *Criccieth Castle*, p. 11.

reference to Cricieth can be found in 1239, when Llywelyn's son Gruffudd was imprisoned there by his half-brother Dafydd, and the commonly held belief that the design of Cricieth's gatehouse was influenced by the design of Beeston's and Montgomery's requires the building of those structures to antedate Cricieth.[43] However, there are more persuasive grounds for endorsing Swallow's suggestion that Cricieth was built slightly earlier, between 1225 and 1235.[44] An *awdl* written shortly after Gruffudd's release from imprisonment in 1234 by Einion ap Madog ap Rhahawd describes him as 'pendefig Cruciaith maith', or lord of extensive Cricieth.[45] The title is a grandiose one; it is hard to see how any poet would have found it a fitting description for the son of a prince if Cricieth was still being built. We are left with the alternative that Cricieth was already in existence and presumably sufficiently well developed as a castle (and perhaps a nascent town) to enable Einion's audience to apprehend this description as lavish. On balance, a start date of the mid-1220s seems likely.

Cricieth's siting likewise requires comment. O'Neil was the first to make the connection between Cricieth and the earlier motte at Dolbenmaen, three miles to the north. O'Neil's argument – that the *cantref* of Eifionydd was overseen by a lord with his seat probably at Dolbenmaen, at a spot overlooking both the principal north–south road through the commote and a crossing of Afon Dwyfawr – is sound and intuitively correct. So too is his inference that the fortification at Dolbenmaen was superseded by Cricieth on the latter's construction.[46] However, the subsequent inference by successive writers – that *all* of the functions fulfilled by Dolbenmaen were subsumed by Cricieth later – is not warranted. In the absence of evidence relating to any other commotal centre in Eifionydd in the mid-thirteenth century, we are justified in thinking that the commote's day-to-day administration was ultimately transferred to Cricieth, even if the date is not certain.[47] But the intention of Cricieth's author cannot have been to guard the north–south road, for it plainly does not do so. Standing three miles south-south-west of the road as the crow flies, Cricieth may have been close enough for patrols to report traffic along the road, but it is most unlikely that troop movements could have been intercepted quickly enough to mount an effective defence of the route (although the castle's presence would have been an obvious threat to supply lines to the rear of any army moving south).

Furthermore, if guarding overland lines of communication in the commote was accorded the same importance during Llywelyn's reign as it was the

---

43.  Avent, *Criccieth Castle*, pp. 2, 12–13.
44.  Swallow, 'Gateways to power', p. 306.
45.  D.F. Evans, 'Castle and town in medieval Wales', in H. Fulton (ed.), *Urban Culture in Medieval Wales* (Cardiff, 2012), p. 185.
46.  O'Neil, 'Criccieth Castle', p. 1.
47.  For a recent rebuttal, however, J. Beverley Smith, 'Llywelyn's hall at Conwy', *AC*, 160 (2011), pp. 207, 215, n. 22.

previous century, one wonders why the prince's new castle was not simply built at Dolbenmaen, rather than at a new site several miles away. While the village's existing motte was clearly unsuitable for the large masonry castle Llywelyn had in mind, there is no reason why the ridge a few hundred yards to the south-west would not have proved an excellent spot for such a construction. Its summit overlooks both road and river in textbook fashion – it constitutes, in fact, the 'other side' of the natural gap described by O'Neil as making the motte's location so suitable for ambuscading passing traffic[48] – and while the approach along the line of the ridge from the north is flatter than would be ideal, one imagines the substantial experience of the Welsh in cutting ditches through bedrock would have been put to good use here.

That the ridge stands bare today disposes us to look beyond the establishment of a new commotal centre for the reason for Cricieth's appearance. The issue certainly exercised O'Neil, who was at a loss to explain why the headland at Cricieth, instead of an inland site, was chosen for Llywelyn's castle. As has been noted, O'Neil regarded the castle's seashore position as irrelevant to its siting, but it is hard to know what other rationale could have obtained for it. It does not appear to have been associated with a town in its earliest years (though Llywelyn may conceivably have sought to create one; it is likely that St Catherine's church was built contemporaneously with the castle).[49] Though the site is commendably suited to such a role, Hogg and King's characterisation of it as a 'state prison' in 1239 seems to imbue it with a status that it never asked for, etymological musings over its name notwithstanding.[50] Nor is it at all easy to argue that the castle was emplaced on the headland for historical reasons – as the successor to an earlier castle, say – for Cricieth was apparently a virgin site.[51]

Assuming that there was no symbolic or ideological value to the site, we may in turn assume that its defensive and visual properties weighed heavily in the balance; and if the principles of corporate emplacement are at all reflective of

48.  O'Neil, 'Criccieth Castle', p. 1.
49.  M.A. Ward, 'St. Catherine's Church, Cricieth', *Transactions of the Caernarfonshire Historical Society*, 58 (1997), pp. 9–10.
50.  A.H.A. Hogg and D.J.C. King, 'Masonry castles in Wales and the Marches: a list', AC, 116 (1967), p. 100. This said, it is interesting that Maredudd ap Rhys Gryg is also on record as having been imprisoned there in 1259, twenty years after Gruffudd's incarceration; Avent, *Cricieth Castle*, p. 3.
51.  Though O'Neil suggested inhabitation during the Iron Age was a possibility: 'Criccieth Castle', pp. 1, 21. Furthermore, Elaine Jamieson has noted that numbers of coastal sites in England exhibiting evidence of Iron Age occupation were subsequently fortified by masonry castles in the medieval era, a situation that may 'possibly indicat[e] that these sites represented places of long-term economic and strategic significance': 'The siting of medieval castles and the influence of ancient places', *Medieval Archaeology*, 63 (2019), p. 350. It is worth noting O'Neil's identification of a possible ancient road running north-east–south-west adjacent to the castle ('Criccieth Castle', p. 20).

Figure 2.1 View from Cricieth over
Bae Tremadog to the south-east.

Llywelyn's agenda, we may further surmise that it was important that the castle be visible to those arriving in Gwynedd by sea via the southern approach. The microlocation at Cricieth had several things going for it. It was an eminently defensible rock jutting out into Cardigan Bay on three sides and, furthermore, a spring on the summit afforded the garrison a water supply in times of siege.[52] It offered impressive sightlines to the south and south-east (Fig. 2.1) – the horizon is almost fifteen miles away at the summit, and even further away as seen from the castle's battlements – and, although one or two other landforms on the southern coast of the Llŷn offered comparable views, such as the headland at Mynydd-Y-Tir to the west, none were so conveniently located for overland access into central Gwynedd.

Construction proceeded along established lines, with rock quarried locally (either from the headland itself or the adjacent hill) and, as at Carndochan, extensive use of galletting, which improved the resilience of the walls.[53] The first phase consisted of the construction of a six-sided inner ward, entrance to which was gained through a twin-towered gatehouse resembling those found at Beeston and Montgomery (Fig. 2.2, 2.3). The D-shaped towers that comprise it offer unambiguous evidence for the use of archers and crossbowmen in the castle's defence, as arrowslits survive at ground level. The entrance they enclose also featured a portcullis. This was a novelty in Gwynedd at the time of construction, but was subsequently adopted in several other castles in the north, including at Dolbadarn, whose fine round tower probably dates from later in Llywelyn's reign, and probably at Y Bere (see below).[54] The only other tower in Cricieth's first phase

---

52. Though Avent, noting the well's inconvenient position inside the entrance passage, concurred with O'Neil that the spring was probably discovered during construction: *Cricieth Castle*, p. 22.
53. O'Neil, 'Cricieth Castle', p. 13.
54. O'Neil, 'Cricieth Castle', pp. 22, 23; for Dolbadarn's portcullis, Williams, *Dolbadarn Castle*, p. 3.

Figure 2.2 Cricieth's inner gatehouse; note the arrowslits at ground level.

is the rectangular tower that straddles the south-east wall. Though its shape appears anachronistic for a thirteenth-century build, a round tower would be unnecessary in circumstances where sapping was impossible due to the seaward-facing wall's construction on solid rock with a sheer drop beneath.[55] The tower, therefore, was probably built as princely accommodation.

This question invites another: what was the castle's intended role beyond issues of security and aggrandisement? Apart from the references to the presence there of leaders of Gwynedd and Deheubarth in the 1230s, 1250s and 1270s, there is precious little to go on in determining who used it. The bardic reference to Gruffudd's dominion over Cricieth is, however, unambiguous, and leads one to wonder if Llywelyn intended that his son would take possession as part of his apanage. It may be that Cricieth's construction was sponsored by Llywelyn late in his reign as an attempt to assign Gruffudd a lordly residence commensurate with his standing within a given sphere of influence. It should be remembered that, as the *edling* or heir to the princeship, Gruffudd's brother Dafydd had almost certainly been bestowed with lands by Llywelyn prior to his death – the court poet Dafydd Benfras's description of Dafydd as *llyw* or lord of

55.  Williams, *Dolbadarn Castle*, p. 14.

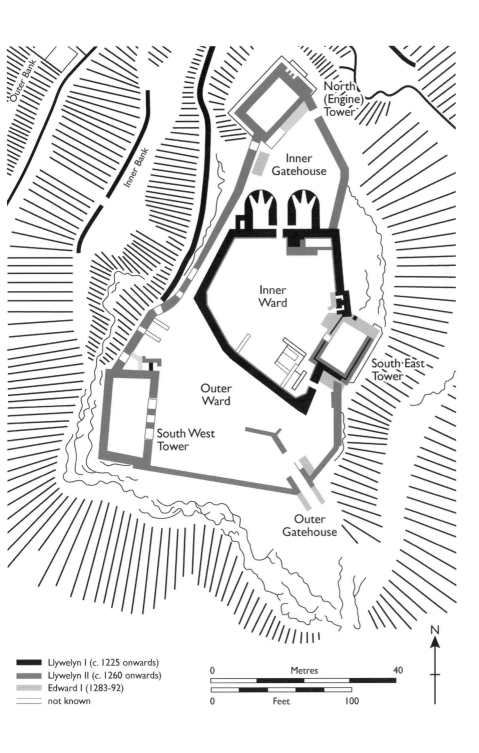

Figure 2.3 Cricieth, plan.

Dinorwig, a mile north of the castle at Dolbadarn,[56] may well be confirmation that, whereas Gruffudd had been given extensive but remote estates in the west, Dafydd enjoyed dominion over lands at the very heart of Venedotian political and economic power. Ensuring an appropriate power balance between the two, with Dafydd enjoying a higher authority and standing than Gruffudd, was no small concern, especially if, as seems likely, the pair were beginning to chafe against one another. Dafydd came of age in 1226, and may soon have been flexing his muscles in terms of governance and administration. It has been plausibly suggested that Dafydd began to take on more and more of the administrative functions of the princeship as Llywelyn neared the end of his life, in effect acting as a regent. His capture and detainment of Gruffudd at Cricieth, which may well have occurred before Llywelyn's death, as several sources suggest,[57] may be an example, as well as a pointed arrogation of his half-brother's territory. Definitive statements as to the location of Dafydd's own power base are elusive in the historical record. A reference in the *Black Book of Wigmore* – dismissed by J.E. Lloyd as unreliable, but rehabilitated by Butler – describing Dolforwyn castle in mid-Wales as having been authored by Dafydd[58] is intriguing, but one is forced to wonder why Llywelyn would install his *edling* so far from the wellsprings of Venedotian power and authority in the north-west. Situating Dafydd in Dinorwig is a more satisfactory solution to this problem, and one which in turn permits us to wonder whether the round tower at Dolbadarn was raised to make of a hitherto modestly built castle a residence fit for the son of a prince. The presence of a well-used fireplace in what would have been the main chamber, as well as the lights in place of slits, the sophisticated entrance arrangements and, according to one analysis, an internal layout demarcating high-status use of the upper level[59] all suggest a building of considerable importance.

The paucity of finds at Dolbadarn requires that we suspend judgement on these points. However, in contradistinction to the sparse archaeological record at (for example) Carndochan, excavations at Cricieth yielded good archaeological evidence indicative of high-status occupation, including finely dressed stone recovered during O'Neil's investigations and a copper-alloy crucifix found in the gatehouse.[60] This pattern of high-quality decorative stone and high-status ceremonial objects is also found at Y Bere and at Deganwy, to which we now turn.

---

56. Rh. M. Andrews, 'The nomenclature of kingship in welsh court poetry 1100–1300 part II: the rulers', SC, 65 (2011), p. 70.
57. LlapG, p. 32 and n. 108.
58. L. Butler, 'Dolforwyn Castle, Montgomery, Powys, Second Report', AC, 144 (1995), pp. 198–9. The authorship of Dolforwyn is fully discussed in chapter 3.
59. C. Ryder, 'The spiral stair or vice: its origins, role and meaning in medieval stone castles', PhD thesis (Liverpool, 2011), pp. 177–81.
60. O'Neil, 'Criccieth Castle', p. 38.

## Deganwy

Alone of the three castles considered in this chapter, Deganwy has been conclusively shown to have been constructed on an ancient site.[61] If reliable, references in *Annales Cambriae* to a castle that can probably be equated with Deganwy demonstrate that a castle existed there in the early medieval period, and this position was refortified by Robert of Rhuddlan in the last quarter of the eleventh century.[62] It appears again in the writings of Gerald of Wales in the late 1180s, and was apparently garrisoned by the Welsh in 1210, when Llywelyn destroyed it to deny Ranulf, earl of Chester its use during an incursion by the latter into Gwynedd.[63] Ranulf had it rebuilt using timber from the nearby Cistercian grange at Creuddyn, and King John used it as a forward base during his campaign of May 1211 against Llywelyn.[64] After the latter's surrender in August 1211, the castle was doubtless one of the many castles the chronicles aver were used by John to administer his newly-won lands. However, it was swiftly recaptured by Llywelyn in 1213, and remained in Welsh possession for the remainder of his reign. Aside from its commanding position, the attractiveness of the site to Llywelyn surely lay in the fact that it was steeped in history. The tradition that Deganwy was the seat of Maelgwn Gwynedd was doubtless vigorous in the early thirteenth century. Llywelyn, forever alert to the possibilities of legitimising his position by dint of association with previous rulers – one thinks of his commissioning of Ewloe – seems to have made much of this link with an illustrious predecessor; the tradition, recorded in lawbooks drawn up during his reign, that explained the place-name Traeth Maelgwn (Maelgwn's Beach) by means of a meeting between Wales' ancient rulers at which the primacy of Gwynedd was asserted by him performed much the same duty as his use of Deganwy.[65] This sort of symbolism enjoyed widespread currency in England at the time, and in similar ways. Elaine Jamieson's recent work on the reuse of ancient sites by medieval castle-builders has drawn attention to the abundant evidence of reoccupation of old sites in medieval England as a method of orientating new institutions against a known cultural background. Ancient places, as Jamieson asserts, 'were more than just crumbling relics of past societies. They represented important points of reference which helped define and maintain the collective identities of local communities.'[66] The rulers of Deheubarth had been similarly aware of the importance of cultivating attractive cultural resonances with a 'more glorious and mythologised version of the past'; the Lord Rhys (d. 1197), for example, had named two of his castles

61. For a general overview of earlier settlement, K. Waddington, *The Settlements of Northwest Wales, From the Late Bronze Age to the Early Medieval Period* (Cardiff, 2013), pp. 128–9.
62. Lloyd, *History of Wales*, p. 383.
63. BYT Pen MS 20, p. 84.
64. BYT Pen MS 20, pp. 84–5.
65. Beverley Smith and Beverley Smith (eds), *A History of Merioneth Vol. 2*, p. 521.
66. Jamieson, 'The siting of medieval castles', p. 369.

Dingeraint (Aberteifi/Cardigan) and Dinefwr – that is, using the ancient cognate *din* (fortress) – harkening back to ancient times of Brythonic supremacy thereby.[67] Gildas' excoriating assessment notwithstanding, Maelgwn's reputation as king of Wales was secure among Llywelyn's contemporaries, and there was no-one more appropriate for the prince to invoke in refortifying the site at Deganwy.

As a previously occupied site, the extent to which Llywelyn was able to dictate Deganwy's emplacement is not demonstrated. Indeed, much of what follows must be prefaced with the disclaimer that, although Deganwy was the site of excavations in the early 1960s, this work did not amount to anything more than, in the lead archaeologist Leslie Alcock's words, 'a reconnaissance in depth, yielding the information on which a large-scale campaign may be based'.[68] Such a sustained campaign of excavations has yet to be embarked on, and so we are left with a very incomplete picture of the castle's history. We know enough, however, to assert that in 1213 the castle was still made of timber, and it is to the subsequent period of Welsh occupation that we should ascribe the initial masonry rebuilding. Excavations revealed the existence of various bits of walling and revetments that have been attributed to Llywelyn, including the curtain wall to the north of what Alcock described as the castle's 'donjon', and possibly also the north-west tower.[69] The principal artefact recovered during these brief investigations was a carved stone head bearing a crown, widely believed to be a likeness of Llywelyn himself, and which had been carefully buried in the soil, presumably by those Welsh whose slighting of the castle following its final capture from Henry III in 1263 all but brought its military life to an end and who were aware that, as Alcock put it, the stone represented 'not a piece of hated English work, but part of the castle of Llywelyn the Great'.[70] Llywelyn imprisoned his son Gruffudd here from 1228 to 1234, though we know nothing further about the episode.[71]

Deganwy's macrolocation is reminiscent of Cricieth's. As Cricieth stands over Bae Tremadog, Deganwy looks out over Bae Conwy, and is well emplaced to observe not only traffic entering and leaving the Conwy estuary but also shipping off the eastern coast of Ynys Môn more generally. It is easily visible from the port at Llanfaes, just over ten miles due west, and the headland at Penmaenmawr, on the other side of the Conwy, looms large to the south-west (indeed, that area may have been appurtenant to Deganwy) (see Fig. 2.4).[72] The microlocation is very good from a defensive point of view, with steep drops on all sides. A hillock due

67. J. Wiles, 'Lordly landscapes in post-conquest Maelienydd (c. 1267–1400)', *The Transactions of the Radnorshire Society*, 86 (2016), p. 68.
68. L. Alcock, 'Excavations at Degannwy Castle, Caernarvonshire, 1961–6', *AJ*, 124 (1967), p. 192.
69. Alcock, 'Excavations at Degannwy Castle', pp. 196–7.
70. Alcock, 'Excavations at Degannwy Castle', p. 197.
71. *LltG*, pp. 131–2.
72. C.O. Jones, 'Dafydd ap Llywelyn, the Sychnant Pass, and Henry III's Welsh campaign of 1245', *Transactions of the Caernarfonshire Historical Society* (forthcoming, 2022).

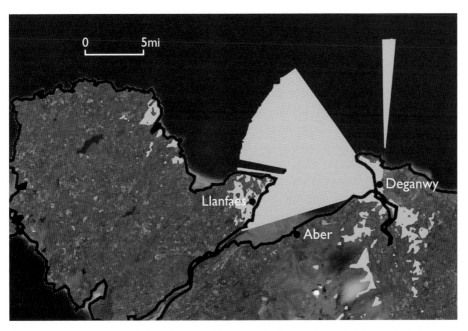

Figure 2.4 Deganwy, viewshed analysis. The large gap in visibility NNW of the castle is due to the prominence of the Great Orme. All of Bae Conwy (due west of Deganwy) is visible, including the port of Llanfaes, as well as the eastern approaches to the Menai Strait. The eastern entrance to the Sychnant Pass (south-west of Deganwy) is also visible, as well as much of the Conwy estuary due south. Analysis created using ArcGIS; height above ground at origin set at six feet; north is at top.

east of that used by Llywelyn represented a possible weakness, inasmuch as it could be used as a siegework by enemy forces. Assessing the seriousness of this deficiency is difficult, however. No fortification of the hillock was attempted by Llywelyn, and it also seems to be the case that the structure known as Mansel's Tower erected on it in the time of Henry III was never completed,[73] leading one to question the extent to which the vulnerability of this prominence to capture was felt to compromise the whole.

The internal layout of the castle will not be known until excavation can be resumed. There are, however, vestiges of what seem to be Welsh features. The most obvious of these are the remains of a D-shaped tower on the northern curtain of similar size to that adjacent to the entrance at Carndochan; the northern revetment, which recalls those at Ewloe and Dolwyddelan; and the building Alcock interpreted as the castle hall, which is rectangular and within the ward, and faces an entrance to the south,[74] as at Ewloe and, later, Dolforwyn.

73.  Alcock, 'Excavations at Degannwy Castle', p. 193.
74.  Alcock, 'Excavations at Degannwy Castle', pp. 194–5.

As Alcock notes, none of this proves a Welsh provenance for these features, and the relative absence of dating evidence uncovered during the excavations – a circumstance he found 'disturbing'[75] – prevents anything other than very tentative conclusions being drawn as to the author of the castle in its earliest masonry phase. What is less in doubt is its strategic and symbolic importance to the princes. In turn, Llywelyn, his son Dafydd and his grandson Llywelyn II expended enormous amounts of energy on slighting the castle and subsequently recapturing it once it was in English possession, and the latter felt it posed such a threat that he had it razed in 1263.[76] This can only have been due to its economic and military importance. The former is indicated in the presence of a settlement in Llywelyn's time as recorded in a document of 1241, as well as (possibly) the remains of building platforms to the north and south-west of the castle. We cannot be certain of this – they may date from the period of English occupation under Henry III – but it has equally been speculated that that settlement may in turn have been located on the site of the original Welsh vill.[77]

Economic activity would, of course, have been stimulated by the castle. However, an additional spur to the economic life of this settlement was the presence of the Cistercian community at Aberconwy, less than two miles to the west. The monastic grange in nearby Creuddyn speaks directly to economic activity, and we may finesse the assertion that the community of monks at Aberconwy was comfortable moving from their initial foundation at Rhedynog Felen in Caernarfonshire to the vicinity of a native Welsh castle, and suggest that such a move might even have been precipitated by Llywelyn in the 1190s.[78] The evidence points in this direction. An 1199 grant to the monks of Aberconwy, though dubious in its present form – it seems to have been penned during Edward I's reign by someone in the monastic community eager to establish the abbey's title to its lands and privileges – may well have been based on authentic documents issued by the prince early in his principate, and makes clear that Llywelyn, in moving the community to the Deganwy area, was emulating the Norman practice of establishing monastic communities in close proximity to military complexes during this early period of his reign.[79]

75.  Alcock, 'Excavations at Degannwy Castle', p. 198.

76.  For Dafydd's 1245 campaign, BYT *Pen* MS 20, p. 107; for Llywelyn II's slighting, BYT *Pen* MS 20, p. 113.

77.  J. Kenney, 'Degannwy Castle, Degannwy: archaeological assessment', Gwynedd Archaeological Trust report 781 (2009), p. 8.

78.  J. Bond, 'The location and siting of Cistercian monasteries in Wales and the west', *AC*, 154 (2005), pp. 56, 72.

79.  For an exhaustive analysis of this document's origins (as well as a similar document supposedly issued contemporaneously), *AWR*, pp. 348–68; Bond, 'The location and siting', pp. 56–7. For a recent survey of the role monastic activity had in stimulating urban growth, M. Fradley, 'Monastic enterprise in town and countryside: two case studies from north-east Shropshire', *Landscape History*, 28 (2006), pp. 5–20.

A ferry across the Conwy was located at Deganwy in medieval times and was almost certainly under Llywelyn's control by the end of the 1190s;[80] and, indeed, the 1199 grant mentioned above makes reference to the rights of the monks to cross the Conwy without paying a toll.

The final aspect of Deganwy's existence under the princes is the distinct possibility that the mouth of the Conwy acted as a harbour for Llywelyn's warships. There is sparse but sufficient evidence to admit the likelihood that Llywelyn, and indeed Llywelyn II, possessed a navy, or something resembling one. Not only are there references in praise poetry to Llywelyn I crossing the Menai with his army in ships in 1194, and a document of King John of 1212 ordering the dispatch of galleys to Wales to attack Llywelyn's vessels, there is also a bardic reference to the harbour of Deganwy, as well as a reference to the deployment of ships by Llywelyn II in the late 1250s.[81] We cannot infer from this that such activity as may be indicated by these references was continuous. However, and as the extensive rebuilding work instituted by Henry III in the late 1240s and early 1250s shows, for all that the Conwy constituted an important barrier to further encroachment in Gwynedd, it was surely also the case that to penetrate as far as Deganwy was to accomplish an important military goal in conflicts with the Welsh, and aids in our understanding of why so many English expeditions viewed Deganwy less as a waypoint and more as a position worthy of capture and retention in its own right – the pivotal factor, one assumes, in Llywelyn II's decision to have it demolished.

## Castell Y Bere

In some ways, Y Bere sits awkwardly with its contemporaries, for although it shares many architectural characteristics with Cricieth in particular – the use of apsidal and rectangular towers, and the presence of finely dressed stone and high-status archaeological finds – it does not conform as closely to the principles of emplacement laid out above. It is neither a coastal castle strictly speaking nor emplaced in a location that would allow it to be seen by large numbers of foreign traders (or so it seems). What evidence there is to illuminate its history under the native princes shows it to have been an important castle, however; it was certainly commenced on a scale exceeding anything Llywelyn had attempted before. Works probably began there in 1221. A castle referred to in the *Brutiau* as having been raised by Llywelyn in Meirionydd during that year is almost certainly

---

80. H.R. Davies, *A Review of the Records of the Conway and the Menai Ferries* (Cardiff, 1942), pp. 1–2; GG, pp. 78–9.

81. For Llywelyn II, LlapG, p. 106, and A.D. Carr, *Medieval Wales* (Basingstoke, 1995), p. 69. When identifying harbours for Llywelyn's vessels, Rhuddlan provides another possibility, having been used by Gruffudd ap Llywelyn (d. 1064), though its usefulness during Llywelyn's reign may have been limited by silting; S. Rees, 'Rhuddlan Castle and the canalization of the River Clwyd', in M. Redknap, S. Rees and A. Aberg (eds), *Wales and the Sea: 10,000 Years of Welsh Maritime History* (Talybont, 2019), p. 108.

Figure 2.5 Y Bere's ward, looking south towards the Middle Tower; the ward's highly uneven ground is evident.

to be identified with it.[82] If those reports are to be followed the proximate cause of Y Bere's commencement was a rift between Llywelyn and his son, Gruffudd: both men prepared forces to do battle and it was only by the intervention of 'wise men', as the *Brutiau* put it, that bloodshed was averted. The episode is dealt with at some length in the *Brutiau*, and the fact that the report of a new castle immediately follows it suggests the former precipitated the latter. This does not, however, explain why the site in the Dysynni valley was chosen for it. The microlocation is, if not optimal, certainly favourable. The rock on which Y Bere stands is a good site for a Welsh masonry castle: approaches from the north, west and east are sheer, and the approach from the south, though less steep, was made easily defensible by means of rock-cut ditches and the siting of two towers, the Middle Tower and the Round Tower, overlooking it during the first phase of construction. Writing with reference to the English campaign of 1282–3, the Osney annalist adds the information that the castle was surrounded by an impassable marsh, and that entry was only possible via narrow causeways.[83] Taken together, these natural obstacles must have done much to augment the castle's masonry defences and, although the ground within the ward is very uneven (Fig. 2.5), the basic requirements of a

82. BYT *Pen* MS 20, p. 98.
83. Walker, 'William de Valence', p. 420 and references therein.

castle, such as the presence of a water supply and the command of the surrounding area, are all present.

Assessing Y Bere's strategic purpose, however, is more complicated than it may seem. None of Llywelyn's castles are well served by contemporary accounts prior to the Edwardian conquest, but in Y Bere's case the lack of early references is almost total. Aside from the above notice of its construction, we are in the dark as to its use by the native Welsh princes. A smattering of documents issued by Llywelyn II (and one by his consort, Eleanor de Montfort) in the 1260s and 1270s from Ystumanner – the commote in which Y Bere stood – may conceivably have been issued while resident in the castle,[84] but the next unambiguous reference to Y Bere's existence occurs during the war of 1282–3, when the garrison, commanded by one Cynfrig ap Madog, was subjected to a ten-day siege by English forces.[85] Its purpose in times of peace, the exact nature of its military role and the additions made to it after Llywelyn I's death are all unknown.

Why was Y Bere emplaced where it is? An ancient routeway that threaded upwards through the valley led north-east to Dolgellau and is considered to have begun at the coast.[86] That Y Bere would have controlled that routeway is obvious, but it is dangerous to suggest that much importance was assigned to guarding this route when Llywelyn was considering the location for his new castle, nor that that constituted the sole reason for Y Bere's emplacement on that spot. Even Richard Avent, so diligent in his analysis and proprietous in his prose, was unable to prevent a note of bewilderment from sounding in his description of Y Bere's location.[87] The routeway seems to have been small and undeveloped: a 1284 account shows that a path had to be cut through the forest which at that time covered the valley floor between Y Bere and Tywyn on the coast, so that the queen's carriage could reach the castle.[88] The strategic importance of this route is somewhat supported by the fact that the motte at Cynfal was raised in the 1140s by Cadwaladr ap Gruffudd further down the valley. However, it is equally true that Cynfal was apparently never refortified after its destruction by Hywel ab Owain Gwynedd shortly afterwards[89] – hardly what one would expect if the motte was intended as a permanent outpost

84. J. Beverley Smith has argued the commotal centre was at Pennal, and this is certainly likely earlier in the century, but the recording of arable land designated to Y Bere in the extent of 1284 (LlapG, pp. 229–30 and references therein) makes it at least conceivable that the commotal centre was moved to the castle, as seems to have occurred at Cricieth.
85. Walker, 'William de Valence', pp. 420–1.
86. Avent, *Dolwyddelan Castle/Dolbadarn Castle/Castell y Bere*, p. 37.
87. Avent, *Dolwyddelan Castle/Dolbadarn Castle/Castell y Bere*, p. 37.
88. E.D. Evans, 'Was there a Borough of Bere?' JMHRS, 10 (1989), p. 293. It may, of course, also be true that traffic up and down the routeway was largely on foot, and so no enlargement of the routeway was necessary during the reigns of the princes; nevertheless, Eleanor of Castile's carriage cannot have been particularly wide, and one wonders as to the state of the path.
89. BYT Pen MS 20, p. 56; Davis, *Castles of the Welsh Princes*, pp. 47–8.

Figure 2.6 Y Bere, oblique aerial view from the west. The hill in the centre of the photograph is Foel Cae'rberllan; Y Bere is situated at the highest point of the thickly wooded ridge directly in front of it. The castle's unsuitability for guarding the north–south route in the valley beyond via the Abergynolwyn defile (to the right of Foel Cae'rberllan) is clear. Photograph taken by Toby Driver, 2009; RCAHMW Catalogue Number: C875382.

overlooking the routeway. For all that Avent asserted that Y Bere's strategic importance lay in its guarding of the Dysynni valley, it is in fact hard to argue with E.D. Evans' opinion that Y Bere is a castle 'ill-served ... by even primitive communications', with 'land routes pass[ing] it by to the east beyond the Cadair Range'.[90] One might counter, as Butler did, that the castle's positioning adjacent to the defile at Abergynolwyn provided the castle's garrison with easy entry into the valley formed by Afon Mathew due east, and hence access to those routes,[91] but this falls foul of *ignoratio elenchi*: a garrison stationed at Y Bere might well have good access to the valley to the east that way, but the castle is plainly poorly emplaced to *monitor* the routes that wend their way through it (Fig. 2.6).

We should therefore problematise Y Bere's macrolocation. Even allowing for the possibility that southern Meirionydd had an importance for the Venedotian economy that is opaque to us today,[92] the strategic explanation for its siting

90.  Evans, 'Was there a Borough of Bere?' p. 293.
91.  Butler, 'Medieval finds from Castell-y-Bere', p. 78.
92.  Ystumanner was, after all, the second richest commote in the lay subsidy roll of 1292–3; K. Williams-Jones (ed. with introduction), *The Merioneth Lay Subsidy Roll 1292–3* (Cardiff, 1976), pp. 21–35.

is insufficient and we must find others. One such explanation may lie in the confrontation between Llywelyn and Gruffudd that occurred immediately prior to the commencement of the castle in 1221. The account contained in the *Brutiau* is worth quoting in full:

> ...strife arose between Llywelyn ab Iorwerth and Gruffudd, his son, because of the cantref of Meirionydd, which the said Gruffudd had subjugated because of the multitude of injuries which the men of that cantref had done to him and his men. And Llywelyn took that subjugation angrily; and he gathered a host and went against Gruffudd and threatened to avenge that attack heavily upon him and upon his men. And Gruffudd, having arrayed his troops ready to fight, boldly awaited the coming of his father. And when wise men on either side saw that there was excessive danger on either side, they urged Gruffudd to surrender himself and all his possessions to his father's will. And also they urged Llywelyn to receive him peacefully and mercifully, and to remit to him all his anger from a good heart. And so it came to pass. However, Llywelyn took from Gruffudd, his son, the cantref of Meirionydd, of which he had gained possession, and the adjoining commote of Ardudwy. And he began to build a castle in it.[93]

Turvey has plausibly suggested that Gruffudd was moved to act in this way because his position as Llywelyn's heir had been finally usurped by his half-brother, Dafydd, who had been named as Llywelyn's *edling* the previous year.[94] Yet it is also true that the above account does not deny that the men of Meirionydd had indeed 'injured' Gruffudd and his men. Building Y Bere would certainly have had the effect of reminding the local inhabitants who was in charge, and thereby bringing one of the most remote (and, it seems, wayward) regions of early thirteenth-century Gwynedd more firmly under Llywelyn's authority. If this is true, it follows that Y Bere would be emplaced in that part of Meirionydd that caused the dissension in the first place. (It would be interesting indeed to know whether the people of the Dysynni valley had a reputation for trouble-making.) Assuming that

---

93.  BYT *Pen MS 20*, p. 98. The ambiguous final line could equally indicate that Llywelyn built a castle in Ardudwy, or elsewhere in Meirionydd, but the scholarly consensus is that Y Bere was meant. A few other possibilities present themselves, including the fortification at Deudraeth; Morris, probably taking his cues from the tradition of the ancient fortification of Caer Collwyn, even implied that the Edwardian castle at Harlech replaced a native Welsh fortress (*The Welsh Wars of Edward I*, p. 219). A sustained (if flawed) attempt has been made by Paul Remfry to resuscitate this idea, though Remfry's suggestion that a substantial part of the fabric of today's castle is of Welsh construction pushes the point far too hard (*Harlech Castle and its True Origins* (n.p., 2013)). Nevertheless, the possibility that a small motte or even a masonry tower was erected at Harlech by a Welsh ruler cannot be completely discounted; A.H. Williams certainly accepted the idea (*An Introduction to the History of Wales, Volume II: The Middle Ages, Part I 1063–1284* (Cardiff, 1948), p. 138, n. 1).

94.  LltG, p. 78.

its presence predated the castle, the positioning of a vaccary at Nantcaw less than a mile away may point to an additional reason for wanting a military presence in this area.[95] The siting of Dolwyddelan and other castles in Gwynedd adjacent to cattle farms has been widely noted,[96] and as cattle continued to be of central importance to the economy throughout Llywelyn's reign – the fine he paid to John following his surrender to the king in 1211 was measured in head of cattle[97] – the prince may have felt it prudent to raise a castle as a layer of protection for a valuable economic resource. It was, perhaps, not for nothing that Llywelyn's successor Llywelyn II would be hailed by Gruffudd ab yr Anad Coch in his eulogy to the prince as the mailcoat of Nantcaw.[98]

And yet there may have been another reason for Y Bere's construction, first put forward in earnest by Ralph Maud in his mercurial essay on the career of Dafydd III. Maud was an unabashed stylist, and his prose has a distinct purplish tinge that sits uncomfortably with the more dispassionate writing style that predominates in Welsh history writing today. It is easy to overlook his blithe assertion of Y Bere as '[Llywelyn's] show-piece, a place one could retreat to, and enjoy', a 'palace of a castle',[99] as so much hyperbole; and yet, for all the formidable military dispositions on show, this might well have some truth to it. The castle's decorative stonework has drawn much praise for its high quality, and included a door frame flanked by sculptures of soldiers holding lances.[100] Floor tiles that probably originated in the castle's chapel bear marked resemblances to similar work at Welsh Cistercian abbeys of the period, and indicate that close attention was paid to architectural detailing. So too does the discovery of fragments of window glass. These date to the late thirteenth century, and perhaps indicate that one of the towers – again, the chapel tower seems the likeliest candidate – had lights.[101] At a time when glassed windows were far from ubiquitous in Wales, these also speak to Y Bere's high status and favoured aspect. The castle must have appealed to King Edward on these grounds, as he retained it and strengthened it following the conquest, and even had an additional *camera* constructed there in 1285, presumably to augment its lordly accommodation.[102]

It may also have appealed on account of what may well have been its symbolic importance. We can place neither Llywelyn I, Dafydd II nor Llywelyn II in the castle at any point in their reigns with any certainty, and yet certain architectural details suggest that, perhaps alone of the castles of Gwynedd, one of its chief functions

95. LlapG, pp. 228, 575.
96. Jones, 'The defences of Gwynedd', p. 39.
97. AWR, pp. 386–7.
98. Clancy, *Medieval Welsh Poems*, p. 172; Evans, 'Castle and town', p. 188.
99. R. Maud, 'David, the last prince of Wales: the ten "lost" months of Welsh history', THSC (1968), p. 58.
100. Butler, 'Medieval finds from Castell-Y-Bere', Merioneth, p. 99.
101. Ibid., p. 91.
102. D.J. Cathcart King, in Beverley Smith and Beverley Smith (eds), *A History of Merioneth Vol. 2*, p. 404.

was ceremonial, an example of what Dixon resoundingly identified as 'the castle as theatre',[103] defined by Marshall as 'a manipulation of the architectural arrangement specifically for the purpose of impressing a contemporary visitor of equal or near-equal status to that of the owner of the castle'.[104] Such an effect was perhaps conceivably meant at Ewloe, where the sudden appearance of the castle within the wood as well as the lengthy walk through woodland that would have been necessary to reach it combined to signify to English visitors their presence in an alien environment in which received notions of castle architecture and emplacement, not to mention ideas of the architectural abilities of their Welsh counterparts, were overturned. A grander effect was achievable at Y Bere, and management of the visitor's experience may well have begun outside the castle. The Osney annalist relates that the castle was surrounded by marshes and was only approachable along certain narrow causeways,[105] a circumstance that lent itself to the exertion of control over the routes along which visitors could be conveyed for purposes of presenting the castle's most impressive aspect. The elaborate entrance arrangements, which included passing through a barbican equipped with a guard house and overlooked by three of the castle's four towers (see below), was presumably intended to further overawe the visitor, as would the abrupt change in elevation – the approach is very steep and, indeed, the barbican is itself situated on a precipitous slope (see Fig. 2.7).[106]

But the most obvious architectural feature that is not purely utile is the staircase leading from the ward to the first floor of the north tower. This tower, which survives today only at basement level, has been identified as the castle's hall largely due to the survival of the base of a pillar in the basement that would have held the weight of a hearth in the floor above, and it has been argued that the eastern end housed a chapel. The intriguing aspect of the tower's construction, however, is that there is no intra-mural stair, a feature found in several places elsewhere in the castle, and indeed at Ewloe and Dolbadarn. The design of staircase that did serve the upper floor displays several oddities. Firstly, it appears to have been altered during construction, for the staircase terminates well short of the north tower and, at the top, one finds oneself looking into an open space below, at the base of which begins a second flight of steps narrower than the first that leads directly to the tower's southern wall.

King noted that the surviving remains reveal no break in construction, and correctly asserts that the open space and the narrower staircase within it were filled in when the second staircase was constructed.[107] The structure that resulted from

103. P.W. Dixon, 'The Donjon of Knaresborough: the castle as theatre', *Château Gaillard*, 14 (1990), pp. 121–39.

104. P. Marshall, 'The ceremonial function of the donjon in the twelfth century', *Château Gaillard*, 20 (2002), p. 141.

105. Walker, 'William de Valence', p. 420.

106. King, in *A History of Merioneth Vol. 2*, p. 398.

107. Ibid., p. 400.

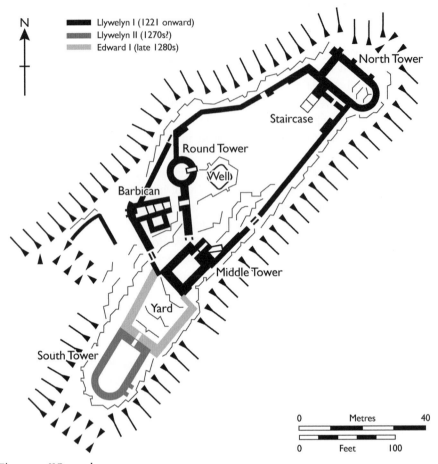

Figure 2.7 Y Bere, plan.

this decision takes up far more space, is wider than the other and juts out into the ward. The question then arises: what was wrong with the first staircase such that it had to be covered over and a new, longer staircase built in its place? Alongside it is another curious feature, a wall in front of the north tower, running parallel to its southern wall and forming a separate room. King noted the lack of a door jamb and identified the surviving room as 'unimportant ... clearly, what mattered was on the upper floor' – in his opinion, a narthex or vestry for the tower's chapel.[108]

However, in light of the large staircase alongside it, as well as the probable use of the tower as a hall, it seems at least conceivable that what these features in fact represent is a ceremonial entrance to that hall, to which a terrace or balcony was added running the length of the north tower's southern wall. Unlike most terraces and similar features at English castles, the terrace would look inward – that is, over

108. *Ibid.*

the castle ward; but in a setting as dramatic and as empty as the Dysynni valley that surely would have been the point. Having ascended the staircase, the climax of the visitor's experience would be to turn around and view at their feet the castle's ward and towers, representing the prince's imposition of their will on the rock, and, beyond it, the thickly forested fastnesses through which they had journeyed to get there – unnavigable except under the prince's protection, impenetrable by nature and by design.

It is tempting to wonder whether the sorts of diplomatic contacts established by the princes in the thirteenth century resulted in the visit of envoys from countries with whom the princes maintained relations, such as France and Scotland, to Y Bere – or, indeed, if Llywelyn's ally, Ranulf of Chester, ever made it as far as Meirionydd in the course of his friendship with the prince. Such visitors would have emerged from the forest to the south to be confronted with a formidable aspect: a masonry castle rising from a craggy boss of rock above a desolate marsh. Hemp saw in Y Bere an attempt to emulate the defences of Deganwy, though this is most unlikely; the tower Hemp invokes to support the argument had not been built at Deganwy by the time Y Bere was raised.[109] However, there are probably broad similarities in construction, inasmuch as the rock of the hill was used to provide stone for the walls – the remains of quarries can be found at both sites, in the centre of the ward at Deganwy[110] and beyond the chapel tower at Y Bere, forming a shallow rock-cut ditch. The entrance is enfiladed 'in copybook fashion', as King puts it (Fig. 2.8),[111] and what remains of the curtain walls show them to have been intelligently situated and constructed, with increases in thickness corresponding to the stretches that were most vulnerable to assault.

How much of Y Bere was built by Llywelyn is not clear. The ward, consisting of an irregular curtain wall linking the apsidal chapel tower at the castle's northern end, the round tower on the western flank and the rectangular middle tower – which probably functioned as a keep for at least part of the castle's life – are all of one build, and were probably erected in the early 1220s over a period of several years.[112] The principal bones of contention are two: the southern tower, which has been speculated to have been an addition by Llywelyn II, and the barbican, which may have also been his work.[113] Both theories are plausible. In the 1220s the concept of bolstering a castle's defences at its entrance by building a barbican – a narrow extension to the entrance projecting beyond the castle walls, allowing assailants to be attacked from above prior to reaching the curtain – was novel,

---

109. Hemp, 'Ewloe Castle', p. 8.
110. Kenney, 'Degannwy Castle', p. 10.
111. *A History of Merioneth Vol. 2*, p. 398.
112. The *Brutiau*, after all, state that Llywelyn *began* building a castle in 1221. King interpreted the appearance of so many straight joints in the castle's fabric as indicative of 'a rather protracted campaign of building, carried out in a piecemeal fashion' (*A History of Merioneth Vol. 2*, p. 403).
113. Pettifer, *Welsh Castles*, p. 115.

Figure 2.8 Y Bere, Middle Tower and Round Tower. The castle's barbican and entrance is at lower left, and would have been effectively enfiladed by these towers.

and it may be argued as an unlikely part of the original design on these grounds. However, in his survey of the castle's architecture King could find no evidence of a definitive break in construction, and it is generally accepted as the work of Llywelyn I.[114] The south tower, meanwhile, has occasioned far more debate, with King and Paul R. Davis favouring a date of construction in the reign of Llywelyn II, while Hugh Brodie has more recently suggested that authorship by Llywelyn I is equally plausible (I incline towards the former; see chapter 3). Even if the south tower was a later build, it is clear from the remains that Y Bere in its earliest form was no trifling construction. Like Cricieth, it made use of the apsidal tower, and the standing masonry at the entrance seems to indicate that a portcullis was installed – one of the Anglo-Norman 'mechanical luxuries' that Hemp so insistently claimed were ordinarily beyond the grasp of Welsh castle builders.[115] The castles erected during Llywelyn's early reign certainly were devoid of them; from Cricieth and Y Bere onwards, they were to be the rule rather than the exception.

---

114. John Kenyon dissented from King's firm conclusion on this point, suggesting the barbican could conceivably have been the work of Edward I: *A History of Merioneth Vol.* 2, p. 403.
115. Hemp, 'Ewloe Castle', p. 6.

# 3

## The castles of Llywelyn II ap Gruffudd (c.1246–82)

When Llywelyn I died in 1240 he was in possession of at least seven substantial masonry castles and perhaps as many as a couple of dozen mottes surmounted by timber or masonry towers. This collection of fortifications constituted an impressive demonstration of his military might and political authority. The next ruler of Gwynedd in a position to add to them was Llywelyn's grandson, also named Llywelyn. Having assumed the leadership of Gwynedd in 1246 after the death of his uncle, Dafydd, Llywelyn II at first ruled in conjunction with his brother Owain and then Dafydd III, but in 1255 both were defeated at the battle of Bryn Derwin and thereafter Llywelyn ruled alone.[1] Two years later he began the first castle works we hear of during his reign, a 'strengthening' or 'restoring', as the source puts it, of Ewloe. Over the next twenty-five years several more would follow, including the construction of a new castle at Sennybridge (Rhyd-y-Briw), near Brecon; the likely sponsorship of Dinas Brân in Powys; and a new build – or perhaps a very extensive overhaul of an old one – at Dolforwyn.[2]

Glanville Jones' celebrated essay on the defences of Gwynedd has been referenced to exhaustion by successive generations of equally celebrated historians; its resilience to criticism – indeed, the reluctance shown by many of his successors to criticise it – is remarkable. Fifty years has now gone by since its publication, however, and it is now starting to show distinct signs of age. In his elevation of the strategic capabilities of the native princes to something more than the work of brave but unthinking chieftains Jones performed a service to history, but his invocation of 'concentric ramparts' and 'military buffer zones'[3] places more weight on the thesis than it can bear. Such terminology imbues the whole affair with the sensibilities of modern-day military historians and requires us to believe that the princes thought of Wales as today's tacticians might have – as a collection of geographical features, of salients and bridgeheads, passes and

1.  LlapG, pp. 72–7.
2.  See infra.
3.  Jones, 'The defences of Gwynedd', p. 34.

plains. Something of the sort may perhaps have obtained in the princes' minds, but in an era before modern cartography, not to say modern methods of warfare, it cannot have done so in so clinical a fashion. Certainly, Llywelyn II's castle-building policy cannot have been conceived as neatly as all that; indeed, from the fragmentary documentary evidence that survives, combined with the architectural evidence available, there are a few possible indications that his plans proceeded on a more *ad hoc* basis, at least in contrast to that of his grandfather. This is hardly surprising given how little of his reign could be thought of as settled, compared with that of the earlier Llywelyn; the prince's foremost biographer's description of it as 'a quest for stability' is apposite.[4]

Nevertheless, a change in strategic emphasis appears to distinguish Llywelyn II's policy from his grandfather's. It is suggested here that Llywelyn II was the author or renovator of six, possibly seven, castles: the internal fabric of Ewloe; the outer ward and associated works at Cricieth; the south tower at Y Bere; Dinas Brân (by proxy); Dolforwyn; Sennybridge; and perhaps part, or even all, of Bryn Amlwg.[5] Four of these castles lay on Wales' eastern border and guarded important routes into Wales. This was a part of Wales in which the princes' built legacy had hitherto been restricted to their sponsorship of abbeys and churches and the possession of timber castles, supplanted now and then by the temporary possession of a masonry castle or two, such as Llywelyn I's capture of Whittington in 1223. The symbolic value of a prince of Wales embarking on such an extravagant castle-building programme in the Marches was surely not lost on the Marcher lords whose lands abutted his, who had seen those lands chipped away to enhance Llywelyn's own. These border castles were places where 'meetings might take place, courts might be held, opponents imprisoned, local notables might gather, to be entertained or to be frightened'.[6] The evidence for such uses – never plentiful at any point during the Age of the Princes – is at its most abundant during Llywelyn II's reign. Ewloe was the meeting place for two high-level conferences between Llywelyn and the officials of Henry III in 1259 and 1260. Also in 1259 Cricieth is recorded as the place of imprisonment of Maredudd ap Rhys of Deheubarth. Sennybridge was the setting for the bringing to heel of a Brecon nobleman, Einion Sais ap Rhys, who was forced to provide sureties for his loyalty to Llywelyn there in 1271. And in 1274 Dolforwyn served as the backdrop for a meeting designed to interrogate the loyalty of Gruffudd ap Gwenwynwyn of Powys, who had allegedly plotted the prince's

---

4.  LlapG, p. 329.
5.  L. Hull, *Castles of Glamorgan* (Almeley, 2007), pp. 136–8 adds that Castell Morgraig, a castle two miles south of Caerffili, may have been erected by Llywelyn II or by his claimed vassal, Gruffudd ap Rhys of the house of Senghenydd (fl. 1267). This claim is based on a doubtful interpretation of architectural evidence; the site has not been excavated and it is prudent to reserve judgement (but see below).
6.  D. Stephenson, 'Empires in Wales: from Gruffudd ap Llywelyn to Llywelyn ap Gruffudd', WHR, 28 (2016), p. 43.

assassination along with Llywelyn's own brother, Dafydd.[7] Such roles could have been discharged by llysoedd, or by timber fortifications, but in the later thirteenth century, an era where masonry castles had emerged as the demonstration par excellence of a ruler's power, Llywelyn may have felt that only castles built in stone would do if he were to achieve the standing of his grandfather.

Into this category, too, might fall the ability to exploit the fiscal possibilities opened up by the founding of towns and markets, activities that Marcher lords were busily engaged on during the late thirteenth century. The only confirmed example of this as inaugurated by a prince of Gwynedd is Dolforwyn, but there are tantalising hints that developments of a similar sort were afoot elsewhere in Gwynedd and Powys. Boroughs were created at Y Bere, Caernarfon and Cricieth after the Edwardian conquest, but in all three cases it appears that there were settlements of some description in place prior to that point. In July 1283 houses in Caernarfon, almost certainly associated with the previous settlement there, were demolished to make way for the new castle and town.[8] Further south a record of compensation paid in 1283–4 for war damage inflicted on houses at Cricieth and Y Bere appears to speak to some sort of pre-existing settlements in both places prior to their fall to the English.[9] Even at diminutive Ewloe it is not inconceivable that a modest local economy focused on iron and coal production began to emerge in the late thirteenth century; a court roll reference in the first decade of the fourteenth century to the manor as a burgus may indicate the intent to formally imbue with that status a settlement whose population at that time has been estimated at around 200.[10] This is, of course, thin evidence, and we can do no better than to speculate. Still, it is provocative to wonder whether Llywelyn II's interest in castles was also occasioned by a desire, or perhaps in the light of his onerous financial responsibilities, a dire need to generate revenue as quickly as possible.

In that sense, these new builds on Llywelyn II's eastern periphery might conceivably be thought of as expeditionary, much as the earliest constructions of Llywelyn I were – they stamped his authority on the regions in which they were emplaced and declared his right to rule. However, the quality of their defences attained a much higher priority, and they were far more sophisticated than those at the earlier castles of Dolbadarn and Dolwyddelan. The rarefied politics of the late thirteenth-century March were rather different from those of early thirteenth-century Gwynedd: in such places as the Brecon region and eastern Powys, the period was one of near-constant low-level conflict, with increasingly powerful Marcher lords such as Roger Mortimer seeking to expand their estates into Wales.[11] As such, Llywelyn's castles in the region were surely envisioned with their

7. Stephenson, 'Ewloe Castle', p. 248; GG, p. 51, n. 51; AWR, pp. 225–6; MP, pp. 144–5.
8. Taylor, The King's Works in Wales, p. 372.
9. A.J. Taylor, 'A fragment of a Dona account of 1284', BBCS, 27 (1977), p. 255.
10. FRO NT/833, K.L. Gruffydd, 'Ewloe and its castle', p. 5.
11. MP, pp. 173–5.

defensive capabilities in mind – as fortifications designed to deter an attack and act as places of passive strength in the event of one – just as much as their visual and symbolic properties. The outstanding example of a princely castle erected to dominate views throughout the surrounding landscape in the Marches is, of course, Dinas Brân near Llangollen; the sophisticated stonework found there led King with justification to describe it as 'surely one of the most splendid of Welsh castles', one 'meant to dazzle and impress [its lords'] guests'.[12] Such an imposing castle – massively built, containing in all probability one of the very few three-storey towers ever erected by the princes of Wales, and highly visible from its hilltop position both up and down the long, loping valleys either side of it[13] – did advertise Llywelyn's power and authority in a region well away from the centres of his lordly authority in the fastnesses of the north-west. But Dinas Brân was also built very strongly indeed, with a massive ditch to its south and east as well as a compact but functional twin-towered gatehouse that would have been considered advanced even among English castles of the mid-thirteenth century. The castle's strength was such that in 1277 the earl of Lincoln averred that there was none stronger anywhere in England or Wales.[14] As the example of Beeston castle in Cheshire demonstrates, building a large and opulent castle designed to impress and overawe did not necessarily equate to making the position much stronger or more defensible, but in Dinas Brân's case it did. The same arguments can also be applied to other castles along the border dating from this period by dint of the evidence relating to the roles they played in war. Aside from the well-documented sieges of Dolforwyn in 1277 and Y Bere in 1283,[15] there are also solid archaeological grounds for thinking that Ewloe and Dinas Brân were subjected to sieges in the wars of 1276–7 and 1282–3 respectively.[16] These may be taken as signs of the importance the English crown attached to their reduction, and precautions that would hardly have been necessary if they were thought of merely as 'little more than haphazard arrangements of towers' or, even more damningly – as another modern commentator has described Ewloe – as 'almost useless', 'a medieval mistake'.[17] The following seeks to view the fruits of the later Llywelyn's

---

12.  King, 'Two castles in northern Powys', pp. 121, 125.

13.  C. Kightly, *Castell Dinas Brân* (Rhuthun, 2003), p. 20.

14.  Edwards, *Calendar of Ancient Correspondence*, p. 83.

15.  LlapG, pp. 413–14; L. Butler, 'Dolforwyn Castle, Montgomery, Powys, First Report: The Excavations 1981–1986', AC, 138 (1989), p. 82; Walker, 'William de Valence', pp. 420–1.

16.  J.F. Sharp and G. Lloyd, 'Notes on excursions 1955', FHSJ, 17 (1957), p. 105 (where it is also suggested that the presumed siegework raised by the forces of Edward I was intentionally left in place after Ewloe's capture to render the castle unusable); for the theorised subjection of Dinas Brân to a siege by English forces led by the earl of Surrey in September 1282, W.B. Jones, 'Medieval earthworks at Dinas Brân, Llangollen', AC, 147 (1998), pp. 238–9. Jones also endorses Sharp and Lloyd's identification of a siegework at Ewloe (Jones, 'Medieval earthworks').

17.  P.R. Davis, *The Forgotten Castles of Wales* (Almeley, 2011), p. 42; RCAHMW Archive 8M/86261/2 (text of Ewloe Castle Nature Trail booklet, 1970).

work – Dinas Brân, Dolforwyn and Sennybridge – as having been constructed with the defence of the Principality as an important, perhaps even central, component in their emplacement.

## Llywelyn's renovation of Ewloe

After the tumultuous opening years of his reign, the first Llywelyn was blessed with relatively stable internal politics within Gwynedd and, in the king of England, a principal opponent preoccupied with (in the case of John) extremely serious divisions within his nobility and (in the case of Henry III) a lengthy and often fractious minority. Llywelyn II, who ascended to the throne in 1246, enjoyed neither advantage. The first decade of his reign was distinguished only by the humiliating circumstance of having to share power with his brother Owain (and, from around 1252 onwards, presumably with his younger brother, Dafydd),[18] as well as a steadfast and relatively ordered March presided over by Henry III. Only after his brothers were defeated at Bryn Derwin was Llywelyn able to act decisively to build his princely authority, embarking on what Welsh sources agree was a spectacular campaign in the Perfeddwlad in late 1256 and early 1257, and thereafter exploiting internal divisions in both Powys and Deheubarth, bringing both under his aegis, along with Builth, Gwerthrynion and a host of other territories in mid-Wales.[19] In 1257 a major campaign sponsored by Henry against the prince met with disaster at Cymerau, where a pitched battle saw the rout of an army under Stephen Bauzan, a prominent knight in the retinue of the Lord Edward.[20] In the following year Llywelyn styled himself *princeps Wallie* for the first time.[21]

Llywelyn's thinking during the latter part of his reign is difficult to gauge. However, three basic precepts of his mindset can be established, of which two shall be examined firstly below. The first of these is that Llywelyn was concerned, even obsessed, with obtaining English recognition of his right to rule over Wales. Such recognition eluded Llywelyn I throughout his reign, and it seems that his grandson felt that the enshrinement of the position of prince of Wales by an English monarch would ensure his own longevity if nothing else.[22] The second is that Llywelyn II placed much emphasis on achieving this through financial means. The earliest formal proposal of this sort which we know of dates from 1259, in which year Llywelyn offered a total of 16,000 marks to be paid in instalments to Henry III in return for recognition of his right to hold his lands and take homage from the other rulers of Wales 'as his grandfather Llywelyn had held them'. Llywelyn further undertook to marry a niece of the king and to give to the king the commotes of Creuddyn and Prestatyn in Gwynedd as part of the deal.

18. Carr, 'The last and weakest of his line', p. 377.
19. LlapG, pp. 72–3, 84–6.
20. LlapG, pp. 98–9.
21. AWR, pp. 79, 499–501.
22. Pryce, 'Anglo-Welsh agreements', pp. 1, 6–7.

The proposal was rejected.[23] Its significance for Llywelyn is clear: if it had won acceptance, Llywelyn's position would resemble his grandfather's, even down to the marriage link with a member of the English royal dynasty. Llywelyn's poets were at the time extolling his virtues in their works and trumpeting his status as a worthy possessor of the crown of Aberffraw.[24] Achieving a lasting and stable peace with the king of England would give real substance to those claims.

The proposal to cede Prestatyn and Creuddyn to the king is indicative of the eagerness with which Llywelyn sought such an accommodation. The significance of these commotes was that the royal castles of Diserth and Deganwy lay in them. Both had been besieged by the Welsh in 1256 and it seems remained in a state of some privation; on their fall in 1263 they were promptly razed by the prince.[25] Their use as bargaining chips in the proposal of 1259 may therefore be viewed as a necessary evil – the retention of two castles by Henry in the Perfeddwlad would have constituted a grave threat to Venedotian security and Llywelyn may well have been thinking of the campaigns of his grandfather, who frequently sought truces with the English crown only to pursue territorial and strategic objectives once his position had improved. However, Llywelyn's willingness to cede their possession also reveals an early sensitivity to the overriding importance of castles in a military context and, by extension, to the security of his patrimony. Although there is no evidence linking Llywelyn with castles anywhere in Wales for the first decade of his reign, after 1256 the historical record is littered with them: Llywelyn can be found assaulting fortifications throughout Wales[26] and was alert to the multiple ways in which castles allowed their possessors to exercise physical and symbolic dominion over the lands in which they stood.

The earliest example of this awareness of which we can be certain is Llywelyn's reoccupation of Ewloe in 1257. As noted above, it can now be established with a fair degree of certainty that Llywelyn's work here did not extend to wholesale additions to the castle – there would have been neither the time nor, in all probability, the financial resources available to Llywelyn in 1257 to accomplish it, and so it is likely that the work done to the castle that year involved repair of damage to the fabric as a result of a decade of neglect following the capitulation of the Welsh at the conclusion of the war in 1246.[27] As far as can be made out, Ewloe played no part in the military campaigns of 1257; there is no record of its capture by Llywelyn, nor of any assault on it by Henry III during his campaign in August and September, as one would expect had its restoration been a recent occurrence. However, it was

23.  AWR, pp. 506–7.
24.  For Ann Parry Owen's translation into English of Llygad Gŵr's poem, in which he describes Llywelyn as 'the crowned one of Aberffraw', LlapG, pp. 336–7, n. 234.
25.  T. Jones (ed.), *Brenhinedd y Saesson, or, The Kings of the Saxons* (Cardiff, 1971), p. 247.
26.  In the *Red Book of Hergest* version of the *Brut* alone, for example, Llywelyn is recorded as capturing Builth in 1260, Deganwy and Diserth in 1263, and Welshpool in 1274; BYT RBH, pp. 251, 255, 261.
27.  Brodie, 'Apsidal and D-shaped towers', p. 234.

being used for meetings between Llywelyn's envoys and those of Henry III in 1259 and again in 1260. Dating repairs to the autumn of 1257 is therefore probably not far wide of the mark.

Ewloe can only have been a priority for Llywelyn for reasons of symbolism and aggrandisement.[28] It remained the commemoration in stone of Owain Gwynedd's victory at Coed Eulo in 1157 – though today's mania for celebrating anniversaries was largely a creation of the Victorians, the fact the victory occurred exactly 100 years previously may conceivably have had some resonance – and there was another, more proximate cause of Llywelyn's interest in Ewloe: its status as an erstwhile possession of Roger de Montalt, lord of Mold. De Montalt had been an implacable opponent of Llywelyn's predecessor, Dafydd II (r. 1240–6), who was required to cede the land of Mold to him under the provisions of the Treaty of Gwerneigron (1241).[29] Mold's lustre – the site of another famous victory by Owain Gwynedd in 1146, as well as Llywelyn I in 1199 – resonated on in the minds of Welsh audiences through praise poetry,[30] and although Dafydd was in no position to dispute the possession of Mold by force of arms following his signing of the treaty, he did have the means and the pretext for conducting a sustained legal campaign to regain it. In March 1242 the king empowered John Lestrange and Henry de Aldithele to hear the claims of Roger de Montalt and Dafydd to the lordship of Mold.[31] We do not know exactly what was argued by the prince's representatives, but the finding of the commission cannot have cheered them. De Montalt was given stewardship of the castle and then in 1244 was made lord of Mold under the following conditions:

> if the king or David or anyone for the king cannot show that his father or grandfather quitclaimed to Llewelyn father of the said David, to his grandfather or the said David their right in the said castle of Mold, then the said Roger shall possess the said castle for ever. If the contrary is shown, then the said Roger shall bind him and his heirs by letters patent to surrender the said castle at the king's mandate, to the king and his heirs, unless in the interval the castle be lost by war or other occupation.[32]

Dafydd would not be reconciled to this decision and besieged Mold during the war of 1244–6; it fell on 28 March 1245.[33] Though probably damaged by its investment – Dafydd had siege engines constructed for the task of reducing

---

28. The following argument is explicated in greater detail in Jones, 'Further thoughts on Ewloe castle'.
29. AWR, pp. 466–7.
30. See, for example, Jones, Gwaith Llywarch ap Llywelyn, poem 25.
31. Calendar of Patent Rolls, Henry III: Volume 3, 1232–1247 (London, 1906), p. 292.
32. Calendar of Patent Rolls, 1232–1247, pp. 426, 442.
33. Christie, Annales Cestrienses, <https://www.british-history.ac.uk/lancs-ches-record-soc/vol14/pp60-79> (accessed 15 February 2020).

nearby Diserth around the same time,[34] and these were doubtless also used at Mold – the castle was nonetheless a very substantial one, with a large bailey; it had been extensively rebuilt on the king's orders in late 1241 and it also boasted some kind of masonry defences by the time of Dafydd's capture of it. It presumably remained in Welsh hands until the collapse of the Welsh following the prince's death in February 1246.[35]

A key element in Ewloe's narrative is that some of the negotiations for Mold were held there. An account preserved in the Welsh Rolls of Edward I records that de Montalt further expounded his claims before Henry III's justices at 'Wapir', which it has been demonstrated was the place-name ordinarily used to refer to Ewloe in this period. When one remembers that Dafydd was forced to cede the Perfeddwlad to Henry in 1241, it becomes clear that the prince, or at least his officials, were put in the humiliating position of having to hear de Montalt's case in the jarringly familiar environs of a castle built by their former lord, but which now resided in the hands of the very parties who now contested Dafydd's most fundamental princely rights.

Llywelyn II's haste to reoccupy Ewloe in 1257 therefore found its impetus not in any supposed pressing need to guard the north-eastern border of the Perfeddwlad but in the far more easily understood impulse to right a grievous wrong of the recent past. It may be safely assumed that de Montalt's position occasioned considerable rancour in Gwynedd in the 1250s, and Llywelyn's seizure of Ewloe can be convincingly framed with this in mind. Of particular interest is the fact that Roger de Montalt seems to have abused his position in order to gain possession of Ewloe – the 1311 inquisition notes that the wood was added to de Montalt's possessions, 'to which it had never belonged', following his assumption of the position of justice of Chester in May 1257.[36] On de Montalt's possession of it, it was turned into a deer park.[37] We are told by the Welsh chronicles that Llywelyn's campaign in the north-east in late 1256 came about due to the pleas of the population, who were suffering under the unjust administration of the region under Llywelyn's future opponent, the Lord Edward; he had visited his lands in the Perfeddwlad that summer.[38] Llywelyn was viewed as delivering the Welsh of the north-east from these depredations, but he also lost no time in using the campaign to settle old scores. The transformation of a hallowed site of victory into a plaything for a minor Marcher lord must have antagonised the prince, who, as Lloyd relates,

34. Edwards, *Calendar of Ancient Correspondence*, p. 22.
35. M. Bevan-Evans, *Mold and Moldsdale*, 3 vols (Flint, 1949), p. 33. Excavations in late 2020 finally revealed the castle's masonry remains.
36. RCAHMW, *Flint*, p. 39.
37. J.E. Lloyd, 'Ewloe', *Y Cymmrodor*, 39 (1928), pp. 1–2.
38. Christie, *Annales Cestrienses*, <https://www.british-history.ac.uk/lancs-ches-record-soc/vol14/pp60-79> (accessed 15 February 2020).

hastened to throw down the fences of the park after the region was regained.[39] It can hardly be coincidental that Ewloe was 'restored' or 'strengthened' in 1257. Arguments for its significance as a border outpost guarding routeways into north-east Wales[40] make little sense – the only such routeway it ever truly guarded was the one through Ewloe wood taken by Henry II in 1157, and which his successors wisely steered clear of – but Butler has noted that presence in the landscape was in itself a virtue: Ewloe allowed the princes to 'exercise a degree of control by limiting westward expansion from Chester, despite its secluded setting'.[41] It also represented a cock of the snook in the direction of a Marcher lord whose hubris in creating a park on the site of one of the most famous Welsh battlefield victories known to history seems to have put Llywelyn's nose well out of joint.

## Cricieth (second phase)

There is more doubt over the significance of Llywelyn's works at Cricieth. As Eifionydd was firmly under his control from 1255 until his death, there is no ready military reason why he saw fit to erect an entirely new outer ward, complete with two substantial towers and a sophisticated new entrance. We may, however, seek an explanation in two directions. The first was the permanent loss of Deganwy in the north. Besieged since 1256, Llywelyn seems to have concluded that it represented too much of a threat to be allowed to remain standing. This stands to reason, as it appears never to have been completed: the remains of the outer bailey and the fortification known as Mansel's Tower lack the anticipated masonry defences on the north and east sides respectively,[42] and there is no evidence to suggest they ever existed. Garrisoning the castle was therefore fraught with difficulties and on its fall in 1263 Llywelyn elected to destroy it, presumably with the idea of defending the newly re-established eastern border with Cheshire to the east instead by means of the castle at Mold (see below), which had been captured during the Perfeddwlad campaign of 1256–7.

This, however, left Llywelyn destitute of one of the princes' most important, and certainly most visible, castles. Its status as a 'corporate' castle has already been noted, and it may be that Llywelyn sought to compensate for the loss by embarking on substantial new works at Cricieth, which now became one of his most lavish residences; the prince is known to have stayed there in 1274.[43] Cricieth may also have supplanted Dolbenmaen as the commotal centre of Eifionydd during Llywelyn's reign. We cannot be sure of the date, but Johnson's suggestion that the westernmost tower of the outer ward may have been built with an administrative role in mind,

39. Lloyd, 'Ewloe', p. 2.
40. Butler, 'Dolforwyn Castle, Powys, Wales', p. 74.
41. Butler, 'Dolforwyn Castle: prospect and retrospect', p. 162.
42. Alcock, 'Excavations at Degannwy Castle', p. 193.
43. AWR, p. 557.

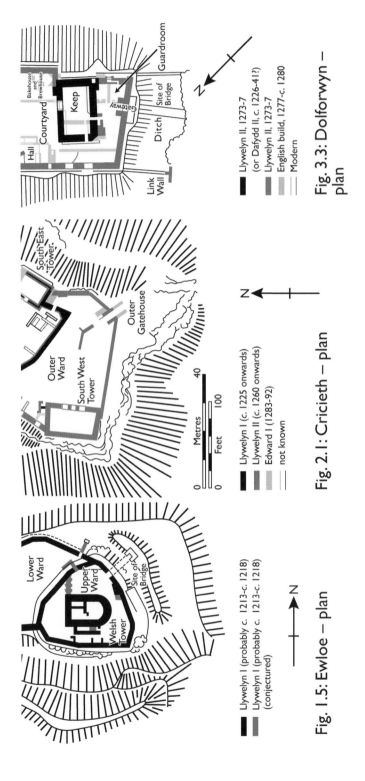

**Fig. 1.5: Ewloe – plan**

Llywelyn I (probably c. 1213–c. 1218)
Llywelyn I (probably c. 1213–c. 1218) (conjectured)

**Fig. 2.1: Cricieth – plan**

Llywelyn I (c. 1225 onwards)
Llywelyn II (c. 1260 onwards)
Edward I (1283–92)
not known

**Fig. 3.3: Dolforwyn – plan**

Llywelyn II, 1273–7 (or Dafydd II, c. 1226–41?)
Llywelyn II, 1273–7
English build, 1277–c. 1280
Modern

Figure 3.1 Comparisons of defensive arrangements at the entrances of Ewloe, Cricieth and Dolforwyn. At each castle, assailants gaining the entrance would be subjected to fire from a tower or wall positioned directly behind the gate, and would then need to turn sharply to the left into a confined space.

though speculative, is worth recounting.[44] We know that Llywelyn II instituted the development of the administrative machinery of royal government for the purposes of raising revenue at least.[45] It is also worth noting that the architectural layout of the outer ward is more complex than has hitherto been assumed. It has recently been argued that the remains of a previously obscure wall north of the outer gatehouse can be interpreted as a gate passage, and that this passage was erected by Llywelyn II in order to obviate the defensive weaknesses caused by the lack of a tower or towers to guard the outer gatehouse.[46] The effect would be to funnel traffic away from the inner ward and in the direction of the west tower; similar arrangements can be observed at Ewloe and Dolforwyn (Fig. 3.1). Yet this layout would also have the advantage of limiting the access of visitors concerned with administrative affairs to the only part of the castle they needed to visit.

The possibility that Cricieth's outer ward was added with a rhetorical purpose in mind should also be admitted. It is worth pointing out that the northern curtain wall was over sixty metres long at the conclusion of the works, was roughly straight and was flanked by two massive towers with the long axes presented to the view from the north. The effect would have been to magnify the castle's enormous size to passersby on the landward side. Liddiard's antedating of the concept of the 'show façade' to the medieval era, as exemplified by his analysis of the assemblages of towers and curtains at Stokesay and Beeston castles, is of relevance here.[47] The former castle dates in its present form to the last years of the thirteenth century, but, as we have seen, Llywelyn I was doubtless familiar with the latter and it probably influenced his works at Cricieth and, conceivably, Deganwy. Llywelyn II, meanwhile, may well have had first-hand experience of a similarly impressive show façade at Dryslwyn, which was certainly in existence by 1245, and at which a second ward had probably been constructed before the end of the 1250s by its lord, Maredudd ap Rhys (Fig. 3.2).[48] The outer ward at Cricieth snakes around the inner ward in the way that it does in order to completely enclose the hilltop, but its author was at liberty to arrange it internally how he liked, defensive requirements notwithstanding. Smaller towers, perhaps of circular or apsidal type, could have sufficed, but the monolithic constructions that were built may owe more than a little to the same need for ostentatious display that is so evident at Dinas Brân (see below).

The work completed at Cricieth by Llywelyn II has been dated to c.1260,[49] though a date around the time of Deganwy's destruction in 1263 would fit equally

44. The idea was endorsed by Lawrence Butler in 'Dolforwyn Castle: prospect and retrospect', p. 160.
45. D. Stephenson, 'From Llywelyn ap Gruffudd to Edward I: expansionist rulers and Welsh society', in Williams and Kenyon (eds), *Impact of the Edwardian Castles*, pp. 10–12.
46. Jones, 'How to make an entrance', pp. 80–9.
47. Liddiard, *Castles in Context*, p. 46.
48. C. Caple, *Excavations at Dryslwyn Castle 1980–95* (Leeds, 2007), pp. 32, 37–8.
49. O'Neil, 'Criccieth Castle', p. 17.

Figure 3.2 Dryslwyn as seen from the south; the remains of the inner and middle wards are visible. After the addition of the outer ward in the late thirteenth century, the southern façade extended even further to the right.

well. Its result was to significantly augment Cricieth's defences, fully enclosing the summit of the hill on which the castle sat and providing additional space for accommodation and outbuildings. The erection of a short screen wall in the outer ward was almost certainly accomplished to provide protection to the inner ward's postern gate in the event that the outer ward was gained by attackers.[50] The suggestion that the enfilading effect achieved by the erection of the two new towers was 'perfect'[51] cannot be admitted, as neither projects beyond the curtain wall, but inward angling of the curtain immediately to the north of the west tower combined with the insertion of multiple arrowslits at this point in the circuit makes good this deficiency. We shall never know if the 'Engine Tower' – that is, the rectangular tower built directly in front of the twin-towered inner gatehouse – accommodated a trebuchet at this point in the castle's history, or whether the use of the tower for this purpose was an Edwardian innovation, though architectural evidence arguably suggests the latter.[52] Even if such a device did not appear during the period of Welsh occupation, Llywelyn's work at Cricieth made it a formidable

50. Jones, 'How to make an entrance', pp. 80–3.
51. O'Neil, 'Criccieth Castle', p. 17.
52. Avent, *Cricieth Castle*, p. 31.

fortress and puts into perspective the haste with which Edward sent an advance force to capture it in March 1283.[53]

## Dinas Brân

Standing less than a mile to the north of Llangollen, for many years Castell Dinas Brân lay somewhat outside the scope of studies of Venedotian castle building, but the recent conjecture that the fortification was sponsored by Llywelyn II[54] is a compelling one, and enables its consideration here. As with so many native Welsh castles, there are several dissenting opinions as to its provenance. Three possible builders have been identified among the leaders of the house of Powys: Gruffudd Maelor (d. 1191), his son, Madog ap Gruffudd (d. 1236), and Madog's son, Gruffudd ap Madog, lord of Bromfield (d. 1269). A recent attempt to assign authorship of the keep to Gruffudd Maelor and the remainder of the castle to Madog[55] is flawed, as the castle's keep, a stout rectangular structure overlooking the castle's entrance, is rather too large and well built to be uncomplicatedly compared with the drystone or poorly mortared stand-alone towers elsewhere in north Wales that are thought to date from the late twelfth century. That Gruffudd Maelor's son Madog might have had a hand in its construction, however, is at least worth considering. Madog was a Powysian lord of some significance. He allied with Ranulf, earl of Chester, during the latter's expedition into Gwynedd in 1210, and correspondence with King John survives demonstrating that he placed great value on securing Madog's adherence during Llywelyn's resurgence in 1212;[56] the northern half of Powys – Powys Fadog – was in fact named after him.[57] Thereafter Madog switched allegiance to Llywelyn I and enjoyed largely stable relations with Llywelyn until the end of his life. Madog may have had the resources to erect a keep, which would amplify the extraordinary architectural statement made by the raising of Valle Crucis abbey a few miles to the west during his reign. While the theory accepted in the early twentieth century that the entire castle was erected by Madog c.1230 pushes the point too hard,[58] erection of the keep by Madog late in his career is conceivable; in fact, Edward Lhwyd recorded an early modern tradition that Madog did indeed reside at the castle in his *Parochalia* (1700).[59] The principal argument in favour of this is the slightly puzzling rock-cut ditch *inside* the castle's ward, effectively separating the keep from the rest of the courtyard; this feature's

53. Taylor, *The King's Works in Wales*, p. 365.
54. *MP*, pp. 234–5.
55. W.B. Jones, 'The building of Castell Dinas Brân, Llangollen', *Clwyd Historian*, 45 (2000), p. 8.
56. *MP*, pp. 107–8.
57. *AWR*, p. 39.
58. Jones, 'The defences of Gwynedd', p. 37. Jones was probably following Hemp and Lloyd, who proposed the same in 1935; Anon., 'Llangollen – report', *AC* (1935), p. 325.
59. R.H. Morris (ed.), E. Lhuyd, *Parochalia ... Issued by Edward Lhwyd*, Archaeologia Cambrensis Supplements; 3 vols (1909–11), Vol. 2, p. 41.

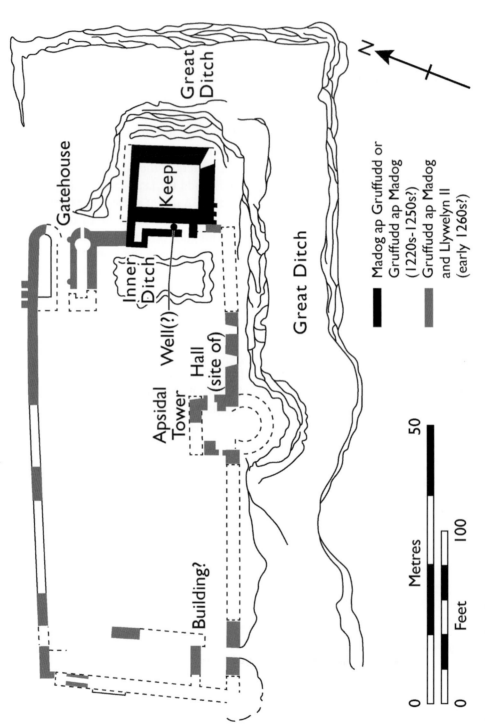

Figure 3.3 Dinas Brân, plan.

function becomes clearer if the keep antedates the construction of the ward, as it would have given vital defence to a stand-alone keep on that side (Fig. 3.3).[60] Arguing against it, however, is the nature of the join between the keep and the northern part of the eastern curtain wall, which seems to suggest that creation of a ward was part of the original plan.[61] No firm conclusions can be drawn, and an open mind should be kept.

The generally accepted date for construction is shortly before 1270, as the castle's only appearance in history prior to the war of 1276–7 dates from that year; this would make it the work of Gruffudd ap Madog. If evidence from the remarkable text known as the *Romance of Fouke le Fitz Waryn* can be admitted, the date of construction may be a little earlier than that. Recent research has suggested a provenance for this text during the period 1258–64, with David Stephenson favouring the latter date based on internal evidence.[62] The *Romance* was for a long time largely dismissed as a semi-legendary narrative no more useful to historians than any similar work of fiction, but recent analyses have demonstrated that, with care, it can be employed to illuminate many episodes in the history of the northern March during the thirteenth century: passages recounting the bestowal of the manor of Ellesmere on Llywelyn I, and his later marriage to a daughter of Fulk fitz Warin, for example, all agree promisingly with the historical record.[63] It is in this light that we should consider a reference early in the *Romance* to a 'Chastiel Bran'. The narrative makes this a fortification of the eleventh century, a detail no more true than the tale of Arthurian derring-do that follows. But for our purposes the salient aspect of this reference is that it would find resonance among the audience for the *Romance*, which primarily consisted of 'the lords of the northern Shropshire marchland' – a grouping that would by the 1260s have included Gruffudd ap Madog, whose wife was Emma Audley, and who had campaigned extensively in the area alongside Llywelyn II in the late 1250s.[64] To these recipients, the insertion of a dramatic episode centred on 'Chastiel Bran' would have been meaningful, particularly if the castle was undergoing or had undergone extensive building works.[65] There is, then, a plausible case – though no more than that – for assigning the bulk of the castle's construction to the late 1250s or early 1260s and envisaging its completion perhaps over the course of several years.

---

60. This is the interpretation favoured by W.B. Jones; for a full explication, and a rebuttal of architectural evidence arguing against it, 'The building of Castell Dinas Brân', p. 6.
61. King, 'Two castles in northern Powys', p. 124.
62. Stephenson, '*Fouke le fitz Waryn*', pp. 28–9.
63. Stephenson, '*Fouke le fitz Waryn*', p. 27; Jones, 'Prydydd Y Moch'.
64. Stephenson, '*Fouke le fitz Waryn*', p. 29.
65. It should be noted that Old Oswestry has been advanced as an alternative identification; see A. Williams, 'Stories within stories: writing history in *Fouke le Fitz Waryn*', *Medium Ævum*, 81 (2012), p. 72, and references therein.

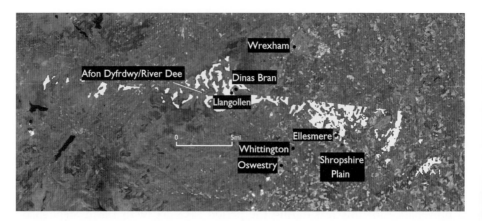

Figure 3.4 Dinas Brân, viewshed analysis. The castle can be widely seen throughout the central portion of Dyffryn Dyfrdwy. It is also visible across a wide swath of land in north-eastern Shropshire to the east: that is, territory that was in previous times considered part of the kingdom of Powys and which remained an aspiration of the lords of Powys. The lordship of the principal Salopian possession of the princes of Wales, Ellesmere (which had been under Llywelyn I's authority almost continuously from 1205 to 1231) is within the viewshed, as is part of Whittington lordship, to which Llywelyn I had possibly laid claim late in his reign, and which would become the possession of Llywelyn II in the 1260s. Analysis created using ArcGIS; height above ground at origin set at six feet; north is at top.

Figure 3.5 Dinas Brân, oblique aerial view from the west. The hill on which the castle sits (centre) is visible from parts of the northern Shropshire Plain to the east for distances of twenty miles. Photograph taken by Toby Driver, 2007; RCAHMW Catalogue Number: C864674.

Characterisations of Dinas Brân as a 'showpiece'[66] for the lords of northern Powys have considerable merit, but the idea that its erection was 'the brave attempt of a waning princely house to reassert its honour and prestige'[67] is less persuasive. It makes more sense to envisage Dinas Brân as the joint enterprise of Gruffudd ap Madog and his overlord, Llywelyn II, and to consider its purpose as twofold: to provide one of Llywelyn's most important vassals with a castle appropriate to his standing and to monitor the Dyfrdwy valley to the south, passage through which afforded entry into the uplands of northern Powys. Its construction may well have spurred the development of the nascent town at Llangollen in the valley below; some sort of settlement was certainly in existence there in 1234, and the grant of a market charter by Edward I in 1284 need not imply a prior lack of market activity.[68] The opulence one would associate with a castle designed to be a status symbol is readily found in the quantities of finely dressed stone on site, including sandstone probably transported down the Dee estuary from the Wirral – itself a detail that argues for a collaborative effort between Gwynedd and Powys in its construction.[69]

None of this, however, explains away Dinas Brân's most startling characteristic: its size. The castle's single ward is an enormous subrectangular structure, the northern and southern curtains of which comprise the longest castle walls found anywhere in native Wales at the time. The castle's aspect would have seemed daunting from the valley floors to the north and particularly the south, as the substantial D-shaped tower and the castle's keep are both positioned on that side. As with Cricieth's outer ward, Dinas Brân's form may have derived from a wish to make it as imposing a presence in the surrounding landscape as possible. Many native Welsh castle sites are situated on the crests of hills, but reaching Dinas Brân's position involves a particularly arduous climb, no matter what direction one approaches from; the comment that transportation of heavy equipment and supplies to the site presented significant logistical problems can hardly be argued with.[70] The site is visible for miles around in every direction; it can even be seen from the Shropshire plain due east (Figs 3.4 and 3.5).

The decision to emplace it on the hill (or indeed, to augment a pre-existing keep rather than begin a new build elsewhere) was surely informed by this, and the similarities with Dryslwyn's emplacement are noticeable. Dryslwyn was situated on a hilltop site and commanded impressive views for many miles up and down the Tywi valley, much as Dinas Brân did over the Dyfrdwy; like Dinas Brân, its

66. Jones, 'The building of Castell Dinas Brân', p. 7.
67. King, 'Two castles in northern Powys', p. 139.
68. *AWR*, p. 709; I. Soulsby, *The Towns of Medieval Wales* (Chichester, 1983), p. 169; *MP*, p. 237 and n. 107.
69. How this material was acquired given the febrile political landscape of the early and mid-1260s is a mystery. Trade in such a sought-after commodity presumably could only have been transacted at a time of peace between Wales and England, which may argue for a slightly later date – after 1267 – for the castle.
70. King, 'Two castles in northern Powys', p. 120.

curtain was built on the break of the hill's slope, 'to make [it] as conspicuous and as effective a defence as possible'.[71] While the architectural features at each site differ, their macrolocations and aspect as seen from their respective valley floors are very similar. There is a good chance that Dryslwyn was known to Llywelyn II. He is on record as entering into an alliance with Maredudd at Caernarfon in 1251, marking the establishment of an alliance between Gwynedd and Deheubarth that would endure for the next half-decade; and although the relationship between the two men soured in 1257, when Llywelyn bestowed on Maredudd's nephew Rhys Fychan lands that Maredudd held belonged to him,[72] Llywelyn spent much of the summer on campaign in Deheubarth, and would have had the opportunity and motive to visit the castle for himself. Excavations during the 1980s and 1990s uncovered considerable evidence of high-status occupancy appropriate to Maredudd's status as the principal ruler of Deheubarth.[73] Had Llywelyn paid a visit, the castle's opulence may well have impelled him to attempt something similar at Cricieth and indeed Dinas Brân.

The castle's defences are complete, if in some respects curious. The apsidal tower is monolithic – it appears to have had three storeys,[74] making it very rare if not unique among native Welsh castles – and well placed to enfilade the southern curtain on which it stands, but the keep is not enclosed, projecting from the curtain on the east. The strangest element is the twin-towered gatehouse, which has no parallel at any other Welsh castle. The inner gatehouse at Cricieth is far more massive and its towers more D-shaped, and Victorian characterisations of it, and Dinas Brân more generally, as exhibiting typically Edwardian features are wishful thinking; 'one might almost [call it] a caricature ... of the [typical] English gatehouse' was King's quizzical assessment of the latter.[75] Then again, it is true that native Welsh castles 'often have idiosyncratic gatehouses adapted to the geography of the site',[76] and Dinas Brân's is no different. As the drop on the northern and western sides of the castle is quite sheer, and the southern side faces the enormous outer ditch, the gatehouse nestles alongside the keep by necessity, the north-eastern corner of the ward being the only position on the castle's rampart which had the space for such a structure. Even here, the ground falls away fairly steeply to the east – an effect that must have magnified the gatehouse's size and bulk. Yet the gatehouse was indispensable to the fabric because of its symbolic importance. Its sophisticated ornamental detailing, which included moulded wall-ribs and imported sandstone (in contrast to the plain mudstone used throughout the rest of the fabric), has been compared to that found in chapels of contemporary

71.  Caple, *Excavations*, p. 349.
72.  LlapG, pp. 99–100.
73.  Caple, *Excavations*, passim.
74.  King, 'Two castles in northern Powys', p. 129.
75.  King, 'Two castles in northern Powys', p. 124.
76.  Caple, *Excavations*, p. 85.

date,[77] and argues very strongly for the structure's importance as proclaiming the lord of Bromfield's power and authority to visitors, underscoring the castle's dual function as a military installation and a statement of lordly agency. The closest parallel is with the twin-towered gatehouse at Bryn Amlwg, which is of very similar size – the difference between the towers' width is less than one and a half metres – and layout. Bryn Amlwg was captured by Llywelyn in 1267 and its gatehouse (and perhaps other parts of the fabric) has been postulated as his work.[78] The case for Venedotian authorship is made below, but, whoever built Bryn Amlwg's gatehouse, their similarity may suggest Dinas Brân emulated its form, or vice versa.

## Dolforwyn

Dolforwyn is often thought of as Llywelyn II's final new castle. In fact, its history may be considerably more complicated. It has long been understood that building commenced in the early 1270s, as indicated in English correspondence, but, as noted in the excavation report, this reading is hardly supported by material finds, of which there are almost none dating from before the castle's fall in 1277.[79] Other interpretations of Dolforwyn's provenance are possible, and the reference in the *Black Book of Wigmore* to the castle having been raised by Dafydd II is worth considering. It is conceivable that the castle's most imposing feature, the rectangular keep, was indeed raised under Dafydd's authority, perhaps during the late 1220s or early 1230s, when Dafydd had come of age and was beginning to issue acts in his own name. That it was the first masonry construction to be built is clear: it occupies the summit of the hill on which Dolforwyn stands and was not bonded with the curtain walls. In this reading, it would have been erected as a stand-alone keep, much as Dinas Brân might have been. (Interestingly, the two structures are extremely similar in proportions and size; their walls are of identical thickness and, although Dolforwyn's keep is two and a half metres longer, its width corresponds with that of Dinas Brân's keep to within thirty centimetres.) The round tower is also considered an early build, and may have been contemporaneous with the keep; however, whereas Butler speculated that the pair may have been built prior to 1273 and communications established between them by a (now lost) wooden palisade,[80] the present writer considers it more likely that the round tower represents the earliest phase of the building works that commenced under Llywelyn II in 1273, and which were incomplete by the time Dolforwyn was besieged in 1277.

Why Llywelyn should have chosen to fortify the site at Dolforwyn can be determined by examining his tempestuous relationship with the lord of southern

77. King, 'Two castles in northern Powys', p. 125.
78. L. Alcock, D.J.C. King, W.C. Putnam and C.J. Spurgeon, 'Excavations at Castell Bryn Amlwg', MC, 60 (1967–8), p. 25.
79. Butler, 'Dolforwyn Castle, First Report', p. 95.
80. Butler, 'Dolforwyn Castle, First Report', p. 95.

Powys, Gruffudd ap Gwenwynwyn. The latter had finally accepted Llywelyn's overlordship in 1263, but the agreement that codified the relationship makes clear Gruffudd's continuing power, and the potential for conflict should contentions arise between the two. Whereas Llywelyn sought to emphasise his right to Gruffudd's homage, Gruffudd doubtless viewed their relations as those of confederates, harkening back to earlier conceptualisations of Welsh political unity.[81] At first, Llywelyn seems to have done his best to ensure Gruffudd's position in southern Powys was bulwarked against the depredations of his Marcher neighbours; a clause in the Treaty of Montgomery in Gruffudd's favour can be interpreted as an insertion designed to allow him to keep lands annexed from Thomas Corbet in 1263.[82] By the early 1270s, however, relations between prince and vassal were souring. The exact cause is unknown, but Gruffudd's witnessing of Llywelyn's attempt to gain and retain control of the commotal lordship of Senghenydd in south Wales against the power of the Clares – a diplomatic and military campaign that was long-lasting, wasteful of limited resources and, ultimately, futile – may have planted seeds of doubt in Gruffudd's mind as to the prince's good judgement.[83] The year after Llywelyn abandoned his claims he began construction of the castle and an associated borough at Dolforwyn. Gruffudd, whose own masonry castle at Welshpool lay just six miles distant, cannot have been happy at the prospect of watching trade being siphoned to Llywelyn's new town; but he may have been even more unnerved by the implication that he could not be trusted to see to the security of the Severn valley on Llywelyn's behalf. In 1274 he was implicated in an assassination plot masterminded by Llywelyn's brother, Dafydd. David Stephenson's sensitive reading of the available sources for this event has teased out the possibility that Gruffudd's involvement in the affair was less serious than Llywelyn eventually made it out to be, Llywelyn's death having been plotted by Dafydd, and by Gruffudd's son, Owain. Only later in 1274 were accusations of his complicity thrown his way, and he fled Wales for England. Llywelyn destroyed Gruffudd's castle at Welshpool shortly thereafter, perhaps for fear of it becoming a focal point for resistance to his wholesale occupation of Gruffudd's lands; his installation of his own officials in positions of power in southern Powys can only have caused disquiet, as did his continued detainment of Owain.[84]

This was the backdrop for Dolforwyn's construction. The castle that resulted, after four seasons of building, is an enigma. The various published descriptions of it, and indeed the roles that have been assigned to it, are so varied and at variance with one another as to stymie all attempts at defining its essential character; even the foremost authority on the structure reversed his position on the quality of its

81. D. Carpenter, 'Confederation not domination: Welsh political culture in the age of Gwynedd imperialism', in Griffiths and Schofield (eds), *Wales and the Welsh*, pp. 23–4.

82. MP, p. 140.

83. LlapG, pp. 339–48.

84. MP, pp. 146–51.

defences.[85] The best that can be said in obviation of this incongruity is that we are looking at an unfinished castle, albeit one that was put into a state of defence in 1277; completion was probably some way off when it fell. That it was intended at least in part to proclaim Llywelyn's direct lordship of southern Powys would seem to be indicated by its most puzzling feature, the southern entrance, which is situated in the middle of the southern curtain (Fig. 3.6). A description of it as being 'under the surveillance of sentries on the south curtain', the implication being that it was adequately protected, protests too much.[86] It is in fact exceptionally poorly defended for a castle of this size, even assuming the existence of a wooden fighting platform above it, and only the steep slope on this side prevented it from making the castle indefensible; as it was, it was immediately stopped up during the period of English occupation.[87] The feature was in the form of an archway with a barrel vault and, although the possibility of its having been a sally port was briefly raised in the excavation report,[88] the structure is rather larger than that of any ordinary postern, and seems to suggest something of more moment than a feature of that sort. As there is no defensive justification for it, the suggestion that it may have been meant to have had some sort of ceremonial function is somewhat attractive.[89] The entrance faces south-east, in the direction of the Severn valley and thenceforth towards the lands held by Roger Mortimer. It would also have been visible to traders approaching the borough on the hill ridge to the south of the castle.

The failure during excavations to discover the ramp that would have afforded access to it,[90] however, invites speculation that, although the entrance had been built, it was not yet in use. The castle's principal entrance is found on the western curtain wall, and here we find yet more evidence of the special attention paid to arrangements for entry. A feature not replicated anywhere in Gwynedd or Powys is the presence of a ditch outside the entrance whose ends are blocked by link walls.[91] We have already seen how the ditches beyond the curtains at (for example) Dinas Brân do not encircle the fortification,[92] but in those cases this is due to the site's natural features, steep drop-offs in one direction rendering further ditching unnecessary. At Dolforwyn, however, the rectangular platform on which the castle

85. Compare Butler, 'Dolforwyn Castle, Powys, Wales', p. 75 ('As the last castle to be built by a native-born ruling prince, Dolforwyn should represent the highest point of their understanding of castle building … . The only feature at Dolforwyn which does not show the highest attainment in defensive planning was the entrance …') with Butler and Knight, *Dolforwyn Castle/Montgomery Castle*, p. 10 ('[Dolforwyn] shows little sign of the more advanced styles of military architecture of the thirteenth century …').

86. Butler, 'Dolforwyn Castle, Montgomery, Powys, Second Report', p. 198.
87. Butler, 'Dolforwyn Castle, Montgomery, Powys, Second Report', p. 198.
88. Butler, 'Dolforwyn Castle, Montgomery, Powys, Second Report', p. 198.
89. Butler and Knight, *Dolforwyn Castle/Montgomery Castle*, p. 29.
90. Butler, 'Dolforwyn Castle, Montgomery, Powys, Second Report', p. 198.
91. Butler and Knight, *Dolforwyn Castle/Montgomery Castle*, p. 25.
92. King, 'Two castles in northern Powys', p. 122.

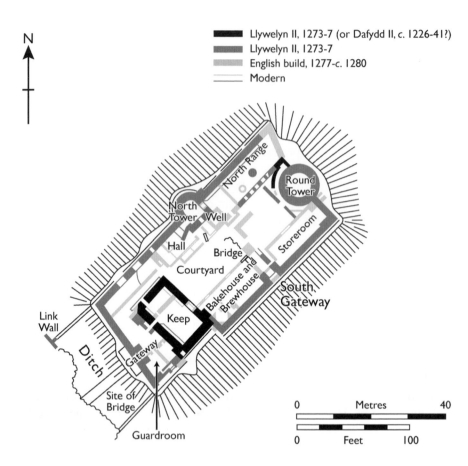

Figure 3.6 Dolforwyn, plan.

sits is level, and the sides of the ditch run the width of the hill ridge, making the ends accessible unless blocked by walls. One wonders whether the link walls thus raised represented the first step towards enclosing the nascent borough to the castle's south-west, as was the case at several places in the March, and indeed at Dryslwyn, at that time under the aegis of Rhys ap Maredudd.[93] Access across the ditch was by means of a bridge, but the entrance, if at all adorned by defences, had nothing more than a fighting platform overhead to fortify it.[94]

However, internal arrangements suggest that, as elsewhere, the architect had taken care to ensure that in the event the gate was forced the castle remained defensible. As Figure 3.1 shows, there are notable similarities between the internal

93. Caple, *Excavations*, pp. 28–30.
94. Butler and Knight, *Dolforwyn Castle/Montgomery Castle*, p. 26.

defensive arrangements of Ewloe, Cricieth and Dolforwyn. At Ewloe attackers gaining entry to the upper ward would find themselves confronted with withering fire from the Welsh Tower directly in front of them, as well as the link wall that established communications between it and the curtain. Hemmed in in this way, they would have no choice but to move round the apsidal end of the tower, only to find their way blocked on the south side of the ward by the edifice of the tower's stair – which at the time was doubtless not open to the elements – and a narrow passageway between the stair and the curtain, which was blocked by a series of walls, the footings of which survive today. At Cricieth the arrangement was almost identical. After forcing the outer gatehouse, attackers did not have the run of the outer ward, but were sandwiched between the southern curtain and an internal dog-leg wall that bisected the ward. The gate passage in which they found themselves was commanded by multiple embrasures in the south-west tower.[95] In both castles, therefore, there were areas in which attackers who had gained the entrance could then be confined and picked off at will.

At Dolforwyn we find a very similar situation – anyone entering by the western gate would be confronted by the long side of the castle's keep, and would then have to turn left and then right in order to finally enter the courtyard, this area of the castle essentially functioning as a gate passage by another name. Combined with a D-shaped tower enfilading the north curtain that may have stood as high as three storeys,[96] the residential round tower commanding the northern approach, some sort of remedy to the issue of the south gateway's securement and a theoretical internal layout that involved the creation of two wards separated by a ditch and link walls, Dolforwyn would doubtless have been perfectly defensible, had Llywelyn had the time to complete it to a good enough standard. He did not – a circumstance that was pivotal in ensuring his position in Powys crumbled during the war of 1276–7 with remarkable speed.

## Defending the Principality: Llywelyn's castles in the war of 1276–7

The military effectiveness of the castles of the princes of Wales can only be measured against their appearances in the so-called wars of Welsh independence, the conflicts of 1276–7 and 1282–3 that between them resulted in the debellation of Llywelyn's Principality of Wales. However, an increasingly common approach has been to deny their viability as bastions of national defence. Addressing the Cambrians in 1977, King suggested that the castles of Llywelyn II 'were not [intended] primarily to resist an invasion in force, but to make his borders secure against erosion and minor violence'.[97] For Derrick Pratt, defending Powys Fadog during the war of 1276–7 was all but impossible; stopping only to pour scorn on the fighting ability

---

95. Jones, 'How to make an entrance', pp. 82–3.
96. Butler, 'Dolforwyn Castle: prospect and retrospect', p. 157.
97. King, 'The defence of Wales, 1067–1283: the other side of the hill', AC, 126 (1977), p. 14.

of the men of Bromfield, Pratt went on to describe Dinas Brân, the 'keystone' to the region's security, as a 'big white elephant'.[98] For Jean-Denis G.G. Lepage the castles' function 'was less one of aggrandizement of the lord ... than as strongholds for an indigenous lord, inside which he protected his subjects in times of attack'.[99] Sean Davies went one step further, averring that 'Welsh rulers never intended their castles to serve as defences against an attack by the English king' and suggesting instead that their primary role in war was to 'serve as local campaign bases from which mobile forces could harass an invading force ... not [to be] held to the last'.[100] This idea flows neatly from the belief, expressed most aptly in the Welsh example by King, that 'While it is not unknown for a castle to block a line of strategic movement, castles were not as a general rule suitable for this purpose.'[101] Welsh attitudes towards the castle, of course, were anything but orthodox, and it is with precisely King's perspective that I wish to argue – Llywelyn II, as he saw his reach extend further even than his grandfather's, is likely to have sought to bolster the defences of his realm by initiating (or strengthening) works at several sites along key lines of communication, with the intention of slowing down or halting the advance of invading armies, including royal ones, at the border of the Principality.

This idea – simple, intuitive and reflective of the dogged manner in which Llywelyn insisted on his princely rights in the mid-1270s – was for a long period the accepted interpretation of the castle's purpose, and many eminent historians endorsed it; A.D. Carr, for instance, was in no doubt that among the roles of the princes' castles was service 'as a defence against an external enemy ... [they were] geared to defence from invasion to the east'.[102] This is not scholarly conceit. Much evidence exists to show that the difficulties involved in traversing the Welsh landscape were real, and loomed large in the strategic planning of the king. In 1277, acutely aware of the reverses suffered by his predecessors, Edward forbade his commanders from taking unnecessary risks with their armies, an order that precluded movement into the vast swathes of territory dominated by hills, mountains and forests unless by way of a road or routeway. Edward's spectacular progress in 1277 was made possible only by means of his prodigious scheme to fell woods and clear new routes through the landscape, the scale of which caught Llywelyn unawares. The salient point, however, is the novelty of Edward's plan – the very fact that he felt it necessary to embark on clearance and the cutting of roads on such a massive scale is testimony to the formidable nature of the Welsh landscape in English eyes. Llywelyn knew and depended on this. It is the reason

98. D. Pratt, 'Anatomy of conquest: Bromfield and Yale 1277–84', *Transactions of the Denbighshire Historical Society*, 56 (2008), pp. 22–3.

99. J.-D.G.G. Lepage, *British Fortifications Through the Reign of Richard III: An Illustrated History* (Jefferson, NC, 2012), p. 216.

100. WS, p. 206.

101. *A History of Merioneth Vol. 2*, p. 386.

102. Carr, *Medieval Wales*, pp. 69–70.

why the construction of castles along his eastern border with the objective of offering meaningful resistance to an invasion army felt to him (and, one presumes, his council) both natural and achievable.

Alternative assessments of the castles' functions tend to elucidate three principal objections to the idea that they were defensive in nature. The first is the notion that native Welsh castles are slight in build and dismissive of basic architectural principles of defence, such that they would be unable to withstand a determined attack by the king. The second is that the idea of retaining territory is at odds with supposedly traditional 'Welsh' methods of fighting, frequently characterised as a type of guerilla warfare that depended on ease and swiftness of movement. And lastly, it is asserted that Llywelyn II must have known that any attempt to hold his castles against the might of the king of England would be pointless, and that he consequently never planned, and certainly never tried, to do so. Offered in support of these arguments is the supposedly occasional investments of Llywelyn's castles in either the wars of 1276–7 or 1282–3 and the diffidence with which those castles that were besieged (such as Dolforwyn and Dolwyddelan) seem to have been held.

All three suppositions suffer not only from the historian's fallacy but also from a simple lack of evidence. This book was written in part to counter the idea that native Welsh castles are lacking in appreciation of the principles of good defence. The solutions they present to such issues as enfilading, entry and internal layout are often odd to eyes used to beholding Anglo-Norman fortifications, but they are the products of their positioning and of limited resources; they are almost always fundamentally sound and their implementation made the castles into viable strongholds. Native Welsh castles *were* weaker and more vulnerable to attack than the Edwardian castles, relatively speaking, but the latter are masterpieces of medieval defence, with few rivals in western Europe in terms of size and design; more or less any other castle would look puny by comparison. As the preceding chapters have shown, the castles of the Llywelyns were perfectly defensible under ordinary circumstances, and were considered so by Marcher lords and by the English kings, who found it necessary to prepare siege towers and engines for use against the princes' castles during the wars of 1244–6, 1276–7 and 1282–3. Surviving documentation relating to Llywelyn II's appointment of constables at three of his castles prior to 1277 shows that they were indeed kept in a state of at least nominal readiness for use,[103] and the prince must have foreseen the possibility that relations with the king would break down, as indeed they did in late 1276. The crisis, which began in 1274 with Llywelyn's refusal to do homage to

---

103. GG, pp. 205, 206, 216. The sixteenth-century manuscript Peniarth 128 (*Llyfr Edward ap Roger*) also records a supposed son of Dafydd II, Llywelyn, as constable of Rhuddlan; AHRC Project on P.C. Bartrum's *Welsh Genealogies* (2010); Gruffudd ap Cynan 05, Welsh Department, Aberystwyth University, <https://cadair.aber.ac.uk/dspace/handle/2160/4951> (accessed 20 January 2021). This individual is not attested in contemporary records.

Edward, could have come as no surprise to the prince, who, though he may have exercised bad judgement, did not reason so poorly that he would have allowed war to begin in the knowledge that he was inviting his own destruction. It follows that he had faith in his castles and his ability as a warlord should diplomacy fail. But neither did he exchange old ways of waging war for a static strategy based on holding strongpoints along his eastern border. What we can discern of his movements in 1276–7 indicates that Llywelyn fought as the princes of Wales had always done: he avoided giving battle, harried when possible and retreated when necessary – the lack of a decisive defeat in the field speaks to the latter – all the while garrisoning his castles in Powys and in all probability Tegeingl and Brecon against attack. Installing such garrisons and attempting to defeat Edward's forces in detail in the fastnesses of Wales were not mutually exclusive strategies.

The widespread acceptance of the last theory – that Llywelyn knew holding his castles was a tactic doomed to failure – is the most mystifying development of all. That his castles were manifestly ineffective in Llywelyn's wars with Edward at first seems to lend credence to the idea. However, the circumstances of the war – the unprecedented scale on which Edward waged it, the faltering loyalties of Llywelyn's lords and the shortfalls in his built defences – mean that we are unable to draw any very definite conclusions about their efficacy. We do know, however, that Llywelyn *did* take steps to hold them, and not empty ones. In the war of 1276–7 he almost certainly installed his own garrison at Dinas Brân at a time when the Powysians had deserted his cause and the security of Powys Fadog was in serious doubt; the siege at Dolforwyn held up an advance through southern Powys until April; Sennybridge has been convincingly identified as the focal point for weeks of determined resistance in the lordship of Brecon; even Ewloe, the curate's egg of native Welsh castles and clearly ill-suited to guard Tegeingl as a region, was apparently pressed into service.[104] These gestures involved the expenditure of men, materiel and provisions, and Llywelyn's supply of all three was finite. He, if not his council, would have made every effort to use them wisely.

It is easy to scoff at Llywelyn's presumption in attempting to hold off Edward's invasion, but we must keep in mind the unexpectedly massive campaign the king waged. Nothing like it had been seen in Britain before. Llywelyn's previous experiences of war with England – Henry III's halting and equivocal expedition of 1257, for example – may well have coloured his judgement, encouraging him to have misplaced faith in his ability to withstand a similar effort. If Edward had come to Wales with a smaller army, of the sort Llywelyn witnessed in the 1250s or even the 1240s, there is a good chance that Llywelyn's attempts to hold his position through a combination of castles and counterattack would have been successful; King's assessment of Dinas Brân, for example – that, if 'held with determination,

---

104. Stephenson, '*Potens et prudens*', p. 428; LlapG, p. 416; D.J.C. King, *Castles and Abbeys of Wales* (London, 1975), p. 10.

the castle could have stood off an English army for as long as supplies lasted'[105] – is worth remembering. Llywelyn probably proceeded with these very ideas of defiance in mind, and little suspected the disaster that awaited him. If he had, he might perhaps have a found a way to reconcile himself to the wound his pride would have sustained by putting his hand in that of the king.

Llywelyn began his preparations for war on the roads and in the fords. Then, as today, controlling roads, routeways and rivers was a crucial component in the waging of war. Roads and paths could be made impassable by the construction of obstacles, holes could be dug in fords (as indeed they were prior to the war) and traffic could be funneled thereby through terrain that made movement difficult and which afforded the possibilities for ambuscade that had served the Welsh so well in previous eras. We have already noted how Henry II was defeated attempting to traverse a routeway through the wood at Ewloe in 1157, and Dafydd II's remarkable battlefield repulse of Henry III's army in north Wales during the summer of 1245 occurred in a mountain pass.[106] Llywelyn II cleaved to the principle of denying good roads to the invader early, as can be deduced from the text of the truce agreed between him and Henry III in August 1260. One of the stipulations of the peace is that 'roads and passes shall not be obstructed, nor woods folded back'.[107] Such references are for obvious reasons hard to come by in wartime; few armies in history go to the trouble of making a note of every road they block and every ford they foul. Nevertheless, these tactics were used again in 1276–7 – a 1288 report detailing the burning by the Welsh of the important bridge over the Severn between Montgomery and Welshpool can only be taken as a reference to preparations to receive an invading army in the war of 1276–7,[108] and shows that, even as he garrisoned his castles, Llywelyn also made sure to attend to the ways of war employed by his predecessors.

It is easy to imagine such tactics sufficing for the *cefnffyrdd* or ridgeways by which the Welsh had traversed the uplands for centuries past, and also for the smaller and less used roads, but the more travelled routes into Wales could be more effectively guarded by fortifications. Having rejected Glanville Jones' concept of an integrated system of defence stretching across sets of concentric hill and mountain ranges by the time of Llywelyn II's reign, we can therefore readmit the theory, or rather, a highly modified version of it, focusing on the idea of a series of castles along the border with England emplaced with defence of key valleys and routeways in mind. The earliest step taken in this direction was the refurbishment and reactivation of Ewloe in the late 1250s, followed by the construction (or

---

105. King, 'Two castles in northern Powys', p. 131.
106. An event that formed an important cornerstone of Humphrey Llwyd's narrative of Dafydd's reign; *Cronica Walliae* (ed. I.M. Williams) (Cardiff, 2002), p. 208. See Jones, 'Dafydd ap Llywelyn'.
107. AWR, p. 508.
108. J. Davies, 'Rhyd Chwima – the Ford at Montgomery – Aque Vadum de Mungumeri', MC, 94 (2006), p. 35.

massive expansion) of Dinas Brân to the south. The addition during the 1260s and 1270s of Dolforwyn, Bryn Amlwg and Sennybridge to this list, all of them within five miles of the border of Llywelyn's Principality, speaks to Llywelyn's determination to stake out his borders. It is even conceivable that the enigmatic castle at Morgraig in southern Senghenydd, situated as it was adjacent to the principal road leading north from Cardiff, was likewise an attempt to secure that territory at a time when Llywelyn was seeking to expand his influence southwards, albeit an abortive one (the castle would appear never to have been finished).[109]

There are two caveats. The first is that this plan was the brainchild not of the first but of the second Llywelyn, and unprecedented in ambition and scope. Jones makes the fortification of the entirety of Wales' eastern border a natural step for the princes of Wales to take, but none of Llywelyn's predecessors adopted such a policy. To embark on such a scheme was audacious and required an extraordinarily brassy neck in the face of such bullish Marcher and crown opposition as Llywelyn II faced in the 1260s and 1270s. There was also Wales' unfavourable physical geography to contend with. In comparative studies of medieval Scotland and medieval Wales, the geographical differences between their respective borders with England are often overlooked. Compared to the size of the country, Scotland's border with England is relatively short and, even after one crosses it, there is over seventy miles of terrain to be traversed before one reaches the Clyde, while over 130 miles separates the border from the Great Glen. Even after the centres of Scottish royal power moved southwards during and after the reign of David I (d. 1153), reaching them was a perilous undertaking for any English army. By contrast, Wales' border with England is long – over 120 miles – and, because the peninsula which forms Wales is broad but not deep, the centres of princely power in Eryri lie no more than forty miles, perhaps a day's travel, distant.[110] Even Llywelyn II's grandfather, blessed with a rather more fractious political scene in

109. Davis, *Castles of the Welsh Princes*, p. 102 makes the reasonable suggestion that Llywelyn sponsored the castle's construction through the lord of Senghenydd, Gruffudd ap Rhys. Given Gruffudd's capture and imprisonment by Gilbert de Clare and the subsequent construction of the massive castle at Caerffili (three miles north of Morgraig) in 1268, this would imply the abandonment of Morgraig as untenable by the latter date. Debate continues over Morgraig's provenance, but the copious use of apsidal towers and the inclusion of a rectangular keep, as at Dolforwyn and Dinas Brân, seem to argue strongly in favour of a native Welsh origin. The use of stone quarried from Ogmore, well to the south-west and outside Llywelyn's (and Gruffudd's) sphere of influence, argues against this, however; Royal Commission on the Ancient and Historical Monuments of Wales, *An Inventory of the Ancient Monuments in Glamorgan Vol. 3 Part 1b: Medieval Secular Monuments: Later Castles From 1217 to the Present* (Cardiff, 2000), p. 199.

110. From the closest point on the modern Wales–England border to – for example – Dolwyddelan castle is just under thirty-four miles as the crow flies; N. Ohler, *The Medieval Traveller* (Woodbridge, 2010), p. 101 suggests that an 'average traveller' going slowly with baggage could conceivably cover twenty to thirty miles a day, and that a horsed traveller 'in a hurry' could cover anywhere between thirty and forty miles.

England and the March and, for a period at least, hefty financial resources, did not attempt to fortify his kingdom in such a way.

Secondly, if Llywelyn's castle-building along the border did indeed comprise an attempt to secure the Principality, his design was almost certainly incomplete by the time war broke out in 1276. Detailed analysis of the road network of medieval Wales lies outside the scope of this book, but it is nevertheless clear that at least one key approach into Gwynedd was not adequately defended by castles: namely, the coastal route in the north-east. We get a good idea of the course of this route from the itinerary of Henry III as recorded by the Chester annalist in 1245 (see Map 3.1). It is likely that Henry followed the Roman road, whose course, it is widely believed, corresponds closely with the modern-day A548; indeed, part of the road was uncovered at excavations near Flint in the early 2000s and again in the 2010s.[111] The unsuitability of Ewloe for the task of guarding this route has already been noticed. It was not large enough nor strong enough to withstand a sustained assault and, in any case, once placed under siege (as it would seem to have been in late 1276) it could be effectively bypassed anyway.

The position at Hen Blas (almost certainly to be identified as Coleshill) would have been far better emplaced to guard the coastal route. Assuming that the A548 continued along the line of the Roman road, the motte stood just under 0.8 miles from it and, furthermore, the signing of a document there in 1261 shows the site was still in use during Llywelyn II's reign.[112] However, the motte there had been levelled by that time, and a princely residence along the lines of the *llysoedd* further west in Gwynedd uwch Conwy built in its place; the prince would have been foolish indeed to place much faith in its ability to withstand an attack by a royal army.[113] Llywelyn was clearly very concerned about the security of Tegeingl, as he besieged and destroyed Hawarden castle in 1265, and may have raided or at least threatened Chester itself, as it is recorded that in 1264 houses were torn down on the city's outskirts and work initiated on a defensive ditch.[114] Llywelyn also insisted on a clause in the Treaty of Montgomery whereby Robert de Montalt was prohibited from building a castle in his lands at Hawarden for sixty years,[115] a point that perhaps constitutes the single most revealing expression of his unease over his north-eastern border. Llywelyn would seem at this time to have held onto Mold, in spite of an undertaking to return it to de Montalt, which may in part explain why Llywelyn subsequently built no new castles in the area – Mold would seem to have been rebuilt in stone in the mid-thirteenth century,[116] and was doubtless

111. Clwyd-Powys Archaeological Trust, 'Pentre Ffwrndan Roman Settlement, Flintshire: Community Excavation and Outreach, 2018–2019', CPAT report 1633–1 (2019), pp. 1–2.
112. *AWR*, p. 520.
113. Leach, 'Excavations at Hen Blas, Second Report', p. 27.
114. Bevan-Evans, *Mold and Moldsdale*, p. 34.
115. *AWR*, p. 537.
116. Bevan-Evans, *Mold and Moldsdale*, p. 28.

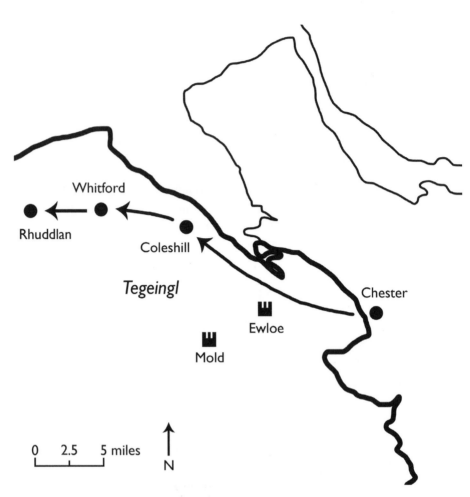

Map 3.1 Macrolocation of Ewloe, showing the route taken by Henry III in 1245.

considered a stronghold of considerable importance, without possession of which an army marching along the coast could be outflanked. Nevertheless, Mold lay five miles to the south-west of the Dyfrdwy and cannot be said to have truly guarded the coastal route either.

This shortcoming in Llywelyn's strategic planning becomes easier to understand in the context of his castle-building policy elsewhere. From his reconquest of the Perfeddwlad in 1256 until his surrender in the war of 1276–7 Llywelyn enjoyed unrivalled supremacy over *pura Wallia*. At first, this seems like a comparatively long period in which the prince might have had the opportunity to build castles at will; and, indeed, we know he had instituted works, albeit of a minor sort, at Ewloe as early as 1257. However, the onerous financial obligations imposed on him by the Treaty of Montgomery (1267), which required the prince to pay the English crown the enormous sum of 5,000 marks in that year and then 3,000 every year until the total of 25,000 marks had been paid, should be taken into consideration. This agreement has been roundly criticised as untenable for a ruler who, according to one rough estimate, could depend on an income of (at most) £5,000 a year at the height of his principate.[117] Evidence of the difficulties Llywelyn encountered in meeting his obligations has been sought in such circumstances as the unprecedented imposition of a tax of three pence on cattle in 1275[118] and the *gravamina* submitted by the men of Gwynedd to the English crown in the late summer of 1283 – that is, after Dafydd III's capture and the conclusion of the war – in which complaints of Llywelyn's seizure of land, imposition of new measures for foodstuffs and extortionate methods of increasing revenue were made.[119] Nor did the shortfalls in Llywelyn's finances go unnoticed: Gruffudd ap Gwenwynwyn, who had fled his lands in southern Powys after being implicated – perhaps unfairly – in a conspiracy against Llywelyn in 1274 spent the following two years repeatedly raiding his former lands of southern Powys from Shropshire alongside several prominent Marcher lords, with the intention of 'depriv[ing] Llywelyn of much of the economic gain that might have accrued to him from his annexation of southern Powys'. These raids were serious affairs: Gruffudd despoiled Cedewain – the very lordship in which Dolforwyn castle stood – as well as the lands around Welshpool and, on one occasion, Arwystli, the cantref through which ran the upper waters of the Severn.[120]

There are several possible indications that Llywelyn's poor financial position may have left its mark on his castle-building policy also. Short of money as the prince undoubtedly was, his policy regarding the security of the border in Tegeingl could be viewed as an attempt to fit his square pegs in the north-east into round holes, as he pressed Ewloe and, perhaps, Mold into service guarding the route of entry from Chester regardless of their unsuitability for the task. However, lack of financial resources may have manifested in other, more tangible ways. It is easy to imagine a situation in which financial strictures on Llywelyn's builders obliged them to cut their coats according to their cloth. The regularity with which accusations of poor building practices such as the use of low-quality mortar have appeared, applied without discrimination to the native Welsh castles of Gwynedd, has effectively obscured the fact that such practices can be seen at only some of the castles raised by the two Llywelyns, and closer inspection seems to bear out the idea that Llywelyn II, perhaps owing to shortness of funds, was forced to skimp on certain aspects of his building programme. The clearest indication of this can be seen in the castle at Dolforwyn. The mortar used throughout the Welsh

---

117. Williams-Jones, *The Merioneth Lay Subsidy Roll*, p. xviii.
118. Edwards, *Calendar of Ancient Correspondence*, p. 105.
119. Ll. Beverley Smith, 'The Gravamina of the community of Gwynedd against Llywelyn ap Gruffudd', BBCS, 31 (1984), pp. 162–4, 171.
120. MP, p. 151.

phase, which is currently dated 1273–7, is of poor quality with a high proportion of sand used, and the extensive damage caused by the investment of 1277 – not mirrored, for example, at the older Y Bere during the lengthier siege of 1283[121] – may reflect the relative weakness of the walls. The really telling indication of lack of funds here is, of course, that the castle was unfinished: a well had yet to be dug, the courtyard is almost destitute of Welsh-built structures, and the south gateway and access ramp were unfinished at the time of the English siege.[122] The only indication of princely expenditure on castles that survives refers to Dolforwyn: between April 1273 and April 1274 the prince's castellan, Bleddyn ap Llywelyn, spent £174 6s 8d on the castle.[123] Architectural details suggestive of works carried out in consecutive building seasons indicate some sort of expenditure over the next three years, but the finished result was markedly less resistant to attack than it might have seemed.

Most of the work carried out by Llywelyn II cannot be as closely dated as Dolforwyn, but the fact that similar problems can be identified at constructions attributed to him may be further evidence of a lack of funds for his castle works. Two architectural peculiarities at Y Bere may provide a further example, the first of which is the south tower. Its authorship has recently been problematised,[124] but if King was correct in dating it to Llywelyn II's reign his suggestion of a construction date in the late 1250s might bear some revision.[125] The tower's noticeably poorer masonry – it is the only part of the castle that has been entirely reduced to its footings (Fig. 3.7)[126] – could be the result of substandard building practices borne out of financial problems late in the reign, as opposed to incompetent work or a deficiency of construction philosophy.

In the same way, we may account for perhaps the most puzzling defensive weakness found in any of the native Welsh castles – the likelihood that the massive link walls that connect the south tower to the rest of the castle were built not by the Welsh but by Edward after the castle's fall (Fig. 3.8). The work is of a different style to the rest of the castle and the walls more massive, and it has been convincingly

121. Repairs to Y Bere following the siege were minor: Walker, 'William de Valence', p. 421. Based on evidence of the steadily improving quality of mortar during successive phases of construction at Dryslwyn, Chris Caple plausibly argues that 'mortar technology had advanced by the third quarter of the 13th century in Wales' (*Excavations at Dryslwyn Castle*, p. 165) – a state of affairs that also weakens the argument that late thirteenth-century constructions in Gwynedd were incompetently built.

122. Butler and Knight, *Dolforwyn Castle/Montgomery Castle*, p. 33; Butler, 'Dolforwyn Castle, Montgomery, Powys, Second Report', p. 191, p. 155; Butler notes (p. 187) that aquiferous rocks are present in the courtyard, but, during excavations, 'none were so moist that they could be tapped [for] drinking water'.

123. Edwards, *Calendar of Ancient Correspondence*, p. 49.

124. Brodie, 'Apsidal and D-shaped towers', p. 232.

125. *A History of Merioneth Vol. 2*, p. 404.

126. *A History of Merioneth Vol. 2*, p. 402.

Figure 3.7 Y Bere, South Tower; the reduction of the tower to its footings is not paralleled elsewhere in the castle, and may be suggestive both of a later date of construction and poorer mortar.

Figure 3.8 Link walls at Y Bere forming the yard between the Middle Tower and the South Tower; the massiveness of the walls compared to those of the South Tower beyond and elsewhere in the castle is evident.

argued that only through assigning it to the period of English occupation can the sums of money spent on augmenting the castle in the 1280s be reconciled to the visible remains.[127]

The apparent lack of communications between the south tower and the ward prior to the English period of occupation is therefore exceptionally odd, and attempts at accounting for it have obliged commentators to assume all sorts of contorted positions.[128] However, the theory King advanced (and rejected as unlikely) to account for it – that the south tower 'was built so late that there was no time to link it with the rest of the castle before the Edwardian conquest'[129] – gains much credence when considered in the light of Llywelyn's financial troubles in the 1270s.[130]

A final possible demonstration of the unfinished and imperfect aspects of Llywelyn's castle-building policy – albeit one that cannot be accepted unhesitatingly – is provided by Bryn Amlwg, the masonry castle on the borders of Ceri that was in Llywelyn's possession from 1267 to 1276.[131] There are reasons for thinking the castle was extensively modified, or perhaps even constructed in its entirety, by Llywelyn II. The two D-shaped towers on its curtain walls and the conjectured first phase of construction of the twin-towered gatehouse have been postulated as Llywelyn's work on typological grounds;[132] the positioning of the round tower in the middle of the short curtain wall at one end of the site strongly resembles Dolforwyn's plan; the similarity of the gatehouse to that at Dinas Brân has already been noted; the curtain walls have been constructed along the break of slope, as at so many other native Welsh castles; and, although the D-shaped towers are smaller than any yet found at a confirmed native Welsh castle, their idiosyncratic positioning in the middle of the curtains is deeply reminiscent of that at Dolforwyn and Dinas Brân, and may well indicate Welsh authorship. It may therefore be instructive that in the D-shaped tower that was excavated at Bryn Amlwg, as well as the curtain on which it sat, we see the same evidence of poor mortar observed at Dolforwyn and Y Bere.

127. King, in *A History of Merioneth* Vol. 2, p. 402.

128. Cf. Davis, *Castles of the Welsh Princes*, p. 43, which envisages the south tower's isolation as an intentional feature. But given its ground-level entrance – a fatal weakness for any structure intended for use as a stand-alone donjon – the characterisation of it as a 'last refuge in the event of a siege' makes no sense.

129. *A History of Merioneth* Vol. 2, p. 404.

130. An alternative suggestion advanced by King was that the Welsh did build curtain walls linking the tower with the rest of the castle, but that they were encased by the thicker English walls built in the 1280s (*A History of Merioneth* Vol. 2, p. 403). This is also possible, and the fact that the English appear to have waited three years before commencing work on the curtain here – even prioritising the construction of a new *camera* in one of the towers over it – may speak in favour of it (Taylor, *The King's Works in Wales*, p. 368). If true, of course, this explanation still supports the idea that Llywelyn was short of money; it seems that nowhere else in the defences were the walls so flimsy that the English felt they needed to undertake major rebuilding.

131. Alcock *et al.*, 'Excavations at Castell Bryn Amlwg', p. 24; *MP*, p. 127.

132. Alcock *et al.*, 'Excavations at Castell Bryn Amlwg', p. 25.

In fact, no traces of lime were found anywhere during excavations except in the gatehouse, and even here the mixture was poor, suggesting what little lime was available was saved for the most important element in the castle's defences.[133]

Based on these examples, we can only go so far; it is a pity that one of the few castles that would seem to have been solely authored by Llywelyn II, and which might conceivably provide support for this interpretation – Sennybridge – remains unexcavated. Nevertheless, the possibility that Llywelyn's financial problems in the later part of his reign manifested in his surviving works should be at least considered. In the face of such seemingly substantial issues with cash flow, it is hard to understand why Llywelyn decided to undertake such an extensive castle-building programme. Caprice should not be written out of Llywelyn's script: his mismanagement of his finances, his rough treatment of the communities under his aegis and, most glaringly, his refusal to do homage to Edward I in 1274 and 1275[134] can variously be interpreted as a collective failure of policy on the part of Llywelyn's council or some more fundamental failing in his own judgement – a failing of imagination, perhaps, as much as policy. It is an axiom that strategists always prepare for the next war with the last war in mind. Llywelyn's castles might well have sufficed if they and their garrisons had been pitted against armies of the size put into the field by Henry III, but against an opponent of Edward I's unprecedented resources and determination they availed him little.

The surviving documentation relating to the war of 1276–7 bears the faint imprint of Llywelyn's bold, but flawed, attempt to hold his kingdom against an English campaign unparalleled in scale. An early advance would seem to have been made by the earl of Warwick, who took charge of the army assembled at Chester on 15 November 1276 and had 'advanced westwards beyond Mold' by 15 December.[135] This would seem to imply the fall of both Ewloe and Mold by the latter date, and the siegework at the former may well date from this period.[136] Thereafter Warwick seems to have consolidated his position for the winter, ensuring no resistance in the easternmost parts of Tegeingl by the time construction began on the first of Edward's 'iron ring' of castles, Flint, in the summer of 1277.

Elsewhere, there are indications of significant resistance in the lordship of Brecon, presumably centred on the castle at Sennybridge, until the early spring of 1277, and in Deheubarth allies of Llywelyn appear to have been engaged in holding the upper Tywi valley for an extended period around the same time.[137] But the fulcrum of Edward's effort was to be found in the middle March, where his

133. Alcock et al., 'Excavations at Castell Bryn Amlwg', pp. 15–16.
134. LlapG, pp. 382–8.
135. FRO NT/833, Gruffydd, 'Ewloe and its castle', p. 4.
136. D.J. Cathcart King was adamant that Ewloe must have been captured by English forces (rather than having been abandoned), though he favoured a date of 1277 for its fall; *Castles and Abbeys of Wales*, p. 10.
137. LlapG, p. 416.

army at Montgomery faced down Llywelyn's positions at Dinas Brân, Dolforwyn, and Bryn Amlwg.[138] Examination of their positions in the landscape supports the idea that the first two, and perhaps Bryn Amlwg as well, were emplaced with the security of the border from Powys Fadog in the north as far south as the lordship of Ceri in mind. Each guarded vital routes into mid-Wales. The northernmost of them, Dinas Brân, overlooked the Dyfrdwy valley, a significant feature because it afforded access to Eryri via Cwm Cynllwyd and the Alwen valley, and one that had seen armed conflict in campaigns earlier in the thirteenth century. Moving south, the next valley encountered is the Tanat, but as the valley is fairly short and terminates in steep uplands it represented an unsuitable entry point for any army and was not fortified. South of the Tanat was the floodplain of the Severn, from which three valleys point westward: the Banwy, the Rhiw and the Severn itself. From the Severn valley several possibilities presented themselves for the invader. The Carno debauched into it near Caersws, and traversing that valley would provide access to southern Meirionydd via the Roman road that ran along it in the direction of Dinas Mawddwy.[139] Securing this route into Gwynedd had, it seems, been an objective of Dafydd II, who besieged the castle at Tafolwern, which lies halfway along its length, in 1244.[140] Alternately, an invading army might simply follow the Severn's path southwards and then turn into the upper Wye; indeed, this seems to have been what occurred in 1277, with Builth secured by Roger Mortimer by 3 May at the latest, when the construction of a castle began there.[141]

Llywelyn's position in south-eastern Powys is summarised in Map 3.2. Following Llywelyn's destruction of Gruffudd ap Gwenwynwyn's castle at Welshpool, the Severn was defended by the castle at Dolforwyn, and on the edge of the Ceri uplands on its southern flank stood Bryn Amlwg. This castle lay less than half a mile from an important ridgeway through Ceri that led in the direction of the Roman road leading north through Caersws as far as the Banwy.[142] It was probably originally erected by an Anglo-Norman lord as a bulwark against Welsh usage of the ridgeways for raiding the Clun valley to the east;[143] such raids continued well into the thirteenth century, such as that led by Dafydd II in the war of 1244–6, which struck as far east as Lydham and ended with an attack on Bacheldre, seven miles to the north-east of Bryn Amlwg.[144]

---

138. But not, apparently, Whittington, which seems to have played no part in the war, and was probably abandoned because of its isolated and untenable position in Shropshire.
139. The earl of Warwick took precisely this route during his campaign in mid-Wales to suppress the revolt of Madog ap Llywelyn in 1295; Edwards, *Calendar of Ancient Correspondence*, p. 143.
140. Edwards, *Calendar of Ancient Correspondence*, p. 21.
141. Taylor, *The King's Works in Wales*, p. 295.
142. W.G. Putnam, 'The Roman road from Forden to Caersws', MC, 57 (1962), pp. 141–9.
143. M. Lieberman, *The Medieval March of Wales: The Creation and Perception of a Frontier, 1066–1283* (Cambridge, 2010), p. 168.
144. F.C. Suppe, *Military Institutions in the Welsh Marches: Shropshire 1066–1300* (Woodbridge, 1994), p. 9.

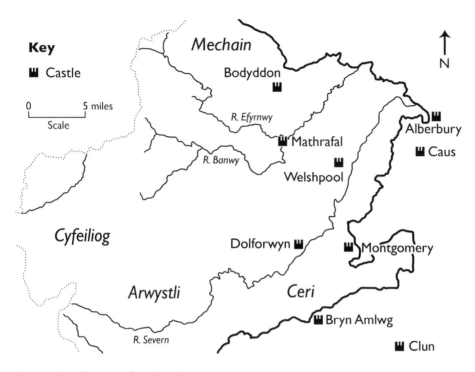

Map 3.2 Fortifications of southern Powys.

An apparent area of weakness is found in Mechain, the lordship to the north of the river Efyrnwy. We hear of no operations in this area by Llywelyn during the war, but he had been present there earlier in his career when he destroyed the motte at Bodyddon in the late 1250s, an event significant enough to earn a mention in the *Brutiau*.[145] There was also the motte-and-bailey castle at Mathrafal, which stood just south of the confluence of the Banwy and the Efyrnwy. However, its status as a defensible fortification in the late thirteenth century is unclear,[146] and nor is there any evidence that Bodyddon was ever refortified. It may be, however, that this area was left undefended by castles because the Berwyn mountains directly behind it, like the uplands above the Tanat, were considered to form an impenetrable barrier against invaders. This idea derives some support from the phlegmatic letter sent to Edward in late November 1282 from Roger Lestrange, who was directing operations in the area after the death of Edward's commander, Roger Mortimer, the previous month. In it Lestrange describes how 'the enemy in his district is beyond Berwen [the Berwyns] and beyond Morugge [Pumlumon], which mountains are so difficult

---

145. BYT Pen MS 20, p. 111.
146. C.J. Arnold and J.W. Huggett, with a contribution by H. Pryce, 'Excavations at Mathrafal, Powys, 1989', MC, 83 (1995), p. 63.

and repellant that no army could safely pass without putting the troops in great peril, and this the king has forbidden.'[147]

The immense importance of south-eastern Powys to the security of the Principality was underscored by the lengthy and bitter disputes over the right of Llywelyn (and Roger Mortimer) to build castles in the region. The raids of Gruffudd ap Gwenwynwyn in the mid-1270s have also already been noticed. The apparent ease with which his parties were able to make these incursions, and Llywelyn's men's inability to oppose them, was brought to the attention of Edward I by Llywelyn, who complained bitterly of their depredations.[148] Edward did nothing to stop them, and may indeed have made a mental note: to him, southern Powys may have begun to look like the soft underbelly of Llywelyn's position. Llywelyn, too, was aware of the precariousness of his situation there: his support from the lords and magnates of the region had been seriously eroded by the intrigues of the mid-1270s and their aftermath, and it is significant that he installed his own officials and men in the region after Gruffudd ap Gwenwynwyn's ejection.[149] He is on record as having been present in southern Powys in the first months of 1277,[150] desperately attempting to shore up resistance to the incursions made by the Marcher lords tasked with reducing the region ahead of Edward's invasion later in the year. An early sign of trouble was the success of Peter Corbet, who quickly reoccupied the Gorddwr – the strip of land east of the Severn and north of Montgomery – thereby placing Dolforwyn within striking distance.[151] Around the same time Gruffudd secured possession of the area around Welshpool, where his castle had been destroyed three years earlier by Llywelyn; the allegiance of his erstwhile tenants followed,[152] leaving Dolforwyn's northern flank in the hands of men hostile to the prince. The assault on the castle duly commenced in early spring and by 31 March it was under siege. Its defenders agreed to yield it if no relief arrived by 8 April and the castle was duly surrendered on that date.[153] During the siege the fabric sustained heavy damage,[154] and building parties were immediately tasked with repairing it. We cannot be sure exactly when Bryn Amlwg fell, but as royal forces in the region were paid off in May resistance had certainly ended before then. The circumstances of its capture are not recorded,

147. Edwards, *Calendar of Ancient Correspondence*, p. 84.
148. AWR, pp. 562–3.
149. BYT Pen MS 20, p. 117.
150. Edwards, *Calendar of Ancient Correspondence*, p. 82.
151. This advance seems to have occurred in the winter of 1276–7; Morris, *The Welsh Wars of Edward I*, pp. 120–1.
152. MP, pp. 152–4.
153. For a full analysis, L. Butler, 'The siege of Dolforwyn castle in 1277', *Château Gaillard*, 19 (2000), pp. 25–6.
154. As early as 3 April Edward was being informed by an observer that the castle 'will need much repair'; Edwards, *Calendar of Ancient Correspondence*, p. 31.

but the discovery of burnt timbers in the castle's round tower during excavations in the 1960s can probably be taken as an indication that it was either fired by its garrison or razed after its capture.[155] By mid-May, Arwystli and Cyfeiliog had been occupied and reduced, the former by tracing the Severn and the latter probably via Dyffryn Carno.[156] A breakthrough further south in the spring by English forces in the Brecon area meant that Llywelyn's position south of Gwynedd had entirely collapsed even before Edward's invasion of north Wales commenced in the summer.

In Gwynedd Llywelyn's forces offered slightly stouter resistance. Given that the earl of Warwick would seem to have been active in Tegeingl from his base in Chester from late November 1276, resistance there was sustained and vigorous; Ewloe seems to have required an investment to secure its surrender[157] and Llywelyn was still in the commote as late as 22 February, on which date he issued a letter whose 'unusually deferential tone' reveals a prince perhaps already chastened by the resoluteness of the English military presence there, probably aware of the wavering loyalty of his men elsewhere along the border and certainly anxious to secure peace at the earliest opportunity.[158] Mold's situation at this time is unclear; it was still in Welsh hands in 1273×4,[159] but whether the castle was gained by means of an assault or investment in 1276–7 only excavation will be able to determine. Meanwhile, Llywelyn seems to have made strenuous efforts to maintain his position in Powys Fadog. The securing of Bromfield was in theory completed by 12 April, on which date Madog ap Gruffudd and his tenants washed their hands of Llywelyn and were received into the king's peace.[160] However, Dinas Brân continued to hold out, and did so until well into the spring; its firing by the garrison on 10 May 1277 (that is, *after* the surrender of the Powysian lords who nominally held it) admits no other conclusion than that its garrison were in the pay of men of Gwynedd, still loyal to the prince of Wales.[161] Its fall removed Llywelyn's final hopes of holding the Perfeddwlad. By late summer Edward had advanced as far as Deganwy and defections of members of Llywelyn's royal government made clear to him the futility of further resistance. By November, he came to terms at Aberconwy.[162]

The enormity and steadfastness of the onslaught unleashed on Llywelyn during the war startles the modern observer, as it must have startled onlookers at the

---

155. Alcock *et al.*, 'Excavations at Castell Bryn Amlwg', p. 16.
156. *LlapG*, pp. 423, 424.
157. It is even possible that such a force was led by Llywelyn's brother Dafydd, who was active as part of the earl's force in late 1276, and who may, as a former member of Llywelyn's retinue, have been familiar with Ewloe and its defensive dispositions.
158. *AWR*, p. 588.
159. *Ibid.*, pp. 554–5.
160. J.G. Edwards (ed.), *Littere Wallie* (Cardiff, 1940), pp. 53–4.
161. Stephenson, '*Potens et prudens*', p. 428.
162. *AWR*, pp. 589–94; *LlapG*, pp. 438–44.

time. Edward invested unprecedented sums of money in arming and victualling three armies, one of which numbered 15,000 at its height; he sanctioned the commencement of enormous building works at Flint, Rhuddlan and elsewhere, works that included the erection of castles on a scale unseen anywhere in Wales up to that point, the repair of castles seized from the Welsh, the dredging and straightening of rivers for ease of navigation and the creation of new roads.[163] No king of England had before attempted such a complex, lengthy and costly operation, and, if the objective was to overawe the populace and their rulers as much as to exert physical control over territory, it worked. Most of Llywelyn's wavering lords were split off from the prince and those who continued to stand by him were surely so thoroughly demoralised by months of unrelenting retreat that, had Edward decided to press beyond the Conwy into the north-west, it is far from certain that they would have offered much additional resistance. Llywelyn's only succour as 1277 ended was that, for logistical and financial reasons, Edward refrained from crossing the Conwy, deciding against what seems to have been his prior policy to remove Llywelyn from power and install his brother Dafydd in his place and in favour of bringing Llywelyn to terms instead.[164] The Eryri massif that so trepidated Edward's father continued to cast its craggy shadows across English lines of advance.

## The war of 1282–3

The Treaty of Aberconwy may not have explicitly removed English recognition of Llywelyn's title, but in every other way his princely status was stripped from him. He lost the territories he had arrogated to himself over the last twenty years, being allowed to retain only Gwynedd uwch Conwy and the homage of five of his lords, and then only during his lifetime; he was obliged to pay the king £50,000 in restitution for war damages and his 'disobedience'; his elder brother, Owain, whom he had detained in prison since 1255, was to be freed with the option of 'recover[ing]' his patrimony if he wishes'.[165] The effect was to reintroduce something like the conditions that existed in Gwynedd following the Treaty of Woodstock concluded thirty years earlier – as Edward's father had subscribed to the maxim *divide et impera*, so too did Edward, by retaining the homage of most of Llywelyn's erstwhile lords and by arranging for Owain's release. The king also rewarded Dafydd for his service in the war with two lordships in the Perfeddwlad, providing him with a power base to rival Llywelyn's (though not as substantial a holding as Dafydd might have hoped for). Most grievously, Llywelyn's status was no longer transmissible – the status of any future heir of his body was, at best, unclear.[166]

---

163. Taylor, *The King's Works in Wales*, pp. 318–20; Evans, 'Conquest, roads and resistance', pp. 287–90.
164. LlapG, pp. 435–6; Prestwich, *Edward I*, pp. 181–2 notes that, by the autumn, Edward was beginning to encounter significant difficulties supplying his army.
165. In the end Owain reconciled to Llywelyn instead, and the prince appears to have granted him an estate on the Llŷn peninsula; BYT Pen MS 20, p. 119; LlapG, p. 441.
166. LlapG, pp. 439–40.

The chastened prince spent the next four and a half years toeing the English line and, when war descended again in 1282, it was not by the prince's hand. This time the instigator was Dafydd, Llywelyn's nominal heir, who attacked and seized Hawarden on 21 March 1282. However, the spate of attacks that erupted across Wales in the next few weeks argues strongly for a concerted campaign against English positions by lords situated across the country co-ordinated by Dafydd.[167] His presence at Llanymddyfri and Carreg Cennen in Deheubarth five days after the capture of Hawarden and his masterminding of the successful assault on Aberystwyth on 9 April[168] indicate his leadership of a war effort motivated by the liberties taken by the English in his own lordships in the Perfeddwlad and elsewhere. Llywelyn's involvement in the war at this point cannot be conclusively determined. A fair number of English chroniclers make him an active party to the revolt from the very beginning. The one closest to the action – the Chester annalist – averred that Llywelyn advised Dafydd to attack Hawarden and participated in the siege of Rhuddlan that followed.[169] But the Hagnaby chronicle's recording of a meeting between Llywelyn and Dafydd, on the one hand, and Reginald de Grey, justice of Chester, and Roger Clifford, on the other, to discuss points of conflict is worth noting. The meeting ended with Dafydd attacking the two lords and his assault on Hawarden followed a short time after.[170] It may be that Llywelyn therefore had some inkling of Dafydd's intentions following this meeting, but as the entry indicates he did not join in Dafydd's attack on the two men he elected to remain aloof from his brother's plans. Similar indications of a belated decision to join in Dafydd's war effort are discernible in Llywelyn's final surviving letters.[171] This would hardly be a surprising course to take. Dafydd was a man who had deserted him on three occasions and fought against him in the previous war, and it is surely significant that, prior to the summer, no attacks are reported as originating from Llywelyn's kingdom above the Conwy. Most importantly, Llywelyn had another reason to stay his hand: his consort, the princess Eleanor de Montfort, was heavily pregnant, and the birth of a son would provide Llywelyn with an heir of his body to take the place of Dafydd. However, Eleanor died giving birth to a daughter on 19 June and Llywelyn seems to have committed to Dafydd's war around this time, perhaps as a result of the loss of his wife and the best hopes he had of siring a male heir.[172]

As Edward made preparations for another campaign into Gwynedd, Dafydd contemplated his position in the north-east. It is hard to know what he hoped to

167. Carr, 'The last and weakest of his line', p. 389.
168. Ibid.
169. Christie, *Annales Cestrienses*, <https://www.british-history.ac.uk/lancs-ches-record-soc/vol14/pp102-121> (accessed 15 February 2020).
170. LlapG, p. 466.
171. A point made with some force as long ago as 1940 by J.G. Edwards: *Littere Wallie*, pp. lxiii–iv.
172. Edwards, *Littere Wallie*, p. 510.

achieve by waging war. The fact that Edward's new castles at Flint and Rhuddlan were besieged from the beginning of the war appears to indicate that his intention was to roll back English occupation of the region, but if that is so the effort was a broken reed almost from the first, as neither fell.[173] In that their continued occupation by English garrisons constituted a grave threat to the rear of Dafydd's forward positions on the border, in 1282 these castles carried out the roles for which they were raised, and the prudent course would have been to cease fighting once their investments had been proven ineffective. Dafydd, displaying perhaps the failure of judgement that typifies his career, did not do so, opting instead to attempt to hold a line stretching from Hawarden in the north to Dinas Brân in Powys Fadog, with his castles at Dinbych and Rhuthun to the west. However, his position soon disintegrated: unable to defend his unfinished castle at Hope (Caergwrle), he slighted it and retreated in mid-June, thereby yielding access to the Alun watershed to the advancing English.[174] Ewloe, if it was ever garrisoned by the Welsh, was abandoned – it was occupied by an English force at the end of June so small as to indicate that no assault was required. An English contingent was present at nearby Hawarden by 4 July. Now Edward was free to advance westwards, and was at Flint by 6 July and Rhuddlan by the eighth.[175] Before him was a short march to the banks of the Conwy, and thenceforth the fastnesses of Eryri.

The importance of Llywelyn's castles in the north-west during the war of 1282–3 is clear. Gwynedd uwch Conwy was clearly understood by the English as key to subjugating Wales, and the centrality of this to Edward's thinking puts into perspective the comments about Llywelyn's castles found in the English chronicles relating to his campaign. The Chester annalist, for example, made a point of the fact that in 1283 Edward captured all the castles of Snowdonia, as did the Osney annalist, and Pierre de Langtoft too made much of Llywelyn's securing of the region, which was such that Edward struggled to find an entry point.[176] Once Llywelyn's castles were seized Eryri would fall and the war would be at an end, and it is no surprise that Edward devoted much attention to securing them. We should acknowledge that, regarding the nature of the fighting in the north-west, we have precious little to go on. Only two castles are confirmed as having been besieged by Edward's forces (though there are indirect grounds for assuming several others were also). There is in addition no certainty over which castles beyond these were defensible in 1282, and the questions of whether or not they were garrisoned, how

173. The siege at Rhuddlan would seem to have been either lifted or abandoned as early as 9 May: Edwards, *Calendar of Ancient Correspondence*, pp. 129–30.
174. Taylor, *The King's Works in Wales*, p. 331.
175. As indicated by Edward's itinerary: T. Stafford, C. West and C. Tomkins, *Mapping the Itinerary of Edward I*, <https://figshare.shef.ac.uk/articles/dataset/Mapping_The_Itinerary_of_King_Edward_I/8948699> (accessed 5 July 2021).
176. Wright, *The Chronicle of Pierre de Langtoft*, Vol. 2, p. 177; H.R. Luard (ed.), *Annales Monastici*, Vol. 4 (London, 1869), p. 292.

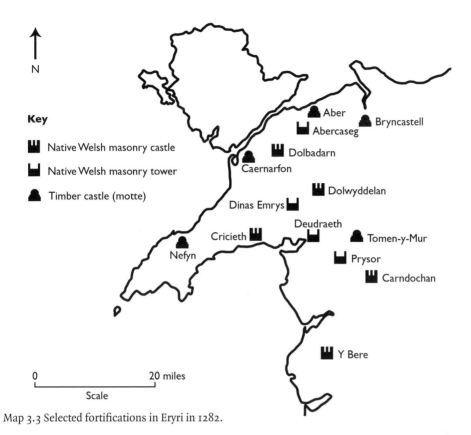

Map 3.3 Selected fortifications in Eryri in 1282.

long they held out and when and how the English assumed control of them are all open. Nevertheless, the notice given to securing the castles by English observers seems to indicate that this was central to Edward's strategic thinking during the campaign, and it is therefore a sound conjecture that such castles as were in Llywelyn's possession were used by him to implement a plan to wage a defensive war of attrition, perhaps with the intention of keeping Edward's men in the field for as long as possible.

Careful consideration of the landscape allows us to make a rough attempt at measuring such a plan's strategic coherence. Map 3.3 shows the fortifications in Llywelyn's possession in Eryri in 1282. The principal fortifications are all found west of the Conwy, and each can be seen as guarding an important route or routes into the massif.

The Conwy formed the historical border separating the region from the Perfeddwlad and constituted an important impediment to the progress of an invading army; we can assume the floodplain was thickly forested, and crossing it anywhere upriver was a dangerous proposition. Nevertheless, the Roman road that ran from Llanelwy (St Asaph) to the ford at Tal-y-cafn, and which continued from the western bank of the Conwy into the Carneddau mountains through the pass known as Bwlch y Ddeufaen, offered a potential access point. In this connection it would be helpful indeed to gain a better understanding of the history of the motte known as Bryncastell during this period. The motte stands on the western bank of the Conwy, less than a mile south of the eastern termination of Bwlch y Ddeufaen.[177] The motte has been speculated as having Norman origins, though a nineteenth-century tradition of an ancient Welsh provenance is recorded.[178] Most interestingly, the remains of a township at Llwydfaen have recently been discovered around 800 metres to the north-east.[179] Determining whether either was occupied in the late thirteenth century would be of considerable interest with respect to Llywelyn's defensive dispositions in 1282; it has certainly been cogently argued that the adjacent *llys* at Gronant was inhabited at that time.[180] To the north the coastline offered another potential route of entry. In Llywelyn's time the coastal route was more dangerous a prospect than it might seem today, with the flat coastal strip narrowing to a natural choke point at the headland at Penmaenmawr; it is not coincidental that the easternmost castle in the area – the now-vanished motte at Dwygyfylchi[181] – lay no more than a mile and a half west of this point. Further west, the motte of the *llys* at Aber guarded both the coast and the western end of Bwlch Y Ddeufaen. The western and eastern ends of the Menai straits were guarded by Caernarfon and Aber respectively, and Nefyn may also have been defended, to monitor traffic in Bae Caernarfon, or perhaps in anticipation of a possible landing on the northern Llŷn.

The four principal valleys through Eryri also contain defensible positions. In the Nant Ffrancon, Nant Peris, Nant Gwynant and Lledr valleys we find masonry fortifications in the guise of standalone towers or fully developed castles at Abercaseg, Dolbadarn, Dolwyddelan and Dinas Emrys respectively. The substantial castle at Y Bere stood in the way of an advance from the south through Meirionydd, and if the above theory that the absence of walls linking the south tower with the castle was due to lack of money and time is correct, it may be that the south tower was begun after the signing of the Treaty of Aberconwy, which abruptly made of Y Bere a frontier castle on Gwynedd's southern border. An excellent example of the apsidal tower in plan, it doubtless enhanced princely accommodation at the castle, allowed for more effective enfilading fire on the castle's barbican and allowed the crossbowmen manning its arrowslits[182] a wider field of fire to the

---

177. RCAHMW, *Caernarfonshire I: East*, p. 27.
178. RCAHMW, *Caernarfonshire I: East*, p. 27 n. 1.
179. T. Driver and D. Hopewell, 'A medieval church and township re-discovered at Llwydfaen, Caerhun, Conwy', *AW*, 48 (2008), pp. 77–81.
180. Beverley Smith, 'Llywelyn's hall at Conwy', p. 211.
181. RCAHMW, *Caernarfonshire I: East*, p. 84.
182. For reasons that are not obvious given the tower's elevated position, King hesitated to ascribe a military purpose to the openings for slits that survive at basement level (*A History of Merioneth* Vol. 2, p. 402).

south than the southern wall of the middle tower: it, and not Dolforwyn, may well represent Llywelyn's final castle works. Further north, Castell Deudraeth was well positioned to guard the crossing of the river Dwyryd; Eifionydd was defended by the massive fortress at Cricieth. Finally, the penetration of Gwynedd from the direction of Powys Fadog was countered by the trio of castles at Carndochan, probably Prysor and perhaps Tomen-y-mur, which guarded the Dyfrdwy valley and Cwm Cynllwyd, the Prysor and Tryweryn valleys, and the southern end of Bwlch Y Gorddinan respectively.

Exactly how many of these castles and towers were garrisoned and saw action in 1282–3 is not known, although we may be able to arrive at a roundabout answer by examining Edward's movements in 1283 and 1284 (see below). In any case, it was these defensive dispositions, or something very much like them, that formed the cornerstone of Gwynedd's defences once the offensives of the summer and autumn had come to an end. How Llywelyn might have fared in espousing this strategy will never be known, as his death at Cilmeri on 11 December 1282 occurred before English forces had gained either the Menai or the Conwy, and Welsh resistance began to collapse shortly thereafter. It is clear, however, that Llywelyn understood that he could not hope to prevail by sitting back and waiting for the onslaught; the campaign during which he died, which began in late November, was conducted in the middle March, well away from Eryri, and suggests that the prince was attempting to bring the army of Montgomery to battle, perhaps with the intent of causing Edward to halt in his advance and divert resources meant for Eryri to that area.[183] The propriety of such a manoeuvre is unclear, and the idea that Llywelyn was lured into embarking on his campaign by trusted allies who had in fact decided on his destruction has been advanced.[184] Even if he had succeeded on inflicting a major defeat on Edward's army in mid-Wales, Llywelyn would have needed many more strokes of luck to see off the king's invasion. Chief among them would have been the maintenance of Eryri as his stronghold. How his castles there might have performed in war with well-motivated and heavily armed garrisons supported by skirmishing parties, as his design surely entailed, will never be known: those who might have led such efforts – 'the flower of his army', as Edward's correspondent Roger Lestrange jubilantly put it[185] – were cut down at Cilmeri.

Nevertheless, some sort of organised defence was put in hand by Llywelyn's successor, Dafydd, and this defence seems to have included a determined attempt to hold Eryri against Edward by means of fortifying its valleys and debauches. Explicit references to armed confrontations are few – Dolwyddelan and Y Bere were besieged in January and April 1283 respectively, and there are reasons for

183. LlapG, p. 558 cogently argues that the decision to move south was an attempt to open a 'second front'.
184. Ibid., pp. 552–9.
185. Edward, *Calendar of Ancient Correspondence*, pp. 83–4.

Table 3.1 Visits by Edward I to native Welsh castle sites, 1283–4.

| Castle | Date of first visit | Subsequent visits of note |
|---|---|---|
| Dolwyddelan | 24 January 1283 | 16–28 May 1283 |
| Aber | 9 July 1283 | 22–30 August 1284 |
| Caernarfon | 12 July 1283 | 1 Apr.–6×7 May 1284; 25 May–8 June 1284; 13–23 and 25 October 1284 |
| Cricieth | 15–17 August 1283 | 24 May 1284, 3 August 1284, 26 October 1284 |
| Llanuwchllyn (Carndochan?) | 22 August 1283 | |
| Deudraeth | 9–10 May 1284 | - |
| Y Bere | 23 May 1284 | 1–4 and 6 November 1284 |
| Tomen-y-Mur | Late May–early June 1284 | - |
| Prysor | 1 July 1284 | - |
| Dolbadarn | 20, 24, 26 June 1284 | 2 July 1284 |
| Abercaseg | 4 July 1284 | - |
| Nefyn | 27 and 29 July 1284 | - |

Source: Stafford et al., *Mapping the Itinerary of Edward I, infra.*

assuming the motte at Caernarfon also required a siege to secure its surrender.[186] The silence of the documentary records regarding the other castles and towers of Eryri has allowed historians to argue that they never saw action in 1282–3, but this is not certain: indeed, Edward's visits to the native Welsh castles through Eryri in 1283 and 1284 may suggest the exact opposite.

Table 3.1 shows the various locations Edward I is known to have visited in 1283 and 1284 that were also the sites of Welsh castles and towers. The reasons for his repeated visits to Caernarfon, Y Bere, Cricieth and Dolwyddelan, all of which were the sites of major building works, are obvious, and his repeated visits to Aber, the most well known of Llywelyn's *llysoedd* on the mainland, are similarly self-explanatory; although the investments of Y Bere and Dolwyddelan are a matter of record, none of his visits to the others necessarily implies fighting in their vicinity. Nor does his visit to Nefyn, which was for the purposes of convening a round table and a tournament, though precisely why Nefyn was chosen for this event is not clear; a royal visit to Tomen-y-Mur for similar reasons has also recently been theorised.[187] In the cases of the towers and smaller castles, explanations for Edward's presence are available which involve nothing more than a desire to break a long journey at a fortified position. This plausibly accounts for his visits to

---

186. Taylor, *The King's Works in Wales*, p. 369, n. 3.
187. S. Lloyd, *The Arthurian Place-Names of Wales* (Cardiff, 2017), p. 47.

Deudraeth and Prysor,[188] and may also neatly explain Edward's fleeting presence at Llanuwchllyn in August 1283; Edward was travelling to the Perfeddwlad at the time, and a stop there would have been expeditious. Llanuwchllyn lies just two miles due west of the castle at Carndochan, and it is probably safe to assume Edward took the opportunity to visit.

Equally, however, Edward may have been motivated by a desire to see for himself the castles that had lately played a part in Llywelyn's downfall. The strongest case to be made for this concerns Edward's visit to the masonry tower at Abercaseg, where he is found on 4 July 1284.[189] In the context of his movements early that month, the Nant Ffrancon valley in which Abercaseg stood was well out of his way. The king is recorded as having been present at Prysor and Dolwyddelan on 1 July, and Dolbadarn (Baladeulyn)[190] on 2 July; the impression given is of a progress north on a beeline towards Caernarfon, where he arrived on 5 July. But the stop at Abercaseg directed his party away from his final destination and entailed leaving the Nant Peris valley entirely and gaining the Nant Ffrancon valley adjacent to it: a significant diversion that would involve either reaching the coastal road and moving upriver or retracing his steps through difficult terrain. Nor, as far as we know, was Abercaseg ever refurbished for military purposes, meaning that there were no works in progress there for Edward to inspect.[191] In other words, the visit to Abercaseg was not a case of Edward seeking lodging for the night in the nearest convenient place, as the tower there was not at all convenient. The corollary is that Edward visited it because, in spite of its anonymity and unprepossessing nature, it was of interest to him. Although the limited excavations carried out there in the 1990s were insufficient to enable an estimate of its construction date, its mortared walls[192] and revetment[193] are strongly reminiscent of the tower at Prysor, perhaps marking it out as being of a similar late twelfth-century date. It was also beautifully placed to dominate its surroundings, being visible for two and a half miles down the Nant Ffrancon valley,[194] and, as the only fortification emplaced to guard the routeway that led through it, it may have seen fierce fighting. Edward's evident desire to visit it is most parsimoniously explained through it having been one of

---

188. C. Taylor, 'The history and archaeology of temporary medieval camps: a possible example in Wales', *Landscape History*, 40 (2019), p. 46.

189. D. Hopewell, 'Ty'n Twr, Bethesda, Archaeological Excavation' (GAT 1173), Gwynedd Archaeological Trust report 86 (1994), p. 6.

190. There is a possibility that these references are to the site known as Baladeulyn in the Nantlle valley; see chapter 1.

191. Some sherds of Saintonge ware were found during excavations, but these are not inconsistent with a late thirteenth-century date; Hopewell, 'Ty'n Twr', ibid.

192. *Ibid.*, p. 5.

193. RCAHMW, NMR Site Files Collection Caernarfonshire Domestic SH 66, NA/CA/93/05 – notes by AJ Parkinson, 8 October 1992, on Ty'n Twr, Bethesda.

194. *Ibid.*

the final bastions of Venedotian resistance in the war.

In a few cases there are documentary references that support the idea that some of the fortifications that appeared in Edward's itinerary were focuses of local resistance. Carndochan, which, as has been noted, was probably visited by Edward, overlooked the upper Dyfrdwy valley. None of Edward's armies is known to have entered this part of the valley in early 1283, as Edward chose to invade Eryri through the upper Conwy. However, a detachment of that army may have made its way up the Dyfrdwy, as the extent of Meirionydd carried out in 1284 showed that the township of Penmaen to the north of Y Bala was laid waste and its men were dead, apparently due to the war; and, furthermore, over two-thirds of the land in the township of Pennant-lliw in which Carndochan stood was also waste due to the war.[195] With evidence of fighting so close to hand, it is hard to imagine Carndochan not playing a part in it. In the same way, one wonders what occasioned the damage to houses at Cricieth that is referred to in the 'dona' account of 1283–4; in the light of (unspecified) repairs carried out there in 1283 and 1284, Taylor's characterisation of a castle damaged either by slighting or by an otherwise unrecorded siege is probably correct.[196]

We cannot see any more clearly than that; only excavations may shed more light on the history of each site. However, the above is sufficient to demonstrate that attempts were made by the Welsh in late 1282 and early 1283 to resist Edward's armies and that, in some cases at least, fortified positions were instrumental in this effort. Some of these fortifications had or may have been raised by Llywelyn I, or perhaps even an earlier ruler, to enhance their prestige and advertise their local pre-eminence – in fact, for expeditionary reasons (see chapter 1). In Gwynedd's time of supreme crisis, however, they were pressed into use as outposts guarding the heart of Eryri. It is an irony that, where direct evidence of garrisoning survives, we can see that it was not Llywelyn who actuated it but his successor, Dafydd; his cleaving to this course may indicate a shared intent discussed between the two leaders. The resoluteness with which his men held their positions, however, varied enormously. The overriding importance of protecting the northern coast that faced the (undefended) island of Ynys Môn surely accounts at least in part for the rash attempt made by Luke de Tany to bridge the Menai, and the ferocious performance of the Welsh during the battle of Moel-y-Don that resulted in the destruction of both the bridge and de Tany's army in November 1282.[197] But at that time Llywelyn was still alive; after his death in December, resistance began to collapse. The first region of Eryri to yield appears to have been the Lledr valley, where Dolwyddelan fell on 18 January 1283 after a three-day siege. The castle's constable seems to have

195. *A History of Merioneth Vol. 2*, p. 711.
196. Taylor, *The King's Works in Wales*, p. 366.
197. Christie, *Annales Cestrienses*, <https://www.british-history.ac.uk/lancs-ches-record-soc/vol14/pp102-121> (accessed 15 February 2020); LlapG, pp. 538–9.

been approached by the English the previous month and bribed to surrender it,[198] and the investment, which inflicted little if any damage on the fabric, may have been to save face among the garrison. Edward was present in the area later in the month, and was on hand to supervise the movement of soldiers northwards, down the Conwy valley. As a bridgehead had been effected at Bangor by the last week of December,[199] Aber was therefore isolated and was probably abandoned around this time.

A bold westward thrust by a vanguard of Edward's army down the Nant Gwynant valley allowed for the securing of Cricieth by 14 March,[200] cutting Dafydd's remaining lands in two; the role of the castles to the south is unknown, though evidence of a fierce fire in the square tower at Carndochan suggests that it was destroyed by either a retreating Welsh garrison or an English force intent on capturing the fortification.[201] The final castles to fall – Y Bere and, it seems, the motte at Caernarfon[202] – were yielded only by means of a siege, but one final detail reveals something of the mindset of their garrisons. At Y Bere, where the siege commenced on 15 April, the leader of the Welsh was the castle's custodian, Cynfrig ap Madog. Even at this time of impending disaster he managed to negotiate the surrender of the castle for the sum of eighty pounds, payable if no relief arrived by 25 April.[203] Two interpretations are possible – either he truly believed that Dafydd might yet relieve his garrison, and the situation could be retrieved, or he was leveraging the strategic importance of Y Bere to cut as lucrative a deal as he could for his fellow men. The former would at least demonstrate that, as the war ended, there remained a few men in Eryri who were willing to serve the prince of Wales; but, given the speed with which Dafydd's position there disintegrated, the beleaguered custodian can hardly be blamed for acceding to the latter.

198. LlapG, p. 574; Prestwich, Edward I, pp. 194–5.
199. Taylor, The King's Works in Wales, p. 357.
200. Taylor, The King's Works in Wales, p. 365.
201. Hopewell, 'Castell Carndochan Excavation Report 2016–17', pp. 26–7. A reference to one Madog ab Iorwerth being granted the castle by Edward I, if valid, may lend further credence to the idea that the king visited and was familiar with the castle; Williams-Jones, The Merioneth Lay Subsidy Roll, pp. 7–8, n. 6.
202. Taylor, The King's Works in Wales, p. 369.
203. Walker, 'William de Valence', p. 421.

# 4

## Conclusion

Generalisation, equivocation and qualification are among the most useful, if the least celebrated, of the tools at the disposal of the historian; the further back in time one goes, the more often one has recourse to them. All the same, it is difficult to find the historian who turns to them with anything but reluctance, if only because human beings like the certainty and finality that comes with a more strident treatment of the past. The preceding offers little in the way of absolute statements of fact about the native Welsh masonry castles of Gwynedd – it has equivocated just as often as it has clarified. In the English example, more could and would have been said from a standpoint of certainty when it comes to thirteenth-century castle-building, but the native royal government of the two Llywelyns is so poorly documented that there are simply too many unknowns to allow theories regarding the provenance and usage of their castles to be advanced with a surer touch.

Indeed, some would say that the difficulties thrown up by the paucity of material relating to the native Welsh castles are insuperable and that even to embark on such an analysis is a fool's errand. The only rebuttal of this point available to us is that the preceding analysis, in spite of its incompleteness and its many fudges and evasions, is a necessary one – the alternative is to allow the facile pronouncements over the form, function and effectiveness of Dolforwyn and Dolwyddelan, of Carndochan and Cricieth, to continue to dictate thinking, as they have done since the time of Lloyd and Hemp. On the chessboard of Welsh history the castles are like overworked knights, forever being pressed into service to provide support for this or that interpretation of the princes' reigns as the need arose – some nothing more than forward bases for skirmishing parties, others the architecturally incompetent conceits of regional magnates with chips on their shoulders, and still others decent if compact attempts at constructing defensible fortresses – until the contradictions inherent in these perspectives cause the entire position to collapse. This will not do. The castles, and no less their authors, deserve more than glib and contradictory assessments of their efficacy, even if it means we have to resort to the balance of probabilities instead of cast-iron certainties more often than we would like when re-examining the princes' architectural legacy.

From the accession of Owain Gwynedd in 1137, the princes of Gwynedd were ascendant in Wales for almost a century and a half, defying challenges to their authority from within and without in spite of substantial shortcomings of manpower and resources. Llywelyn I and Dafydd II in particular acquitted themselves on the European stage with considerable poise – indeed, the numerous diplomatic ingenuities, audacious imaginative leaps and steely grasp of *realpolitik* exhibited by Dafydd II inclines one to the view that, had he not died young, he would today be remembered as a quite exceptional ruler.[1] Both men were also formidable warlords, as was Llywelyn II; and if the latter displayed errors of judgement in the dealings with Edward I that ultimately led to his downfall, he, like his predecessors, was a worthy, competent ruler in all aspects of his principate for the first two decades of his reign. To draw any other conclusion where these princes' ability to rule is concerned is obtuse at best and playing to the broadest stereotypes of Welsh backwardness at worst.

The criticism levelled at the castles they raised is similarly unsustainable. Attempts to impose a single paradigm of use on to castles as varied in design, construction and deployment as Y Bere, Dolwyddelan and Dinas Brân smack of facile and reductionist thinking and have led far too many commentators to offer withering comment on their defensive capabilities, as though their military strength comprised the sole measure of their usefulness, or the princes were to blame for the profound structural deficiencies – be they demographic, geographical or material – that hobbled their attempts at statehood. This approach fundamentally misconstrues the purpose and functioning of these castles. Rulers who waste finite financial and material resources on useless fortifications are very shortly stripped of their power to rule: the essential truth of the longevity of the house of Gwynedd cannot be expressed any more simply than that and, whatever their shortcomings, it at least renders these castles purposeful structures.

In the eyes of English monarchs and Marcher lords alike, that purposefulness extended into the military sphere and, as the preceding has sought to show, there is abundant evidence of the considerations that were thought necessary to make when planning expeditions into and invasions of Gwynedd. The princes did not ascend to their position by being stupid in military matters, and their will to resist conquest was recognised in England for what it was. In the end, only the full, concentrated might of Edward I sufficed to break the princes' power; until that moment came they dominated Wales and defended their patrimony with vigour. Gwynedd, as Liddiard puts it, was 'a hard nut to crack'[2] – by dint of its impenetrable forests and mountainous aspect, but also because of the many castles and mottes that dotted the landscape. They worked to protect Gwynedd

---

1.   B.G.E. Wiedemann, '"Fooling the court of the lord Pope": Dafydd ap Llywelyn's petition to the Curia in 1244', *WHR*, 28 (2016), p. 232.

2.   Liddiard, *Castles in Context*, p. 56.

in various ways, not all of which were immediately, or even principally, military. Their siting was the product of the exigencies of the moment. The tripartite model advanced here represents an attempt to understand the various lines of reasoning that motivated the princes. Expeditionary emplacement was designed to demonstrate authority; corporate emplacement was intended to expand influence; defensive emplacement was designed to preserve *pura Wallia*'s independence. Not every castle fits so neatly into that schema, and the theories put forward in this book are just that; their merits can be debated. But the carefree way in which native Welsh castles have hitherto been treated demands some comprehensive reassessment of the sort presented here. Given that the castle-building policies of the princes of Wales are entirely opaque, there will be elements of the above analysis that are incorrect in degree or interpretation. But some sort of reasoning resembling that put forth here surely obtained in the minds of the two Llywelyns; the subtle changes of emphasis in emplacement from period to period cannot but be reflective of shifting strategic and political agendas.

So too are the ways in which castles assigned a role in one period found themselves repurposed in another. The manner in which the corporate castle of Y Bere – plush, ornate in execution, meant for display – was suddenly thrust into the forefront of conflict in 1283 has been recounted, but there were almost certainly earlier reassignments of roles. The most persuasive candidate is Dolbadarn, where the differences in scale, proportion and construction between its outsized, well-mortared round tower and its diminutive drystone walls are exceptional. The tower's superior architecture strongly suggests it postdates all other construction.[3] It may be thought of as an attempt to convert this previously unprepossessing castle into a residence commensurate (in terms of its princely accommodation at least) with the corporate castles being built by Llywelyn elsewhere late in his reign. The possibility that it was meant as the nucleus of Llywelyn's son Dafydd's power base as lord of Dinorwig has already been noted. We may even go further, and endorse Spencer Gavin Smith's recent suggestion that the surrounding landscape was modified around the same time to create a 'little park', and that the castle grounds themselves may have contained a herber garden, built for the edification of Llywelyn I's consort Joan. Admittedly, the case for the former is based on (very late) place-name evidence and that for the latter on circumstantial evidence heavily reliant on access analysis only[4] (though pollen analysis may yet be revealing). It does, however, have the advantage of explaining the peculiar arrangement of Dolbadarn's northern end, which, unlike the southern end, is not capped by a tower (Fig. 4.1); and it would also fit in very well with our understanding of the enhanced importance and prominence of the role of the consort during the first Llywelyn's reign. Joan – or, indeed, one of

3.    RCAMHW, *Caernarfonshire II: Central*, pp. 166–7 suggests the round tower and courtyard were 'contemporary ... or nearly so', but the warrant – the alleged 'slightness' of the castle without such a tower – is slender.
4.    Smith, 'Dolbadarn Castle', pp. 69–70.

Figure 4.1 Joan's reputed 'hall' and 'garden' at Dolbadarn.

her successors, Isabella de Briouze or Eleanor de Montfort; gardens were recorded at Nefyn and Caernarfon directly after the conquest[5] – may even have had a leading role in creating such spaces within castles and, as has been speculated, might have had the northern part of the castle, including the building widely interpreted as its hall, assigned to her for the use of her officers and household apart from the prince's own retinue. As Creighton and Liddiard note, 'studies of the uses and manipulation of space [in castles] must broaden their horizons beyond the walls of the structures with which they are immediately concerned to consider how settings too were zoned in social terms'.[6] The argument that Dolbadarn's round tower may have been 'zoned' by dint of the spiral staircases it contains may be brought to bear in this connection.[7] If Smith's thesis can be supported, the effect of the round tower's erection and the appearance of a park and garden at Dolbadarn was transformational, signifying a radical change in the castle's function that made it the focus of a compact but impressive modified landscape at the very heart of the prince's domain.

From this viewpoint, we can discern more clearly the factors that have so persistently confounded the understanding of historians in regard to the native Welsh castles. All too often, their critical faculties wilted in the heat of three powerful tyrannies. The first was the tyranny of scale. The relationship of native Welsh castles

5.   Swallow, 'Living the dream', p. 179, Smith, 'Dolbadarn Castle', p. 69.
6.   Creighton and Liddiard, 'Fighting yesterday's battle', p. 166.
7.   Ryder, 'The spiral stair or vice', pp. 177–81.

to their environs was often interpreted in glib ways that either accentuated their smallness, or, in the rush to mould such places into long-held cultural stereotypes of Welsh idiosyncrasy, made of them whimsical caricatures of their English counterparts – the extraordinary contrast between them and the neighbouring Edwardian castles making this last a particularly attractive, because intuitive, stance to adopt. The tyranny of architecture, meanwhile, similarly obliged commentators to view the fabric and emplacement of strongholds such as Dolforwyn and Y Bere through a lens better suited to the appreciation of Anglo-Norman and English castles, a set of fortifications that cleaved to an altogether different set of building and emplacement principles. The resultant assessments of the castles' architecture exaggerated or concocted defensive deficiencies while ignoring or downplaying the frequently tangible and often innovative solutions to problems of defence. The final tyranny was that of the map. All too often, castle guidebooks and academic monographs on medieval Wales alike have featured maps of the nation studded with the locations of Welsh castles.[8] Such visual representations serve to efface chronological difference and impose on the reader an agenda that takes as its starting point the role of the castle as a place of war and treats all native Welsh castles, no matter who authored them, how old they are or how radically they were modified, as cut from the same cloth and serving identical functions as military strongholds. It has been written of conflict landscapes that they 'are often multi-temporal, and they include features used, reused and modified in different periods'.[9] What is true of the landscape – one thinks of the vale of Montgomery, the district around Y Bala or the lowlands of Deheubarth in the Welsh connection – is also true of the castle sites considered in this volume. In assessing their form and function, the personal and political circumstances of their authors can hardly be excised from consideration.

There remains the question of the native Welsh castles' performance in the wars of the late thirteenth century. The later Llywelyn's appreciation of his situation should be queried. His grandfather appears to history as a realist: he grasped opportunities as they came his way, bided his time in periods of uncertainty and took calculated risks. Llywelyn II followed a similar path in the early years of his principate – he could hardly have done otherwise, given the unfavourable circumstances in which he came to power – but we may venture that as time went on such pragmatic values succumbed to a sense of idealism, perhaps even wishful thinking. His lofty ideas of paying his way to independence in the aftermath of the Second Barons' War seem to have been grounded in overly optimistic estimates of his financial clout. Llywelyn placed massive territorial and governmental expansion in the here and now as collateral against the immense

8.   See, for example, Jones, 'The defence of Gwynedd'.
9.   D. Mlekuž, U. Košir and M. Črešnar, 'Landscapes of death and suffering: archaeology of conflict landscapes of the Upper Soča Valley, Slovenia', in B. Stichelbaut and D. Cowley (eds), *Conflict Landscapes and Archaeology from Above* (Farnham, 2016), p. 128.

debts such enterprises accrue as time goes on. He appears to have gambled on attaining a stable orbit by assembling a grand confederacy composed of magnates from Powys, Deheubarth and further afield as the island of Britain's third polity, maximising his income from these territories by means of networks of local officials charged with effecting efficient taxation of the populace and adopting belligerent attitudes towards the Marcher lords on his eastern and southern flanks in the 1260s and 1270s. The contradictions inherent in this project have recently been subjected to probing analysis.[10] However, it is this aspect of Llywelyn's worldview that most convincingly refutes the idea that his castles were never meant to constitute 'defences against the power of the English king'.[11] The military function of the castles dating from the early thirteenth century that he inherited reflected the earlier Llywelyn's lower horizons, but by the 1270s both the social and political milieu of *pura Wallia* – at that historical moment referred to more correctly as the Principality – had been transformed. Llywelyn II's ambitions to act as overlord of the other kingdoms and lordships of *pura Wallia* found its justification in the house of Gwynedd's uninterrupted (if uneven) exercise of leadership; this ideology relied on shared cultural, racial, linguistic, geopolitical and socioeconomic characteristics. In this respect his outlook was doubtless no different to that of his immediate predecessors. But where his political ideology resembled theirs, his experience was manifestly different, for he had witnessed the fraught political scene in the 1240s – the swiftness with which Llywelyn I's polity had collapsed after his death and the enormous problems Dafydd II encountered in attempting to reconstitute it.[12] These setbacks involved the denial of many lands appurtenant to Gwynedd to other Welsh rulers and, from 1241 until 1244, the loss of the Perfeddwlad – a circumstance Llywelyn inherited and must have felt acutely for the first decade of his reign, as the population of his patrimonial lands in the north-east lived under an English administration. As a result, the prince – certainly exercised, and perhaps chagrined, by the encroachment on his patrimonial lands, and wary of a repeat – spent much of his later reign testing the length of his arm. His obtuse insistence on securing the homage of Maredudd ap Rhys of Deheubarth, his ill-fated campaign to annex Senghenydd and his construction of the castle at Sennybridge all point to a man whose worldview involved ensuring his grip on power was strong and felt throughout the Principality, whose conceptualisation of his own power made him an equal of the king of Scots and the king of England, the man of the latter only in name.[13] His castles reflected that mentality. They may have been smaller and less numerous than many of those in the Marcher lordships, but inasmuch as they were built to see to the defence

---

10.   Stephenson, 'Empires in Wales', p. 54.

11.   *WS*, p. 205.

12.   G.A. Williams, 'The succession to Gwynedd, 1238–47', *BBCS*, 20 (1964), pp. 393–413.

13.   *LlapG*, pp. 348–50, 350–5, 416–17.

of Llywelyn's realm they can only have been intended to withstand any and all assaults Llywelyn could envisage, including the attacks of the king.

We can appreciate the point more fully in another way. It has been claimed that such castles as Llywelyn had built in the border regions were meant in times of war to function as nothing more than 'local campaign bases from which mobile forces could harass an invading force'.[14] Implicit in this idea is that the war thus framed is not a war of conquest. It involves accepting both that invasions of one's territory will be a regular occurrence and that one's borders are inherently pervious and open to disputation from time to time by one's lordly neighbours. This may well have been the principle on which Llywelyn I operated. Yet by the mid-1260s at the very latest Llywelyn II had set his sights on freeing himself from precisely these concerns. For all that the Treaty of Montgomery skirts around issues of Welsh jurisdiction over Maelienydd, and indeed the geographical extent of Llywelyn's domain,[15] it had one undeniable merit, which was that it was concluded between Llywelyn and the king of England – the advantage to Llywelyn being that he could approach the king for redress in case of encroachment on his territory (as indeed he subsequently did).[16] Having at last achieved the recognition of his authority that eluded his predecessors, Llywelyn II sought a lasting dominion over his Principality, and that involved defending its borders as stoutly as the king of England would defend his; a situation where Marcher lords constantly nibbling away at the edges of his territory would be an affront to his new-found status as prince of Wales and would make a mockery of Henry's declaration in the Treaty of Montgomery that, in conceding the prince's title, he wished 'to magnify the person of Llywelyn'.[17] Merely harassing such forces as presumed to invade his lands would no longer do. The scale on which Dinas Brân and Dolforwyn in particular were built argues very strongly for a custodial function commensurate with Llywelyn's authority and eminence as the leader of the Welsh and the protector of their lands against any who would dispute their autonomy; and Llywelyn would have been foolish not to recognise that, in a scenario where relations between the English crown and Gwynedd were not so harmonious, those opponents might include the king himself, and raised his castles with such an eventuality in mind. One might even take the conclusions of Stephenson a step further and suggest that, in elevating Wales to the status of the third polity of the island of Britain, Llywelyn placed himself in an ideological straitjacket from which he could not extricate himself. Dafydd II, Llywelyn I and even Owain Gwynedd had all employed the tactic of yielding when necessary at war with the English king, ensuring their own survival at the expense of the concession of territory and a measure of authority. It was the diplomatic equivalent of a fighting retreat, the age-old tactic of a people

---

14.  WS, p. 206.
15.  Stephenson, 'A treaty too far?' p. 20.
16.  AWR, pp. 561–2, 574–5.
17.  Stephenson, 'A treaty too far?' p. 31.

disadvantaged by lack of numbers and resources in the face of an enemy whose ranks abounded in both; not for nothing was the Welsh soldier of Gerald of Wales' time associated with the Parthian shot.[18] However, Llywelyn II staked everything on holding his ground, a philosophy that found expression through his erection of castles up and down the Welsh border. For reasons of prestige and perhaps personal pride he seems to have been unable to recognise that his position was not so strong that he could flout the principles that had served his ancestors so well; where they had cleaved to the ancient Chinese rule 'wait at leisure while the enemy labours', Llywelyn preferred 'not one step back'. The Welsh considered themselves a people; that peoplehood was expressed territorially and required Llywelyn II to insist on his hereditary right to rule the Wales in which they lived, entirely and without hindrance. That was, it seems, how the prince saw it, and it provides an explanation for his alacrity – some would say rashness – in laying claim to the homage of lords well beyond the boundaries of his princely predecessors' kingdoms,[19] issuing haughty protestations of his princely rights to the king of England and his most powerful magnates[20] and raising castles he could not pay for.

This being the case, we must reject the idea that, with the exception of Dolforwyn, Llywelyn II did not defend his castles or that his castles were intended only as 'places of last retreat'.[21] Davies correctly states that these castles were not 'held to the last';[22] however, this can be viewed not so much as a deliberate policy on Llywelyn's part but as a result of the wavering confidence of the garrisons he (and later Dafydd) placed in them in the face of unprecedented and overwhelming military might. The Welsh annalist was sensitive to this very point, stating that the defenders at Dolforwyn surrendered in 1277 through lack of water, instead of (as seems clear in the English sources) negotiating a surrender[23] – a more noble remembering of their actions, perhaps, and one that preserved the impression of a steadfast fidelity to their prince. To assert that stockpiles of supplies were limited in native Welsh castles and that, by extension, they were never meant to be subjected to lengthy sieges is to argue from silence. While Dolwyddelan certainly seems to have been short of supplies following its brief siege in January 1283, it appears to have been a special case, its surrender almost certainly having been agreed prior to the arrival of the English by its traitorous castellan.[24] There is no way of determining the situation at, say, Ewloe in 1276 or Caernarfon and Dinas Brân (and, conceivably, Cricieth) in 1282 and 1283; and, intriguingly, there was a handsome surplus of food at Y Bere on its fall in April of that year, so much so

18. Thorpe, *The Journey through Wales/The Description of Wales*, pp. 233–4.
19. LlapG, pp. 342–4.
20. AWR, p. 554.
21. J. Black, *Fortifications and Siegecraft: Defense and Attack through the Ages* (London, 2018), p. 47.
22. WS, p. 206.
23. Butler, 'The siege of Dolforwyn castle', pp. 25–6, and n. 5.
24. LlapG, p. 574.

that the occupying force felt obliged to offer renumeration for it.[25] None of this requires us to invoke notions of token shows of defence prior to a swift surrender, still less to accept that 'Llywelyn [II] knew he could never hold his castles against a royal expedition.'[26] If he did not intend to fortify his territory from Edward, the most dangerous threat to his authority, then who?

On viewing castles such as Dolforwyn, Dinas Brân and Sennybridge, all three of them on the borders of Wales and overlooking the lower ground to the east and south-east, one is struck by the hubris of their siting, and it is easy to discern in them the weight of expectation settling on the shoulders of Llywelyn II as he contemplated his grandfather's achievements and his own need to equal or even surpass them. Stretched thin as his resources were, his downfall may seem inevitable, especially after the concluding of the Treaty of Montgomery, 'the point at which, for Llywelyn's principality, the rot set in',[27] as it has recently been described. It need not have been so. Avoidance of unnecessary expenditures – including, perhaps, a prudent withdrawal from his easternmost lands in the March, much as Dafydd II or Llywelyn I might have authorised in similar circumstances – combined with a more diplomatic handling of the political situation in Powys in particular and the ambitions of his brothers and a willingness to bend to Edward when the need arose could have averted disaster. Llywelyn – by temperament, one is inclined to conclude – could do none of these things, and so it was left to Edward to break the Welsh butterfly on his wheel.

In this way, the castles the king raised to subjugate the Welsh came into being. They have been described as 'in many respects ... largely useless – in isolated positions that did not actually control the surrounding territory at all', and as 'white elephants'.[28] They were not. Capturing them proved beyond the abilities of Llywelyn II or Dafydd III, and nor could they be reduced to ineffectiveness by investing them. For all that they lay empty later in their careers, they did what they were meant to do and secured Wales for the English. In so doing they achieved a kind of hegemony over their landscape, standing as quintessential examples of medieval castle architecture (which, of course, they are). So too, in their way, however, are the castles of the two Llywelyns. If the likes of Caernarfon, Harlech and Conwy represent the apotheosis of castle-building, standing as demonstrations of what can be achieved with abundant resources, Dolbadarn, Cricieth and Dolforwyn constitute exemplars of what can be done with few. That they were built at all was an assertion of the Venedotian will to power, and that they continue to inspire fascination and admiration today is an indication of the remarkable skill, thoughtfulness, energy and ambition that went into their construction.

25. Walker, 'William de Valence', p. 421. The food comprised bread, mead, wheat, oats and flour, and was valued at over eight pounds.
26. WS, p. 206.
27. Stephenson, 'A treaty too far?' p. 30.
28. J.D. Davies, *Britannia's Dragon: A Naval History of Wales* (Stroud, 2013), p. 26.

# Bibliography

## Primary sources

*Calendar of Patent Rolls, Henry III: Volume 3, 1232–1247* (London, 1906).

Christie, R.C. (ed.), *Annales Cestrienses Chronicle of the Abbey of S. Werburg, At Chester* (London, 1887).

Edwards, J.G., *Calendar of Ancient Correspondence concerning Wales* (Cardiff, 1935).

Edwards, J.G. (ed.), *Littere Wallie* (Cardiff, 1940).

Fisher, R. (ed.), *Richard Fenton's Tours in Wales* (*Archaeologia Cambrensis* supplement, 1917).

Gruffydd, K.L. 'Ewloe and its castle', FRO NT/833, unpublished essay.

Hughes, H.D., *Hynafiaethau Llandegai a Llanllechid* [Antiquities of Llandegai and Llanllechid] (1866; repr. Groeslon, 1979).

Jenkins, D. (ed. and transl.), *The Law of Hywel Dda* (Llandysul, 2000).

Jones, D.G. (ed.), *Prydnawngwaith Y Cymry a gweithiau eraill gan William Williams* [*Prydnawngwaith a Cymry* and other works by William Williams] (Bala, 2011).

Jones, E.M. (ed.) with the support of Jones, N.A., *Gwaith Llywarch ap Llywelyn 'Prydydd Y Moch'* [The Work of Llywarch ap Llywelyn 'Prydydd Y Moch'] (Cardiff, 1991).

Jones, T. (ed.), *Brut Y Tywysogyon* [Chronicle of the Princes] (*Peniarth MS 20 version*) (Cardiff, 1952).

Jones, T. (ed.), *Brut Y Tywysogyon* [Chronicle of the Princes] (*Red Book of Hergest version*) (Cardiff, 1973).

Jones, T. (ed.), *Brenhinedd y Saesson, or, The Kings of the Saxons* (Cardiff, 1971).

Jones, T., '"Cronica de Wallia" and other documents from Exeter Cathedral Library MS. 3514', BBCS, 12 (1946), pp. 27–44.

Llwyd, H., *Cronica Walliae* (ed. I.M. Williams) (Cardiff, 2002).

Luard, H.R. (ed.), *Annales Monastici*, Vol. 4 (London, 1869).

Maxwell, H. (ed.), *The Chronicle of Lanercost 1272–1346* (Glasgow, 1913).

Morris, R.H. (ed.), E. Lhuyd, *Parochialia ... Issued by Edward Lhwyd*, Archaeologia Cambrensis Supplements; 3 vols (1909–11).

Pennant, T., *Tours of Wales*, 2 vols (London, 1778; repr. 1810).

Smith, L.T. (ed.), *The Itinerary in Wales of John Leland* (London, 1906).

Williams-Jones, K. (ed. with introduction), *The Merioneth Lay Subsidy Roll 1292–3* (Cardiff, 1976).

Wright, T. (ed.), *The Chronicle of Pierre de Langtoft*, Vol. 2 (Cambridge, 2012).

## Secondary sources

Anon., 'Llangollen – report', AC, (1935), pp. 319–75.

Alcock, L., 'Excavations at Degannwy Castle, Cernarvonshire, 1961–6', AJ, 124 (1967), pp. 190–201.

Alcock, L., King, D.J.C., Putnam, W.C. and Spurgeon, C.J., 'Excavations at Castell Bryn Amlwg', MC, 60 (1967–8), pp. 8–27.

Alexander, J.W., *Ranulf of Chester: A Relic of the Conquest* (Athens, GA, 1983).

Allen, M., 'Silver production and the money supply in England and Wales, 1086–c.1500', *Economic History Review*, 64 (2011), pp. 114–31.

Andrews, Rh. M., 'The nomenclature of kingship in welsh court poetry 1100–1300 part II: the rulers', SC, 25 (2011), pp. 53–82.

Arnold, C.J. and Huggett, J.W., with a contribution by Pryce, H., 'Excavations at Mathrafal, Powys, 1989', MC, 83 (1995), pp. 59–74.

Avent, R., *Castles of the Princes of Gwynedd* (London, 1983).

Avent, R., *Criccieth Castle* (Cardiff, 1989).

Avent, R., *Dolwyddelan Castle/Dolbadarn Castle* (Cardiff, 1994).

Avent, R., *Dolwyddelan Castle/Dolbadarn Castle/Castell Y Bere* (Cardiff, 2004).

Beeston, A.F.L., 'In the steps of Gerallt Cymro', THSC (1988), pp. 11–28.

Besly, E., 'Short Cross and other medieval coins from Llanfaes, Anglesey', *British Numismatic Journal*, 65 (1995), pp. 46–83.

Bevan-Evans, M., *Mold and Moldsdale*, 3 vols (Flint, 1949).

Beverley Smith, J., *Llywelyn ap Gruffudd: Prince of Wales* (Cardiff, 1998).

Beverley Smith, J., 'Llywelyn's hall at Conwy', AC, 160 (2011), pp. 205–18.

Beverley Smith, J., 'Magna Carta and the Charters of the Welsh Princes', *English Historical Review*, 99 (1984), pp. 344–62.

Beverley Smith, J. and Beverley Smith, Ll. (eds), *A History of Merioneth Vol. 2: The Middle Ages* (Cardiff, 2001).

Beverley Smith, Ll., 'The Gravamina of the community of Gwynedd against Llywelyn ap Gruffudd', BBCS, 31 (1984), pp. 158–76.

Black, J., *Fortifications and Siegecraft: Defence and Attack through the Ages* (London, 2018).

Bond, J., 'The location and siting of Cistercian monasteries in Wales and the west', AC, 154 (2005), pp. 51–79.

Bramley, K.A. et al. (eds), *Gwaith Llywelyn Fardd I ac Eraill o Feirdd y Ddeuddegfed Ganrif* (Cardiff, 1994).

Brodie, H., 'Apsidal and D-shaped towers of the Princes of Gwynedd', AC, 164 (2015), pp. 231–43.

Burton, J. and Stöber, K., *Abbeys and Priories of Medieval Wales* (Cardiff, 2015).

Butler, L., 'The castles of the Princes of Gwynedd', in Williams and Kenyon (eds), *Impact of the Edwardian Castles*, pp. 27–36.

Butler, L., 'Dolforwyn Castle, Montgomery, Powys, First Report: The Excavations 1981–1986', AC, 138 (1989), pp. 78–98.

Butler, L., 'Dolforwyn Castle, Montgomery, Powys, Second Report: The Excavations 1987–1994', AC, 144 (1995), pp. 133–203.

Butler, L., 'Dolforwyn Castle, Powys, Wales: excavations 1985–1990', *Château Gaillard*, 15 (1992), pp. 73–82.

Butler, L., 'Dolforwyn Castle: prospect and retrospect', in Kenyon and O'Conor (eds), *The Medieval Castle*, pp. 149–62.

Butler, L., 'The siege of Dolforwyn castle in 1277', *Château Gaillard*, 19 (2000), pp. 25–6.

Butler, L. and Knight, J.J., *Dolforwyn Castle/Montgomery Castle* (Cardiff, 2004).

Butler, L.A.S., 'Medieval finds from Castell-Y-Bere, Merioneth', *AC*, 123 (1974), pp. 78–113.

Caple, C., *Excavations at Dryslwyn Castle 1980–95* (Leeds, 2007).

Carlin, M. and Crouch, D. (eds and transls), *Lost Letters of Medieval Life: English Society, 1200–1250* (Philadelphia, PA, 2013).

Carpenter, D., 'Confederation not domination: Welsh political culture in the age of Gwynedd imperialism', in Griffiths and Schofield (eds), *Wales and the Welsh*, pp. 20–8.

Carr, A.D., 'The last and weakest of his line: Dafydd ap Gruffydd, the last Prince of Wales', *WHR*, 19 (1999), pp. 375–99.

Carr, A.D., *Medieval Wales* (Basingstoke, 1995).

Carr, A.D. and Carr, G., *Cestyll Gwynedd* [Castles of Gwynedd] (Cardiff, 1985).

Chapman, F.G.W., 'Notes on the castles of Harlech and Cricieth', *Journal of the British Archaeological Association*, 34 (1878), pp. 159–67.

Clancy, J.P., *Medieval Welsh Poems* (Dublin, 2003).

Clwyd-Powys Archaeological Trust, 'Pentre Ffwrndan Roman Settlement, Flintshire: Community Excavation and Outreach, 2018–2019', CPAT report 1633–1 (2019).

Cox, R., 'Asymmetric warfare and military conduct in the Middle Ages', *Journal of Medieval History*, 38 (2012), pp. 100–25.

Creighton, O., *Castles and Landscapes: Power, Community and Fortification in Medieval England* (London, 2002).

Creighton, O. and Liddiard, R., 'Fighting yesterday's battle: beyond war or status in Castle Studies', *Medieval Archaeology*, 52 (2008), pp. 161–9.

Crouch, D., *Medieval Britain c. 1000–1500* (Cambridge, 2017).

Davies, G., 'Traddodiadau a Hynafiaethau Llanuwchllyn' [Traditions and antiquities of Llanuwchllyn], *Cylchgrawn Cymdeithas Hanes a Chofnodion Sir Feirionnydd/JMHRS*, 3 (1958), pp. 151–60.

Davies, H.R., *A Review of the Records of the Conway and the Menai Ferries* (Cardiff, 1942).

Davies, J., 'Rhyd Chwima – the Ford at Montgomery – Aque Vadum de Mungumeri', *MC*, 94 (2006), pp. 23–36.

Davies, J.D., *Britannia's Dragon: A Naval History of Wales* (Stroud, 2013).

Davies, R.R., *The Age of Conquest: Wales 1063–1415* (Oxford, 1991).

Davies, R.R., *The Revolt of Owain Glyn Dŵr* (Oxford, 1995).

Davies, S., *War and Society in Medieval Wales 633–1283* (Cardiff, 2004).

Davies-Cooke, T.B., 'Ewloe Castle', *AC*, 5th series, 8 (1891), pp. 1–7.

Davis, P.R., *Castles of the Welsh Princes*, 2nd edn (Talybont, 2011).

Davis, P.R., *The Forgotten Castles of Wales* (Almeley, 2011).

De Lewandowicz, M., 'A survey of Castell Prysor, Meirionnydd', *AW*, 38 (1998), pp. 36–42.

Denholm-Young, N. (ed.), *Vita Edwardi Secundi: The Life of Edward the Second* (Oxford, 1957).

Dixon, P.W., 'The donjon of Knaresborough: the castle as theatre', *Château Gaillard*, 14 (1990), pp. 121–39.

Driver, T. and Hopewell, D., 'A medieval church and township re-discovered at Llwydfaen, Caerhun, Conwy', *AW*, 48 (2008), pp. 77–81.

Edwards, J.G., 'Henry II and the fight at Coleshill: some further reflections', WHR, 3 (1967), pp. 251–63.

Elis-Williams, D., 'St. Gwyddelan's Church and the medieval geography of Dolwyddelan', AW, 54 (2015), pp. 109–24.

Evans, D.F., 'Castle and town in medieval Wales', in H. Fulton (ed.), *Urban Culture in Medieval Wales* (Cardiff, 2012), pp. 183–204.

Evans, D.F., 'Conquest, roads and resistance in medieval Wales', in V. Allen and R. Evans (eds), *Roadworks: Medieval Britain, Medieval Roads* (Manchester, 2016), pp. 277–302.

Evans, E.D., 'Was there a Borough of Bere?' JMHRS, 10 (1989), pp. 290–8.

Evans, G., *The Fight for Welsh Freedom* (Talybont, 2000).

Evans, N., 'Finding a new story: the search for a usable past in Wales, 1869–1930', THSC, new series, 10 (2004), pp. 144–62.

Fradley, M., 'Monastic enterprise in town and countryside: two case studies from north-east Shropshire', *Landscape History*, 28 (2006), pp. 5–20.

Gillingham, J., 'The context and purposes of the *History of the Kings of Britain*', Anglo-Norman Studies, 13 (1990), pp. 99–118.

Gillingham, J., 'The Early Middle Ages (1066–1290)', in K.O. Morgan (ed.), *The Oxford History of Britain*, rev. edn (Oxford, 2001), pp. 120–92.

Gower, J., *The Story of Wales* (Croydon, 2012).

Gresham, C., 'The development of Criccieth Castle', *Transactions of the Caernarfonshire Historical Society*, 34 (1973), pp. 14–22.

Griffiths, R., 'The revolt of Rhys ap Maredudd, 1287–88', WHR, 3 (1966), pp. 121–43.

Griffiths, R.A. and Schofield, P.R. (eds), *Wales and the Welsh in the Middle Ages: Essays presented to J. Beverley Smith* (Cardiff, 2011).

Gruffydd, K.L., *Maritime Wales in the Middle Ages: 1039–1542* (Wrexham, 2016).

Hemp, W.J., 'Castell Y Bere', AC, 97 (1942), pp. 120–2.

Hemp, W.J., 'Ewloe Castle and the Welsh Castle plan', Y Cymmrodor, 39 (1928), pp. 4–19.

Hemp, W.J., *Ewloe Castle* (London, 1929).

Henken, E., *National Redeemer: Owain Glyndŵr in Welsh Tradition* (Cardiff, 1996).

Higham, R. and Barker, P., *Timber Castles* (Exeter, 2004).

Hogg, A.H.A., 'Castell Carndochan', *Cylchgrawn Cymdeithas Hanes a Chofnodion Sir Feirionnydd*/JMHRS, 2 (1955), pp. 178–80.

Hogg, A.H.A. and King, D.J.C., 'Masonry castles in Wales and the Marches: a list', AC, 116 (1967), pp. 71–132.

Hopewell, D., 'Castell Carndochan: survey and excavation 2014–17', AC, 169 (2020), pp. 177–207.

Hopewell, D., 'High status medieval sites: Castell Carndochan Excavation Report 2015–16', Gwynedd Archaeological Trust (2016).

Hopewell, D., 'High status medieval sites: Castell Carndochan Excavation Report 2016–17', Gwynedd Archaeological Trust (2017).

Hopewell, D., 'Ty'n Twr, Bethesda, Archaeological Excavation' (GAT 1173), Gwynedd Archaeological Trust report 86 (1994).

Hughes, H., 'Criccieth Castle', AC, 60 (1905), pp. 200–10.

Hughes, H. and North, H.L., *The Old Churches of Snowdonia* (1908; repr. Capel Curig, 1984).

Hull, L., *Castles of Glamorgan* (Almeley, 2007).

Hurlock, K., *Wales and the Crusades c. 1095–1291* (Cardiff, 2011).

Insley, C., 'The Wilderness Years of Llywelyn the Great', *Thirteenth Century England*, 9 (2003), pp. 163–73.

Jamieson, E., 'The siting of medieval castles and the influence of ancient places', *Medieval Archaeology*, 63 (2019), pp. 338–74.

Johns, C.N., *Castell Cricieth/Cricieth Castle*, 2nd edn (1984; London, 1970).

Johnstone, N., 'Llys and Maerdref: the royal courts of the Prince of Gwynedd', SC, 34 (2000), pp. 167–201.

Jones, B., 'Documents relevant to Wales before the Edwardian conquest in the Vatican archives', in P. Skinner (ed.), *The Welsh and the Medieval World: Travel, Migration and Exile* (Cardiff, 2018), pp. 215–40.

Jones, C.O., 'Dafydd ap Llywelyn, the Sychnant Pass, and Henry III's Welsh campaign of 1245', *Transactions of the Caernarfonshire Historical Society* (forthcoming, 2022).

Jones, C.O., 'Further thoughts on Ewloe castle', AC, 170 (2021), pp. 237–50.

Jones, C.O., 'Gwenwynwyn, the silver mine at Carreghofa, and the supremacy of Powys', CMCS, 79 (2020), pp. 47–59.

Jones, C.O., '"Ho, oh! What castle is this": Flint and the quincentenary of Richard II's arrest', FHSJ, 41 (2018), pp. 145–57.

Jones, C.O., 'How to make an entrance: an overlooked aspect of native Welsh masonry castle design', *Journal of the Mortimer History Society*, 1 (2017), pp. 73–89.

Jones, C.O., 'Prydydd y Moch, Ellesmere, and Llywelyn ab Iorwerth's Shropshire campaigns', AC, 169 (2020), pp. 165–76.

Jones, C.O., *The Revolt of Madog ap Llywelyn* (Llanrwst, 2008).

Jones, C.O., 'A rupture, sudden and unaccountable? King John's Welsh incursion of 1209 reconsidered', WHR, 30 (2020), pp. 1–18.

Jones, G., 'The defences of Gwynedd in the thirteenth century', *Transactions of the Caernarfonshire Historical Society*, 30 (1969), pp. 29–43.

Jones, J.E. and Stockwell, A., 'Tomen Castell, Dolwyddelan, Gwynedd, North Wales: excavations at an early castle site', AW, 54 (2015), pp. 73–90.

Jones, N.A. and Feer, E., 'A poet and his patrons: the early career of Llywelyn Brydydd Y Moch', in F. Fulton (ed.), *Medieval Celtic Literature and Society* (Dublin, 2005), pp. 132–62.

Jones, O., 'Historical writing in medieval Wales', PhD thesis (Bangor, 2013).

Jones, T., *A History of the County of Brecknock*, Vol. 1 (London, 1805).

Jones, T.V., 'Review of *National redeemer: Owain Glyndŵr in Welsh tradition* by Elissa R. Henken', WHR, 19/1 (1998), pp. 151–5.

Jones, W.B., 'The building of Castell Dinas Brân, Llangollen', *Clwyd Historian*, 45 (2000), pp. 1–8.

Jones, W.B., 'Medieval earthworks at Dinas Brân, Llangollen', AC, 147 (1998), pp. 234–9.

Jones Pierce, T., 'Aber Gwyn Gregin', *Transactions of the Caernarfonshire Historical Society*, 23 (1962), pp. 37–43.

Kenney, J., 'Degannwy Castle, Degannwy: Archaeological Assessment', Gwynedd Archaeological Trust Report 781 (2009).

Kenyon, J., '"Those proud, ambitious heaps": whither castle studies?' AC, 166 (2017), pp. 1–31.

Kenyon, J.R. and O'Conor, K. (eds), *The Medieval Castle in Ireland and Wales: Essays in Honour of Jeremy Knight* (Dublin, 2003).

Kightly, C., *Castell Dinas Brân* (Rhuthun, 2003).

King, D.J.C., *Castles and Abbeys of Wales* (London, 1975).

King, D.J.C., 'The defence of Wales, 1067–1283: The other side of the hill', AC, 126 (1977), pp. 1–16.

King, D.J.C., 'Two castles in northern Powys: Dinas Brân and Caergwrle', AC, 123 (1974), pp. 113–39.

King, D.J.C. and Spurgeon, C.J., 'The mottes in the vale of Montgomery', AC, 114 (1965), pp. 69–86.

Leach, G.B., 'Excavations at Hen Blas, Coleshill Fawr, Near Flint – Second Report', JFHS, 18 (1960), pp. 13–60.

Lepage, J.-D.G.G., *British Fortifications Through the Reign of Richard III: An Illustrated History* (Jefferson, NC, 2012).

Lewis, C.P., 'Gruffudd ap Cynan and the Normans', in K.L. Maund (ed.), *Gruffudd ap Cynan: A Collaborative Biography* (Woodbridge, 1996), pp. 61–78.

Liddiard, R., *Castles in Context: Power, Symbolism and Landscape, 1066 to 1500* (Macclesfield, 2005).

Liddiard, R. and Williamson, T., 'There by design? Some reflections on medieval elite landscapes', AJ, 165 (2008), pp. 520–35.

Lieberman, M., *The Medieval March of Wales: The Creation and Perception of a Frontier, 1066–1283* (Cambridge, 2010).

Lloyd, J.E., 'Ewloe', *Y Cymmrodor*, 39 (1928), pp. 1–3.

Lloyd, J.E., *A History of Wales*, 2 vols (London, 1911).

Lloyd, S., *The Arthurian Place-Names of Wales* (Cardiff, 2017).

McDonald, R.A., *Manx Kingship in its Irish Sea Setting, 1187–1229* (Dublin, 2007).

Marshall, P., 'The ceremonial function of the donjon in the twelfth century', *Château Gaillard*, 20 (2002), pp. 141–51.

Maud, R., 'David, the last prince of Wales: the ten "lost" months of Welsh history', THSC, pt 1 (1968), pp. 43–62.

Medhurst, J., *A History of Independent Television in Wales* (Cardiff, 2010).

Mlekuž, D., Košir, U. and Črešnar, M., 'Landscapes of death and suffering: archaeology of conflict landscapes of the Upper Soča Valley, Slovenia', in B. Stichelbaut and D. Cowley (eds), *Conflict Landscapes and Archaeology from Above* (Farnham, 2016), pp. 127–46.

Morris, J.E., *The Welsh Wars of Edward I* (Oxford, 1901).

Neaverson, E., *Medieval Castles in North Wales* (Liverpool, 1947).

Ohler, N., *The Medieval Traveller* (Woodbridge, 2010).

O'Keefe, T. and Coughlan, M., 'The chronology and formal affinities of the Ferns donjon, Co. Wexford', in Kenyon and O'Conor (eds), *The Medieval Castle*, pp. 133–48.

Olson, K., '"Ar ffordd Pedr a Phawl": Welsh pilgrimage and travel to Rome, *c.* 1200–*c.* 1530', WHR, 24 (2008), pp. 1–40.

O'Neil, B.J.St.J., 'Criccieth Castle, Caernarvonshire', AC, 98 (1944–5), pp. 1–51.

Oram, R., *Alexander II, King of Scots 1216–1249* (Edinburgh, 2012).

Owen, E., 'Arvona Antiqua', AC, 22 (1867), pp. 102–8.

Owen, H.W. and Morgan, R., *Dictionary of the Place-Names of Wales* (Llandysul, 2007).

Parker, W., 'Gwynedd, Ceredigion and the political geography of the Mabinogi', *Cylchgrawn Llyfrgell Genedlaethol Cymru/NLWJ*, 23 (2002), pp. 365–9.

Pettifer, J., *Welsh Castles* (Woodbridge, 2000).

Pierce, T.J., 'The Old Borough of Nefyn 1355–1882', *Transactions of the Caernarfonshire Historical Society*, 18 (1957), pp. 36–53.

Platt, C., 'Revisionism in Castle Studies: a caution', *Medieval Archaeology*, 51 (2007), pp. 83–102.

Pounds, N.J.G., *The Medieval Castle in England and Wales: A Social and Political History* (Cambridge, 1990).

Pratt, D., 'Anatomy of conquest: Bromfield and Yale 1277–84', *Transactions of the Denbighshire Historical Society*, 56 (2008), pp. 17–58.

Prestwich, M., *Edward I* (Berkeley, CA, 1988).

Prestwich, M., 'Welsh infantry in Flanders in 1297', in Griffiths and Schofield (eds), *Wales and the Welsh*, pp. 56–69.

Pryce, H. (ed.), *The Acts of Welsh Rulers 1120–1283* (Cardiff, 2005).

Pryce, H., 'Anglo-Welsh agreements, 1201–77', in Griffiths and Schofield (eds), *Wales and the Welsh*, pp. 1–19.

Pryce, H., *J.E. Lloyd and the Creation of Welsh History: Renewing a Nation's Past* (Cardiff, 2011).

Pryce, H., 'Negotiating Anglo-Welsh relations: Llywelyn the Great and Henry III', in Weiler (ed.) with Rowlands, *England and Europe in the Reign of Henry III*, pp. 13–29.

Pryce, H., *Tywysogion* [Princes] (Cardiff, 2006).

Putnam, W.G., 'The Roman road from Forden to Caersws', *MC*, 57 (1962), pp. 141–9.

Redknap, M., 'Some medieval brooches, pendants and moulds from Wales: a short survey', *AC*, 143 (1996), pp. 92–138.

Rees, S. 'Rhuddlan Castle and the canalization of the River Clwyd', in M. Redknap, S. Rees and A. Aberg (eds), *Wales and the Sea: 10,000 Years of Welsh Maritime History* (Talybont, 2019), pp. 108–9.

Remfry, P., *Harlech Castle and its True Origins* (n.p., 2013).

Renn, D. and Avent, R., *Flint Castle/Ewloe Castle* (Cardiff, 2001).

Roderick, A.J., 'Marriage and politics in Wales, 1066–1282', *WHR*, 4 (1968), pp. 3–20.

Royal Commission on the Ancient and Historical Monuments of Wales, *An Inventory of the Ancient Monuments in Anglesey* (London, 1937).

Royal Commission on the Ancient and Historical Monuments of Wales, *An Inventory of the Ancient Monuments in Caernarfonshire I: East* (London, 1956).

Royal Commission on the Ancient and Historical Monuments of Wales, *An Inventory of the Ancient Monuments in Caernarfonshire II: Central* (London, 1960).

Royal Commission on the Ancient and Historical Monuments of Wales, *An Inventory of the Ancient Monuments in Glamorgan Vol. 3 Part 1b: Medieval Secular Monuments: Later Castles From 1217 to the Present* (Cardiff, 2000).

Royal Commission on the Ancient and Historical Monuments of Wales, *An Inventory of the Ancient Monuments of Wales and Monmouthshire II: Flint* (London, 1912).

Ryder, C., 'The spiral stair or vice: its origins, role and meaning in medieval stone castles', PhD thesis (Liverpool, 2011).

Savory, H.N., 'Excavations at Dinas Emrys, Beddgelert (Caern.), 1954–56', *AC*, 109 (1960), pp. 13–77.

Sharp, J.F. and Lloyd, G., 'Notes on excursions 1955', *FHSJ*, 17 (1957), pp. 95–106.

Smith, S.G., 'Dolbadarn Castle, Caernarfonshire: a thirteenth-century royal landscape', *AW*, 53 (2014), pp. 63–72.

Soulsby, I., *The Towns of Medieval Wales* (Chichester, 1983).

Stafford, T., West, C. and Tomkins, C., *Mapping the Itinerary of Edward I*, <https://figshare.shef.ac.uk/articles/dataset/Mapping_The_Itinerary_of_King_Edward_I/8948699>.

Stephenson, D., 'Empires in Wales: from Gruffudd ap Llywelyn to Llywelyn ap Gruffudd', WHR, 28 (2016), pp. 26–54.

Stephenson, D., 'Events at Nefyn c. 1200 – the plundering of King John's Irish hounds and hawks', CMCS, 75 (2018), pp. 39–43.

Stephenson, D., '*Fouke le Fitz Waryn* and Llywelyn ap Gruffudd's claim to Whittington', SHA, 77 (2002), pp. 26–31.

Stephenson, D., 'From Llywelyn ap Gruffudd to Edward I: expansionist rulers and Welsh society', in Williams and Kenyon (eds), *Impact of the Edwardian Castles*, pp. 9–15.

Stephenson, D., *The Governance of Gwynedd* (Cardiff, 1984).

Stephenson, D., 'Llywelyn the Great, the Shropshire March and the building of Montgomery castle', SHA, 80 (2005), pp. 52–8.

Stephenson, D., 'Madog ap Maredudd, *rex Powissensium*', WHR, 24 (2008), pp. 1–28.

Stephenson, D., *Medieval Powys: Kingdom, Principality and Lordships, 1132–1293* (Woodbridge, 2016).

Stephenson, D., '*Potens et Prudens*: Gruffudd ap Madog, Lord of Bromfield 1236–1269', WHR, 22 (2005), pp. 409–31.

Stephenson, D., 'A reconsideration of the siting, function and dating of Ewloe castle', AC, 164 (2015), pp. 245–53.

Stephenson, D., 'A Treaty too far? The impact of the Treaty of Montgomery on Llywelyn ap Gruffudd's Principality of Wales', MC, 106 (2018), pp. 19–32.

Stephenson, D., 'Welsh lords in Shropshire', SHA, 77 (2002), pp. 32–7.

Stephenson, D. and Jones, C.O., 'The date and the context of the birth of Dafydd ap Llywelyn', FHSJ, 39 (2012), pp. 21–32.

Suppe, F.C., *Military Institutions in the Welsh Marches: Shropshire 1066–1300* (Woodbridge, 1994).

Swallow, R., 'Gateways to power: the castles of Ranulf III of Chester and Llywelyn the Great of Gwynedd', AJ, 171 (2014), pp. 289–311.

Swallow, R., 'Living the dream: the legend, lady and landscape of Caernarfon Castle, Gwynedd, North Wales', AC, 168 (2019), pp. 153–95.

Taylor, A., *The Welsh Castles of Edward I* (Oxford, 1986).

Taylor, A.J., 'A fragment of a Dona account of 1284', BBCS, 27 (1977), pp. 253–62.

Taylor, A.J., *The King's Works in Wales 1277–1330* (London, 1974).

Taylor, C., 'The history and archaeology of temporary medieval camps: a possible example in Wales', *Landscape History*, 40 (2019), pp. 41–56.

Taylor, H., *Historic Notices of Flint* (London, 1883).

Thorpe, L. (transl.), *Gerald of Wales: The Journey through Wales/The Description of Wales* (London, 1978).

Titow, J., 'Evidence of weather in the account rolls of the Bishopric of Winchester 1209–1350', *Economic History Review*, 12 (1960), pp. 360–407.

Treharne, R.F., 'The Franco-Welsh Treaty of Alliance in 1212', BBCS, 18 (1958–60), pp. 60–75.

Turvey, R., *Llywelyn the Great* (Llandysul, 2007).

Turvey, R., *The Lord Rhys: Prince of Deheubarth* (Llandysul, 1997).

Waddington, K., *The Settlements of Northwest Wales, From the Late Bronze Age to the Early Medieval Period* (Cardiff, 2013).

Walker, R.F., 'William de Valence and the army of west Wales, 1282–1283', WHR, 18 (1997), pp. 407–29.

Ward, M.A., 'St. Catherine's Church, Cricieth', *Transactions of the Caernarfonshire Historical Society*, 58 (1997), pp. 7–34.

Warren, W.L., *Henry II* (Berkeley, CA, 1977).

Weiler, B.K.U. (ed.) with Rowlands, I.W., *England and Europe in the Reign of Henry III (1216–72)* (Routledge, 2002).

Wiedemann, B.G.E., '"Fooling the court of the lord Pope": Dafydd ap Llywelyn's petition to the Curia in 1244', WHR, 28 (2016), pp. 209–32.

Wiles, J., 'Lordly landscapes in post-conquest Maelienydd (c. 1267–1400)', *The Transactions of the Radnorshire Society*, 86 (2016), pp. 65–86.

Wilkinson, L., 'Joan, wife of Llywelyn the Great', *Thirteenth Century England*, 10 (2005), pp. 81–94.

Williams, A., 'Stories within stories: writing history in *Fouke le Fitz Waryn*', *Medium Ævum*, 81 (2012), pp. 70–87.

Williams, A.H., *An Introduction to the History of Wales, Volume II: The Middle Ages, Part I 1063–1284* (Cardiff, 1948).

Williams, D., *Dolbadarn Castle* (Cardiff, 1990).

Williams, D.M. and Kenyon, J.R. (eds), *The Impact of the Edwardian Castles in Wales* (Oxford, 2010).

Williams, G.A., 'The succession to Gwynedd, 1238–47', BBCS, 20 (1964), pp. 393–413.

# Index